# PREFACE for teachers and parents

This thesaurus contains two main types of entry.

1  There are entries which give *synonyms* for the common words in a child's vocabulary. Where appropriate, opposites are also given. Example sentences or phrases put each word in a meaningful context.

2  There are *topic entries* which give lists of words which are not synonyms but which are related to the headword. For example, various kinds of animal are listed under **animal**; musical terms are given under **music**; and so on. These entries will be helpful to individual children who just need a jog to the memory to find the word they were looking for; they also provide opportunities for them to explore and discuss the vocabulary of a particular topic.

The arrangement of the thesaurus is simple and user-friendly. Each entry is self-explanatory: there are no abbreviations or cryptic devices. The headwords, which comprise all the words children are likely to look up as starting-points for a word-search, are arranged in simple alphabetical sequence, avoiding the need for a separate index (a common but awkward and confusing feature of some other thesauruses). The more discussable entries - topic entries, and entries for headwords with a particular complex range of senses or usages - are enclosed in boxes. This will encourage young readers to browse.

The English language is infinitely variable and adaptable. Ultimately, children's awareness of this variety and adaptability will come not from a book like this, but from their experience of language in use. I hope, therefore, that they will be encouraged to see the thesaurus not just as a book to refer to, but as a book which raises questions about vocabulary - and about language in general - which they will want to discuss with teachers, parents, and other experienced users of our language.

This large print edition has an attractive layout, special cream paper and clear black print. It is designed for those who find an uncluttered page easier to read.

The headword list in this thesaurus is derived from that of *The Oxford Young Readers' Dictionary*, to which this book will make an ideal companion volume.

Alan Spooner

# USING THIS THESAURUS

A thesaurus helps you find words to make your language more interesting, and to help you say exactly what you want to say. It gives you words which have the same meaning as the word you thought of. These are called *synonyms*.

It may give you words which mean the *opposite* of the word you thought of.

It will often give you words which are useful when you are talking or writing about a particular *topic*.

Remember that a thesaurus does not give you explanations or definitions of what words mean. If you want to know what a word means, you need to look it up in a dictionary like *The Oxford Young Readers' Dictionary*.

# IN THIS THESAURUS YOU WILL FIND...

## Headwords
The words you look up are printed in heavy black type, so that they are easy to find.

## Examples
Sentences or phrases showing how you might use the word are printed in ordinary type.

## Synonyms
Words which mean the same as the word you look up are the *synonyms*. These are words you might use instead of the word you look up. They are printed in bold black type.

## Antonyms
If the word you look up has a useful opposite, it comes after the synonyms.

## Numbers
When a word has more than one meaning, or if it is used in more than one way, we number the different uses.

## Related words
Sometimes we give lists of words which are specially interesting. These entries are in the boxes. Many of these are not lists of synonyms, but lists of words related to a topic.

# The OXFORD Young Readers' THESAURUS

Compiled by
Alan Spooner

OXFORD
UNIVERSITY PRESS

Oxford University Press, Great Clarendon Street, Oxford, OX2 6DP

Oxford  New York
Athens  Auckland  Bangkok  Bogotá
Buenos Aires  Calcutta  Cape Town  Chennai  Dar es Salaam
Delhi  Florence  Hong Kong  Istanbul  Karachi
Kuala Lumpur  Madrid  Melbourne
Mexico City  Mumbai  Nairobi  Paris  São Paulo  Singapore
Taipei  Tokyo  Toronto  Warsaw

and associated companies in
Berlin  Ibadan

*Oxford* is a trade mark of Oxford University Press
© Alan Spooner 1999

First published 1999
1 3 5 7 9 10 8 6 4 2

A CIP catalogue record for this book is available from the British Library

*The Oxford Young Readers' Thesaurus* is based on the text of *The Oxford Junior Thesaurus*

ISBN 0 19 910 534 0
Printed in Great Britain by
St Edmundsbury Press

Do you have a query about words, their origin, meaning, use, spelling, pronunciation, or any other aspect of the English language? Then write to OWLS at Oxford University Press, Great Clarendon Street, Oxford OX2 6DP.

All queries will be answered using the full resources of the Oxford Dictionary Department.

**Headwords**
The words you look up are printed in heavy black type, so that they are easy to find.

**Examples**
Sentences or phrases showing how you might use the word are printed in ordinary type.

**Related words**
Sometimes we give lists of words which are specially interesting. These entries are in the boxes. Many of these are not lists of synonyms, but lists of words related to a topic.

**bolt** *verb*
1  Remember to bolt the back door.
   OTHER VERBS YOU MIGHT USE ARE  **to bar**   **to fasten**   **to lock**
2  The horse bolted.
   OTHER VERBS ARE  **to escape**   **to run away**
For other words, see **run**
3  Don't bolt down your food!
   OTHER VERBS ARE  **to gobble**   **to gulp**

**book** *noun*
        VARIOUS KINDS OF BOOK ARE
        **album   annual   atlas   diary   dictionary
        directory   encyclopedia   hymn book   novel
        paperback   story book   thesaurus**

**bottom** *noun*
1  the bottom of a wall.
   OTHER WORDS YOU MIGHT USE ARE  **base   foot   foundation**
The opposite is **top**
2  the bottom of the sea.
   ANOTHER WORD IS **bed**
The opposite is **surface**

**Numbers**
When a word has more than one meaning, or if it is used in more than one way, we number the different uses.

**Antonyms**
If the word you look up has a useful opposite, it comes after the synonyms.

**Synonyms**
Words which mean the same as the word you look up are the synonyms. These are words you might use instead of the word you look up. They are printed in bold black type.

# Aa

**abandon** *verb*
1  It's cruel to abandon a pet.
OTHER VERBS YOU MIGHT USE ARE   **to desert     to forsake     to leave**
2  We abandoned the game when it rained.
OTHER VERBS ARE   **to cancel     to give up     to postpone**

**able** *adjective*
1  Are you able to play tomorrow?
OTHER WORDS YOU MIGHT USE ARE   **allowed     free**
2  Jo is an able tennis player.
OTHER WORDS ARE   **capable     clever     skilful     talented**

**abolish** *verb*
I wish they would abolish tests.
OTHER VERBS YOU MIGHT USE ARE   **to end     to get rid of     to remove**

**accept** *verb*
1  Please accept this gift.
OTHER VERBS YOU MIGHT USE ARE   **to receive     to take**
2  I accept that it was my fault.
OTHER VERBS ARE   **to admit     to agree     to believe**

**accident** *noun*
1  OTHER WORDS YOU MIGHT USE ARE   **collision     crash     mishap**
WORDS YOU MIGHT USE FOR A VERY SERIOUS ACCIDENT ARE   **calamity     catastrophe     disaster**
2  We met by accident.
OTHER WORDS ARE   **chance     coincidence**

**accompany** *verb*
Dad accompanied us to school.
A PHRASE YOU MIGHT USE IS **to go with**

**account** *noun*
Jo wrote an account of the match.
OTHER WORDS YOU MIGHT USE ARE   **description     report     story**

## accurate *adjective*
1  Is your watch accurate?
OTHER WORDS YOU MIGHT USE ARE  **correct**  **right**
2  Give me an accurate account of what happened.
OTHER WORDS ARE  **exact**  **precise**  **true**

## ache *noun* and *verb*
For other words, see **pain**

## achievement *noun*
It was a great achievement to win by four goals.
OTHER WORDS YOU MIGHT USE ARE  **accomplishment**  **feat**  **success**

## act *verb*
1  She acted quickly to put out the fire.
PHRASES YOU MIGHT USE ARE  **to do something**  **to take action**
2  Jo likes to act in plays.
OTHER VERBS YOU MIGHT USE ARE  **to appear**  **to perform**
To act without using words is **to mime**
3  He was acting like an idiot.
ANOTHER VERB IS **to behave**

## action *noun*
1  The film was full of action.
OTHER WORDS YOU MIGHT USE ARE  **activity**  **excitement**
2  It was a kind action to dig Mr Brown's garden.
OTHER WORDS ARE  **act**  **deed**

## active *adjective*
1  Our puppy is very active.
OTHER WORDS YOU MIGHT USE ARE  **energetic**  **lively**
2  Mum is active in charity work.
OTHER WORDS ARE  **busy**  **involved**  **working**

## activity *noun*
1  What activities do you enjoy?
OTHER WORDS YOU MIGHT USE ARE  **hobby**  **job**  **project**  **task**
2  The shops are full of activity when the sales are on.
OTHER WORDS ARE  **action**  **bustle**  **excitement**

## actual *adjective*
Is that the actual tree Robin Hood lived in?
OTHER WORDS YOU MIGHT USE ARE  **genuine**  **real**

## add  *verb*
1  Add the milk and the sugar.
OTHER VERBS YOU MIGHT USE ARE　**to combine　to mix　to put together**
2  We added the numbers together.
For other words you might use when you do maths, see **mathematics**
The opposite is **subtract**

## additional  *adjective*
OTHER WORDS ARE　**extra　more**

## admire  *verb*
1  We admired the firemen's skill.
OTHER VERBS YOU MIGHT USE ARE　**to praise　to respect　to wonder at**
2  I admired the view.
OTHER VERBS ARE　**to appreciate　to enjoy　to like**

## admit  *verb*
1  Jo admitted that she was wrong.
OTHER VERBS YOU MIGHT USE ARE　**to accept　to confess　to own up**
2  They only admit you if you have a ticket.
OTHER VERBS ARE　**to allow in　to let in**

## adore  *verb*
Jo's dog adores her.
OTHER VERBS YOU MIGHT USE ARE　**to idolize　to love　to worship**

## adult  *noun*
ANOTHER WORD IS **grown-up**

## advance  *verb*
As the army advanced, the enemy ran away.
OTHER VERBS YOU MIGHT USE ARE　**to approach　to come near
to move forward　to progress**
The opposite is **retreat**

## advantage  *noun*
It's an advantage to have the wind behind you when you run.
ANOTHER WORD IS **help**

## advertise  *verb*
They advertised a new car on TV.
OTHER VERBS YOU MIGHT USE ARE　(*informal*) **to plug　to promote
to publicize**

## advertisement *noun*
OTHER WORDS YOU MIGHT USE ARE     *(informal)* **ad** or **advert**     **commercial**     **poster**

## advice *noun*
My advice is to save your money.
OTHER WORDS YOU MIGHT USE ARE     **recommendation**     **suggestion**

## advise *verb*
What did the doctor advise?
OTHER VERBS YOU MIGHT USE ARE     **to recommend**     **to suggest**

## aeroplane *noun*
For other machines that fly, see **aircraft**

## affect *verb*
The weather affects my mood.
OTHER VERBS YOU MIGHT USE ARE     **to alter**     **to change**     **to influence**

## afraid *adjective*
The dog is afraid of thunder.
OTHER WORDS YOU MIGHT USE ARE     **frightened**     **scared**     **terrified**

## aggressive *adjective*
That dog looks rather aggressive.
OTHER WORDS YOU MIGHT USE ARE     **hostile**     **rough**     **violent**
The opposite is **friendly**

## agree *verb*
1 Mum agreed that I was right.
OTHER VERBS YOU MIGHT USE ARE     **to accept**     **to admit**
2 We agreed to go shopping.
OTHER VERBS ARE     **to arrange**     **to consent**     **to decide**

## aid *verb*
For other verbs, see **help**

## aim *verb*
1 Aim the gun at the target.
OTHER VERBS YOU MIGHT USE ARE     **to direct**     **to point**
2 We aimed to arrive by tea-time.
OTHER VERBS ARE     **to intend**     **to plan**     **to try**     **to want**

**aircraft** *noun*

VARIOUS KINDS OF AIRCRAFT ARE

aeroplane   air-liner   balloon   glider   helicopter
jet   jumbo jet   plane

## alarm *noun*

1 An alarm goes if there is a fire.

OTHER WORDS YOU MIGHT USE ARE **signal   siren   warning**

2 The storm was so bad that the animals were filled with alarm.

OTHER WORDS ARE **dismay   fear   fright   panic   terror**

## alarm *verb*

The thunder alarmed the animals.

OTHER VERBS YOU MIGHT USE ARE **to frighten   to scare   to upset**

## alert *adjective*

A sentry must be alert.

OTHER WORDS YOU MIGHT USE ARE **attentive   awake   observant
watchful**

## allow *verb*

You are allowed to drive when you have passed a test.

OTHER VERBS YOU MIGHT USE ARE **to authorize   to license   to permit**

## ally *noun*

For other words, see **friend**

## alter *verb*

For other verbs, see **change**

## amaze *verb*

The conjuror's tricks amazed us.

OTHER VERBS YOU MIGHT USE ARE **to astonish   to astound   to surprise**

## amazing *adjective*

For other words, see **extraordinary**

## ambition *noun*

Sam's ambition is to be a pilot.

OTHER WORDS YOU MIGHT USE ARE **aim   goal   objective   wish**

**ambush** *verb*
The soldiers ambushed the enemy.
OTHER VERBS YOU MIGHT USE ARE **to attack    to jump out on    to take by surprise    to trap**

---

**ammunition** *noun*
KINDS OF AMMUNITION ARE
**bullet    cannonball    hand grenade    missile    shell**
For other words, see **weapon**

---

**amount** *noun*
OTHER WORDS YOU MIGHT USE ARE **quantity    total**

**amuse** *verb*
While we waited for the bus I tried to amuse the others.
OTHER VERBS YOU MIGHT USE ARE **to cheer up    to divert    to entertain**

**amusing** *adjective*
an amusing joke.
OTHER WORDS YOU MIGHT USE ARE **comic    funny    humorous    witty**

**ancient** *adjective*
For other words, see **old**

**anger** *noun*
He showed his anger by slamming the door.
OTHER WORDS YOU MIGHT USE ARE **annoyance    fury    rage    temper**

**angry** *adjective*
Mum was angry when Jo broke the window.
OTHER WORDS YOU MIGHT USE ARE **annoyed    cross    furious    in a temper    infuriated    irate    (*informal*) mad    vexed**
The opposite is **pleased**

**animal** *noun*, see opposite page

**announce** *verb*
1 Jo announced that she was ready.
OTHER VERBS YOU MIGHT USE ARE **to declare    to report    to state**
2 The DJ announced our record.
ANOTHER VERB IS **to introduce**

# animal *noun*

OTHER WORDS YOU MIGHT USE ARE
**beast**          **creature**

A word you might use for a big animal you don't like is **brute**

DIFFERENT CLASSES OF ANIMAL ARE
| | | | |
|---|---|---|---|
| **amphibian** | **bird** | **fish** | **mammal** |
| **reptile** | | | |

ANIMALS THAT FARMERS KEEP ARE
| | | | |
|---|---|---|---|
| **bull** | **cow** | **goat** | **horse** |
| **ox** | **pig** | **sheep** | |

ANIMALS PEOPLE KEEP AS PETS ARE
| | | | |
|---|---|---|---|
| **cat** | **dog** | **donkey** | **ferret** |
| **gerbil** | **guinea pig** | **hamster** | **horse** |
| **mouse** | **rabbit** | **rat** | **tortoise** |

WILD ANIMALS YOU MIGHT SEE IN BRITAIN ARE
| | | | |
|---|---|---|---|
| **badger** | **bat** | **deer** | **dormouse** |
| **fox** | **hare** | **hedgehog** | **mole** |
| **otter** | **shrew** | **squirrel** | **stoat** |
| **vole** | **weasel** | | |

OTHER WILD ANIMALS ARE
| | | | |
|---|---|---|---|
| **antelope** | **ape** | **baboon** | **bear** |
| **beaver** | **bison** | **buffalo** | **camel** |
| **cheetah** | **chimpanzee** | **dromedary** | **elephant** |
| **elk** | **giraffe** | **gorilla** | **grizzly bear** |
| **hippopotamus** | **hyena** | **jackal** | **jaguar** |
| **kangaroo** | **koala** | **leopard** | **lion** |
| **llama** | **mongoose** | **monkey** | **moose** |
| **panda** | **panther** | **platypus** | **polar** |
| **bear** | **porcupine** | **reindeer** | **rhinoceros** |
| **skunk** | **snake** | **tiger** | **wallaby** |
| **wolf** | **zebra** | | |

ANIMALS THAT LIVE IN THE SEA ARE
| | | | |
|---|---|---|---|
| **dolphin** | **fish** | **octopus** | **porpoise** |
| **seal** | **sea lion** | **turtle** | **walrus** |
| **whale** | | | |

## announcement *noun*
The head read some announcements.
OTHER WORDS YOU MIGHT USE ARE **notice statement**

## annoy *verb*
The wasps were annoying me.
OTHER VERBS YOU MIGHT USE ARE **to bother to irritate to pester to torment to trouble to upset to worry**

## answer *noun*
1 an answer to a question.
OTHER WORDS YOU MIGHT USE ARE **reply response**
2 the answer to a problem.
OTHER WORDS ARE **explanation solution**

## anxious *adjective*
1 Mum gets anxious if I'm late.
OTHER WORDS YOU MIGHT USE ARE **concerned nervous worried**
2 We were anxious to start.
OTHER WORDS ARE **eager keen**

## apologize *verb*
I apologized for being rude.
A PHRASE IS **to say sorry**

## appeal *verb*
The sick man appealed for help.
OTHER VERBS YOU MIGHT USE ARE **to ask to beg to plead**

## appear *verb*
1 He appeared out of the mist.
OTHER VERBS YOU MIGHT USE ARE **to arrive to come out to turn up**
2 You appear tired.
OTHER VERBS ARE **to look to seem**

## appetite *noun*
1 an appetite for food.
OTHER WORDS YOU MIGHT USE ARE **greed hunger**
2 an appetite for adventure.
OTHER WORDS ARE **desire longing passion wish**

## appointment *noun*

The head can't see us this afternoon because she has another appointment.

> OTHER WORDS YOU MIGHT USE ARE     **arrangement     engagement     meeting**

## approach *verb*

I got nervous when the big dog approached me.

> A PHRASE IS **to come near**

## appropriate *adjective*

£10 was an appropriate price.

> OTHER WORDS YOU MIGHT USE ARE     **fitting     proper     right     suitable**

## approve *verb*

Did you approve of what I did?

> OTHER VERBS YOU MIGHT USE ARE     **to admire     to like     to praise**

## approximately *adverb*

The trip costs approximately £10.

> OTHER WORDS YOU MIGHT USE ARE     **about     nearly     roughly**

## area *noun*

1  The playground is a large area.
> OTHER WORDS YOU MIGHT USE ARE     **expanse     surface**

2  Uncle Tom lives in a nice area of London.
> OTHER WORDS ARE     **district     neighbourhood     part     region**

## argue *verb*

Jo and Sam are good friends: they don't often argue.

> OTHER VERBS YOU MIGHT USE ARE     **to disagree     to quarrel**

## argument *noun*

1  We had an argument about who was going to pay.
> OTHER WORDS YOU MIGHT USE ARE     **disagreement     dispute     quarrel**

2  There has been a lot of argument in the paper about a bypass.
> OTHER WORDS YOU MIGHT USE ARE     **controversy     debate**

## arm *noun*

For other parts of the body, see **body**

## arrange *verb*
1 Jo arranged the books on the shelf.
OTHER VERBS YOU MIGHT USE ARE **to set out    to sort    to tidy**
2 We arranged a trip to the sea.
OTHER VERBS ARE **to decide on    to fix    to organize    to plan**

## arrest *verb*
The police arrested the suspect.
OTHER VERBS YOU MIGHT USE ARE **to capture    to catch    to detain**
**to take into custody**

## arrive *verb*
1 When will Granny arrive?
OTHER VERBS YOU MIGHT USE ARE **to appear    to come    to turn up**
The opposite is **depart**
2 We arrived home for dinner.
OTHER VERBS ARE **to come    to get to    to reach**

## art *noun*
KINDS OF ART ARE
**collage    drawing    embroidery    modelling
needlework    painting    photography    pottery
sculpture    sewing    sketching    weaving**

DIFFERENT ARTISTS ARE
**painter    photographer    potter    sculptor    weaver**

## artificial *adjective*
1 Sam wore an artificial beard in the play.
OTHER WORDS YOU MIGHT USE ARE **false    pretend**
2 This dress is made of artificial material.
OTHER WORDS ARE **man-made    synthetic**
The opposite is **genuine**

## ask *verb*
1 What did you ask?
OTHER VERBS YOU MIGHT USE ARE **to enquire    to find out    to inquire**
2 The criminal asked to be given another chance.
OTHER VERBS ARE **to beg    to implore    to plead    to request**
3 My friends asked me to go out.
ANOTHER VERB IS **to invite**

**assist** *verb*
For other verbs, see **help**

**assistant** *noun*
You can't do that job on your own: you need an assistant.
    OTHER WORDS YOU MIGHT USE ARE   **helper**   **partner**
Someone who helps a person with an official job is a **deputy**.
Someone who helps a person commit a crime is an **accomplice**.

**assorted** *adjective*
For other words, see **various**

**astonish** *verb*
The player's skill astonished us.
    OTHER VERBS YOU MIGHT USE ARE   **to amaze**   **to astound**   **to surprise**

**athlete** *noun*
    OTHER WORDS YOU MIGHT USE ARE   **sportsman**   **sportswoman**
For various sports, see **sport**

**attach** *verb*
    WAYS TO ATTACH THINGS ARE   **to bind**   **to connect**   **to fasten**   **to fix**
    **to glue**   **to join**   **to link**   **to stick**   **to tie**

**attack** *verb*
1  The soldiers attacked the enemy.
    DIFFERENT WAYS TO ATTACK ARE   **to ambush**   **to assault**   **to bomb**
    **to bombard**   **to charge**   **to raid**
2  Two men attacked him in the street.
    OTHER VERBS YOU MIGHT USE ARE   **to mug**   **to set on**
The opposite is **defend**

**attempt** *verb*
Jo attempted to swim ten lengths.
    OTHER VERBS AND PHRASES ARE   **to endeavour**   **to exert yourself**
    **to make an effort**   **to try**

**attend** *verb*
1  We attended the school concert.
    PHRASES YOU MIGHT USE ARE   **to be present at**   **to go to**
2  Are you attending to me?
    OTHER VERBS YOU MIGHT USE ARE   **to listen**   **to pay attention**

**attract** *verb*
The bright lights attracted us.
OTHER VERBS YOU MIGHT USE ARE **to appeal to    to fascinate
to interest**

**attractive** *adjective*
1  an attractive person.
OTHER WORDS YOU MIGHT USE ARE **beautiful    charming
glamorous    good-looking    handsome    likeable    pleasant
pretty**
The opposite is **ugly**
2  an attractive idea.
OTHER WORDS ARE **appealing    interesting    pleasing    tempting**
The opposite is **boring**

**audience** *noun*
The audience enjoyed the play.
OTHER WORDS YOU MIGHT USE ARE **listeners    spectators**

**author** *noun*
ANOTHER WORD IS **writer**
For other words, see **write**

**available** *adjective*
Our magazine is now available.
OTHER WORDS YOU MIGHT USE ARE **on sale    ready**

**average** *adjective*
It was an average kind of day.
OTHER WORDS YOU MIGHT USE ARE **middling    normal    ordinary
typical    usual**
The opposite is **extraordinary**

**avoid** *verb*
Sam avoided the washing-up.
OTHER VERBS YOU MIGHT USE ARE **to dodge    to escape    to get out of
to shirk**

**awake** *adjective*
I was awake all night because of the storm.
OTHER WORDS YOU MIGHT USE ARE **alert    conscious**
The opposite is **asleep**

**award** *noun*
Jo got an award for swimming ten lengths.
OTHER WORDS YOU MIGHT USE ARE **badge** **medal** **prize** **reward** **trophy**

**aware** *adjective*
Jo was aware that Mum would worry if she was late.
ANOTHER WORD IS **conscious**

**awful** *adjective*
For other words, see **bad**

**awkward** *adjective*
1 Ducks look awkward when they walk on dry land.
ANOTHER WORD IS **clumsy**
2 Are you trying to be awkward?
OTHER WORDS ARE **difficult** **uncooperative**
3 The visitors came at an awkward time.
ANOTHER WORD IS **inconvenient**

# Bb

**baby** *noun*
ANOTHER WORD IS **infant**
A baby just starting to walk is a **toddler**.

**back** *noun*
I had to wait at the back of the queue.
OTHER WORDS ARE **end** **rear** **tail end**
The opposite is **front**

**back** *verb*
Dad backed the car into the gate.
ANOTHER VERB IS **to reverse**

**bad** *adjective*

THIS WORD HAS MANY USES. HERE ARE SOME OF THE WAYS YOU CAN USE IT, AND SOME OTHER WORDS YOU COULD CHOOSE

1 a bad deed.
**criminal   cruel   evil   immoral   sinful villainous   wicked   wrong**

2 a bad child.
**disobedient   mischievous   naughty**

3 a bad player.
**hopeless   incompetent   rotten   useless**

4 a bad accident.
**appalling   awful   dreadful   frightful   horrible serious   severe   shocking   terrible**

5 a bad piece of work.
**careless   incorrect   poor   shoddy   useless weak   worthless**

6 bad food.
**decayed   mouldy   rotten   smelly**

7 a bad smell.
**nasty   objectionable   offensive   revolting sickening   unpleasant**

8 a bad habit.
**dangerous   harmful   nasty   unhealthy**

9 I feel bad today.
**feeble   ill   poorly   sick   unwell**

The opposite is **good**

**badge** *noun*
a school badge.
OTHER WORDS YOU MIGHT USE ARE   **crest   emblem   sign   symbol**

**bad-tempered** *adjective*
OTHER WORDS YOU MIGHT USE ARE   **angry   cross   grumpy   irritable short-tempered**
The opposite is **cheerful**

**bag** *noun*
For other words, see **container**

**bake** *verb*
For other ways to cook things, see **cook**

# ball *noun*

THINGS SHAPED LIKE A BALL ARE    **globe**    **sphere**

For other shapes, see **shape**

# ban *verb*

They banned smoking on the buses.

OTHER VERBS YOU MIGHT USE ARE    **to forbid**    **to make illegal**    **to prohibit**

# band *noun*

1 Robin Hood lived with a band of outlaws.

ANOTHER WORD IS **gang**

2 Jo plays the guitar in a band.

OTHER WORDS ARE    **group**    **orchestra**

For more words to do with music, see **music**

3 A wooden barrel has bands of metal round it.

OTHER WORDS ARE    **hoop**    **loop**    **ring**

# bang *noun*

1 We heard a loud bang.

OTHER WORDS YOU MIGHT USE ARE    **blast**    **boom**    **crash**    **explosion**

For other sounds, see **sound**

2 I got a nasty bang on the head.

OTHER WORDS ARE    **blow**    **bump**    **hit**    **knock**

# banish *verb*

The traitor was banished from his country.

OTHER VERBS ARE    **to exile**    **to expel**    **to send away**

# bank *noun*

We sat on a grassy bank.

OTHER WORDS YOU MIGHT USE ARE    **embankment**    **slope**

# banner *noun*

The people in the procession waved banners.

OTHER WORDS YOU MIGHT USE ARE    **flag**    **standard**    **streamer**

# banquet *noun*

OTHER WORDS ARE    **dinner**    **feast**    (*informal*) **spread**

For other words, see **meal**

## bar *noun*
1 a wooden bar.
   OTHER WORDS YOU MIGHT USE ARE **beam** **rail** **rod**
2 an iron bar.
   ANOTHER WORD YOU MIGHT USE IS **girder**
3 a bar of chocolate.
   ANOTHER WORD IS **block**

## bare *adjective*
OTHER WORDS YOU MIGHT USE ARE **naked** **nude** **unclothed**
**uncovered** **undressed**

## barely *adverb*
Sam was so tired that he could barely keep his eyes open.
OTHER WORDS YOU MIGHT USE ARE **hardly** **only just** **scarcely**

## barrel *noun*
For other containers, see **container**

## barren *adjective*
The desert was completely barren.
OTHER WORDS YOU MIGHT USE ARE **bare** **lifeless** **sterile**

## barrier *noun*
They put up a barrier to keep the crowd off the field.
OTHER WORDS ARE **barricade** **fence** **railings** **wall**

## base *noun*
1 Dad used cement to make a firm base for the shed.
   ANOTHER WORD IS **foundation**
2 Don't sit near the base of the cliff.
   OTHER WORDS YOU MIGHT USE ARE **bottom** **foot**
3 After a long march, the soldiers returned to their base.
   OTHER WORDS ARE **depot** **headquarters**

## bashful *adjective*
The little boy was too bashful to say 'thank you'.
OTHER WORDS YOU MIGHT USE ARE **modest** **shy** **timid**

## basic *adjective*
I know the basic facts, but I've still got a lot to learn.
OTHER WORDS ARE **chief** **essential** **important** **main**
**principal**

## basin *noun*
OTHER WORDS ARE    **bowl    dish**

## basket *noun*
For other kinds of container, see **container**

---

### bat *noun*
The special bat you use in tennis is a **racket**.
The stick you hit the ball with in golf is a **club**.

---

### bath *noun*
SPECIAL KINDS OF BATH ARE
**Jacuzzi    sauna    shower**

---

## battle *noun*
For other words, see **war**

## bay *noun*
OTHER WORDS YOU MIGHT USE ARE    **cove    estuary    gulf    inlet**

## beach *noun*
Jo and Sam spent a happy day at the beach.
OTHER WORDS YOU MIGHT USE ARE    **sands    shore**
For other words, see **seaside**

## beam *noun*
1 a beam of wood.
OTHER WORDS YOU MIGHT USE ARE    **bar    plank**
2 a beam of light.
OTHER WORDS ARE    **ray    shaft**

## beam *verb*
He beamed when he heard my voice.
OTHER VERBS YOU MIGHT USE ARE    **to grin    to laugh    to look happy
to smile**

## bear *verb*
1 Will this branch bear my weight?
> OTHER VERBS YOU MIGHT USE ARE   **to carry**   **to hold**
> **to support**
2 She bore the pain bravely.
> OTHER VERBS ARE   **to endure**   **to put up with**   **to stand**
> **to suffer**

## beast *noun*
> OTHER WORDS YOU MIGHT USE ARE   **animal**   **creature**
> ANIMALS THAT MAKE YOU AFRAID ARE   **brute**   **monster**

## beat *verb*
1 We beat our opponents 6-0.
> OTHER VERBS YOU MIGHT USE ARE   **to conquer**   **to defeat**
> **to outdo**   **to overcome**   (*informal*) **to thrash**
2 It's cruel to beat animals.
For other verbs, see **hit**
3 Dad beat some eggs to make an omelette.
> OTHER VERBS ARE   **to mix**   **to stir**   **to whisk**
4 When I run my heart beats fast.
> OTHER VERBS ARE   **to knock**   **to pound**   **to throb**

## beautiful *adjective*
1 a beautiful bride.
> OTHER WORDS YOU MIGHT USE ARE   **attractive**   **charming**
> **elegant**   **glamorous**   **good-looking**   **gorgeous**
> **handsome**   **lovely**   **pretty**
The opposite is **ugly**
2 beautiful weather.
> OTHER WORDS ARE   **enjoyable**   **fine**   **good**   **nice**
> **pleasant**

## beckon *verb*
Sam beckoned to me to join him.
> OTHER VERBS YOU MIGHT USE ARE   **to make a sign**   **to signal**

## become *verb*
In time the little shoot will become a big tree.
> PHRASES YOU MIGHT USE ARE   **to change into**   **to grow into**
> **to turn into**

**bed** *noun*
PARTS OF A BED ARE
**base     headboard     mattress**

A bed with a base and a mattress is a **divan**.
Two beds one above the other are **bunks**.
A bunk on a ship is a **berth**.
An old-fashioned bed with curtains round is a **four-poster**.

THINGS YOU USE TO MAKE A BED ARE
**bedclothes** or **bedding**

DIFFERENT KINDS OF BEDCLOTHES ARE
**bed linen     bedspread     blanket     counterpane
coverlet     duvet     eiderdown     pillow     pillowcase
quilt     sheet**

**bee** *noun*
KINDS OF BEE ARE     **bumble-bee     drone     queen bee**

**begin** *verb*
When does the film begin?
OTHER VERBS YOU MIGHT USE ARE     **to commence**     (*informal*) **to get going
to start**
The opposite is **end**

**behave** *verb*
1 Sam behaved strangely today.
ANOTHER VERB IS **to act**
2 Our teacher told us to behave.
A PHRASE IS **to be good**

**behaviour** *noun*
Our teacher praised our good behaviour.
OTHER WORDS ARE     **conduct     manners**

**belief** *noun*
1 It's my belief that ghosts don't exist.
OTHER WORDS YOU MIGHT USE ARE     **opinion     view**
2 We had a special service where people with different religious beliefs said prayers together.
OTHER WORDS ARE     **creed     faith     religion**

## believe *verb*
1 You can't believe all he says.
OTHER VERBS YOU MIGHT USE ARE   **to accept   to rely on   to trust**
2 I believe he cheated.
OTHER VERBS ARE   **to consider   to feel sure   to think**

---

### bell *noun*
DIFFERENT WAYS BELLS SOUND ARE
**chime   clang   jangle   jingle   peal   ping   ring   tinkle   toll**

---

## belongings *noun*
Be sure to take your belongings when you get off the train.
OTHER WORDS YOU MIGHT USE ARE   **possessions   property   things**

## bench *noun*
1 a bench to sit on.
OTHER WORDS YOU MIGHT USE ARE   **form   seat**
2 a carpenter's bench.
ANOTHER WORD IS **table**

## bend *noun*
a bend in the road.
OTHER WORDS YOU MIGHT USE ARE **corner   curve   turn   twist**

## bend *verb*
1 The blacksmith bent the metal into fantastic shapes.
OTHER VERBS YOU MIGHT USE ARE   **to coil   to curl   to curve   to distort   to fold   to twist   to wind**
2 He was so tall that he had to bend to go through the door.
OTHER VERBS ARE   **to bow down   to crouch   to duck   to stoop**

## bet *verb*
ANOTHER VERB IS **to gamble**
KINDS OF BETTING ARE   **lottery   the pools**

## bewildered *adjective*
We were bewildered by all the different traffic signs.
OTHER WORDS YOU MIGHT USE ARE   **confused   muddled   puzzled**

## **bewitched** *adjective*
I was bewitched by the magical music.
OTHER WORDS ARE    **charmed    enchanted    spellbound**

## **biased** *adjective*
The referee was biased.
OTHER WORDS YOU MIGHT USE ARE    **one-sided    prejudiced    unfair**

## **big** *adjective*
1 a big person. a big thing.
OTHER WORDS YOU MIGHT USE ARE    **colossal    enormous    fat    giant    gigantic    great    huge    large    massive    monstrous    tall**
2 a big hall.
OTHER WORDS ARE    **roomy    spacious    vast**
3 a big event.
OTHER WORDS ARE    **grand    impressive    spectacular**
4 a big decision.
OTHER WORDS ARE    **important    serious**
The opposite is **small**

## **bill** *noun*
Keep the bill to prove how much you paid.
OTHER WORDS YOU MIGHT USE ARE    **account    receipt**

## **bind** *verb*
They bound the prisoner's hands.
OTHER VERBS YOU MIGHT USE ARE    **to secure    to tie**

## **bird** *noun*, see next page.

## **bit** *noun*
1 I don't want it all, only a bit of it.
OTHER WORDS YOU MIGHT USE ARE    **chunk    crumb    dollop    fraction    morsel    part    piece    portion    section**
2 Mum told Jo to sweep up every bit of the broken mug.
OTHER WORDS ARE    **chip    fragment    speck    splinter**
3 I picked up the bits of paper and put them in the rubbish bin.
ANOTHER WORD IS **scrap**

## **bite** *verb*
The dog tried to bite me!
OTHER VERBS YOU MIGHT USE ARE    **to nip    to snap at**
For other words, see **eat**

# bird *noun*

A male bird is a **cock**.
A female bird is a **hen**.

WORDS FOR A YOUNG BIRD ARE
**chick          fledgling      nestling**

SOME BIRDS KEPT AS PETS ARE
**budgerigar    canary        cockatoo      macaw
parakeet      parrot**

BIRDS KEPT ON A FARM ARE **poultry**

KINDS OF POULTRY ARE
**chicken       duck          goose         turkey**

COMMON BRITISH GARDEN BIRDS ARE
**blackbird     bullfinch     chaffinch     goldfinch
greenfinch    robin         sparrow       starling
thrush        tit           wren**

SOME BIRDS YOU MIGHT SEE OR HEAR IN THE BRITISH COUNTRYSIDE
ARE
**crow          cuckoo        curlew        dove
grouse        jackdaw       jay           lapwing
lark          linnet        magpie        martin
nightingale   partridge     peewit        pheasant
pigeon        raven         rook          skylark
swallow       swift         wagtail       warbler
woodpecker    yellowhammer**

SOME BIRDS OF PREY ARE
**buzzard       eagle         falcon        hawk
kestrel       kite          osprey        owl
sparrowhawk**

BIRDS THAT LIVE NEAR WATER ARE
**coot          duck          flamingo      goose
grebe         heron         kingfisher    moorhen
pelican       swan**

SOME SEA BIRDS ARE
**cormorant     puffin        seagull       tern**

OTHER BIRDS ARE
**ostrich       peacock       penguin       stork
vulture**

## bitter *adjective*
1 a bitter taste.
OTHER WORDS YOU MIGHT USE ARE   **acid   harsh   sharp   sour**
2 a bitter wind.
OTHER WORDS ARE   **biting   piercing**
For other words, see **cold**
3 a bitter quarrel.
OTHER WORDS ARE   **angry   resentful   spiteful**

## black *adjective*
OTHER WORDS ARE   **dark   inky   pitch-black   sooty**

---

## blade *noun*
THINGS WITH A SHARP BLADE ARE
**axe   dagger   knife   razor   scissors   shears   sword**

---

## blame *verb*
When she saw the mess, Mum blamed me!
OTHER VERBS YOU MIGHT USE ARE   **to accuse   to criticise   to scold**

## blank *adjective*
1 a blank piece of paper.
OTHER WORDS YOU MIGHT USE ARE   **clean   unmarked   unused**
2 Fill in the blank spaces.
ANOTHER WORD IS **empty**

## blast *noun*
1 a blast of cold air.
For other words, see **wind**
2 the blast of a bomb.
OTHER WORDS ARE   **bang   boom   explosion**

## blaze *verb*
OTHER VERBS YOU MIGHT USE ARE   **to burn   to flame   to flare up**
For other words, see **fire**

## bleak *adjective*
a bleak hillside.
OTHER WORDS YOU MIGHT USE ARE   **bare   cold   exposed   miserable   windswept   windy**

## blend *verb*
Dad blended the ingredients to make a cake.
> OTHER VERBS YOU MIGHT USE ARE **to beat   to combine   to mix   to stir together   to whisk**

## blessed *adjective*
> OTHER WORDS ARE **holy   sacred**

## blind *adjective*
> OTHER WORDS YOU MIGHT USE ARE **sightless   visually handicapped**

## block *noun*
a block of concrete.
> OTHER WORDS ARE **chunk   lump   slab**

## block *verb*
1 A flock of sheep blocked the road.
> ANOTHER VERB IS **to obstruct**
2 The roads were blocked with traffic.
> OTHER VERBS YOU MIGHT USE ARE **to clog   to jam**

## bloom *verb*
Roses bloom in the summer.
> OTHER VERBS YOU MIGHT USE ARE **to blossom   to flower**

## blossom *noun*
In spring we have masses of blossom on our apple tree.
> OTHER WORDS ARE **blooms   flowers**

## blow *noun*
Sam got a nasty blow on the head.
> For other words, see **hit**

## blow *verb*
The wolf tried to blow the pigs' house down.
> ANOTHER VERB IS **to puff**

**to blow up a tyre**
> ANOTHER VERB IS **to inflate**

**to blow up with a loud bang**
> OTHER VERBS YOU MIGHT USE ARE **to burst   to explode   to go off**

## blunt *adjective*
The opposite is **sharp**

## blurred *adjective*
a blurred photograph.
OTHER WORDS YOU MIGHT USE ARE   **cloudy   faint   fuzzy   hazy
misty   unclear   unfocused**
The opposite is **clear**

## blush *verb*
She blushed when the teacher praised her work.
OTHER VERBS YOU MIGHT USE ARE   **to flush   to go red   to redden**

## boast *verb*
He boasted that he was best at everything.
ANOTHER VERB IS **to brag**

---

### boat *noun*
OTHER WORDS ARE
**craft   ship   vessel**

DIFFERENT KINDS OF BOAT ARE

| | | | |
|---|---|---|---|
| **aircraft carrier** | **barge** | **battleship** | **canoe** |
| **cruiser** | **destroyer** | **dinghy** | **ferry** |
| **galleon** | **house boat** | **junk** | **launch** |
| **lifeboat** | **liner** | **motor boat** | **oil tanker** |
| **paddle steamer** | **punt** | **raft** | **rowing boat** |
| **sailing boat** | **speed-boat** | **steamer** | **submarine** |
| **tanker** | **trawler** | **tug** | **warship** |
| **yacht** | | | |

---

## body *noun*, see next page

## bodyguard *noun*
OTHER WORDS YOU MIGHT USE ARE   **guard**   (*informal*) **minder   protector**

## bog *noun*
OTHER WORDS ARE   **marsh   quicksands   swamp**

## boil *verb*
1 Is the water boiling?
ANOTHER VERB IS **to bubble**
2 Jo put the potatoes on to boil.
For other ways to cook things, see **cook**

## body *noun*

Another word for the body of a dead person is **corpse**.
Another word for the body of a dead animal is **carcass**.
The main part of your body, not including the head, arms, and legs, is the **trunk**.

PARTS OF YOUR TRUNK ARE
**abdomen** or **tummy**   **back**   **bottom** or **buttocks**   **breast**   **chest**   **navel** or **tummy button**   **nipples**   **shoulders**

THE INNER ORGANS OF YOUR BODY INCLUDE
**bladder**   **bowels**   **glands**   **heart**   **intestines**   **kidneys**   **liver**   **lungs**   **ovaries**   **stomach**   **womb**

Your **arteries** take blood from the heart to other parts of the body, and your **veins** take blood back to the heart.

Your **muscles** are the parts you use when you move.
The **nerves** take messages to and from the brain.
Your **sexual organs** are your **penis** or **vagina**.

PARTS OF YOUR HEAD ARE
**brain**   **cheeks**   **chin**   **ears**   **eyes**   **forehead**   **gums**   **hair**   **jaw**   **lips**   **mouth**   **nose**   **nostrils**   **scalp**   **teeth**   **throat**   **tongue**

Your arms and legs are your **limbs**.

PARTS OF YOUR ARM ARE
**elbow**   **hand**   **shoulder**   **wrist**

PARTS OF YOUR HAND ARE
**fingers**   **fingernails**   **knuckles**   **palm**   **thumb**

PARTS OF YOUR LEG ARE
**ankle**   **calf**   **foot**   **knee**   **shin**   **thigh**

PARTS OF YOUR FOOT ARE
**heel**   **instep**   **toe**   **toenails**

Your bones are your **skeleton**.

THE MAIN BONES OF YOUR HEAD ARE   **jaw**   **skull**

IMPORTANT BONES IN YOUR BODY ARE
**backbone** or **spine** or **vertebrae**   **pelvis**   **ribs**

THE MAIN JOINTS IN YOUR BODY ARE
**ankle**   **elbow**   **hip**   **knee**   **knuckle**   **neck**   **shoulder**   **vertebra**   **wrist**

## bold *adjective*

1 a bold deed.
For other words, see **brave**
2 bold handwriting.
   OTHER WORDS YOU MIGHT USE ARE     **big     clear     large**

## bolt *verb*

1 Remember to bolt the back door.
   OTHER VERBS YOU MIGHT USE ARE     **to bar     to fasten     to lock**
2 The horse bolted.
   OTHER VERBS ARE     **to escape     to run away**
For other words, see **run**
3 Don't bolt down your food!
   OTHER VERBS ARE     **to gobble     to gulp**

## bone *noun*

For other words you might use, see **body**

---

## book *noun*

VARIOUS KINDS OF BOOK ARE

**album     annual     atlas     diary     dictionary
directory     encyclopedia     hymn book     novel
paperback     story book     thesaurus**

---

## boot *noun*

For other things you wear on your feet, see **shoe**

## bore *verb*

to bore a hole through something.
   OTHER VERBS YOU MIGHT USE ARE     **to drill     to pierce**

## boring *adjective*

a boring television programme.
   OTHER WORDS YOU MIGHT USE ARE     **dreary     dry     dull     monotonous
tedious     tiresome     uninteresting     wearisome**
The opposite is **interesting**

## borrow *verb*

If someone lets you use something for a time, you borrow it.
If you give something to someone to use, you lend it.

## boss *noun*
For other words, see **chief**

## bother *verb*
Is the loud music bothering you?
> OTHER VERBS YOU MIGHT USE ARE **to annoy** **to disturb** **to irritate** **to pester** **to trouble** **to upset** **to worry**

## bottle *noun*
For other kinds of container, see **container**

## bottom *noun*
1 the bottom of a wall.
> OTHER WORDS YOU MIGHT USE ARE **base** **foot** **foundation**

The opposite is **top**
2 the bottom of the sea.
> ANOTHER WORD IS **bed**

The opposite is **surface**
3 the bottom that you sit on.
> OTHER WORDS ARE **backside** **behind** **buttocks**

## boulder *noun*
There were some huge boulders on the beach.
> OTHER WORDS ARE **rock** **stone**

## bounce *verb*
The ball bounced off the wall.
> ANOTHER VERB IS **to rebound**

## bound *verb*
The dog bounded over the gate.
> OTHER VERBS YOU MIGHT USE ARE **to jump** **to leap** **to spring**

## bound *adjective*
**bound to**
It's bound to rain if we go out.
> PHRASES ARE **certain to** **sure to**

**bound for**
The rocket is bound for the moon.
> PHRASES YOU MIGHT USE ARE **aimed at** **going towards**

## boundary *noun*
> OTHER WORDS YOU MIGHT USE ARE **border** **edge** **frontier** **limit**

## bouquet *noun*
a bouquet of flowers.
OTHER WORDS YOU MIGHT USE ARE          bunch          posy          spray

## bowl *noun*
OTHER WORDS YOU MIGHT USE ARE          basin          dish          tureen

## bowl *verb*
For other verbs, see **throw**

## box *noun*
OTHER WORDS YOU MIGHT USE ARE          carton          case          chest          crate

## brains *noun*
Use your brains!
OTHER WORDS YOU MIGHT USE ARE          intelligence          mind          reason
**understanding**

## branch *noun*
a branch of a tree.
OTHER WORDS YOU MIGHT USE ARE          bough          limb

## brand *noun*
Which brand of butter do you buy?
OTHER WORDS YOU MIGHT USE ARE          kind          make

## brave *adjective*
OTHER WORDS YOU MIGHT USE ARE          bold          courageous          daring
**fearless          heroic          plucky**
The opposite is **cowardly**

## bravery *noun*
OTHER WORDS YOU MIGHT USE ARE          courage          daring          heroism
**valour**

## bread *noun*
DIFFERENT FORMS IN WHICH YOU BUY BREAD ARE
**baguette          French stick          loaf          roll
sliced bread**

For different kinds of bread, see **food**

## break *noun*

1 a break in a pipe. a break in the fence.

OTHER WORDS YOU MIGHT USE ARE   crack   cut   gap   hole   leak   opening   slit   split   tear

2 a break in a game.

OTHER WORDS ARE   half time   interval   lull   pause   rest

---

### break *verb*

DIFFERENT WAYS THINGS BREAK ARE

to chip   to collapse   to crack   to crumble   to decay   to fall apart   to fracture   to shatter   to snap   to splinter   to split

DIFFERENT WAYS YOU CAN BREAK THINGS ARE

to crush   to demolish   to destroy   to drop   to smash   to squash   to wreck

---

## breed *noun*

What breed of dog is that?

OTHER WORDS YOU MIGHT USE ARE   kind   species   variety

## breed *verb*

Most birds breed in the spring.

OTHER VERBS YOU MIGHT USE ARE   to produce young ones   to reproduce

## bridge *noun*

KINDS OF BRIDGE ARE   fly-over   viaduct

## brief *adjective*

OTHER WORDS YOU MIGHT USE ARE   concise   little   short

The opposite is **long**

## bright *adjective*

1 bright lights.

OTHER WORDS YOU MIGHT USE ARE   brilliant   colourful   dazzling   flashing   gleaming   glittering   shining   shiny   sparkling

2 a bright boy.

OTHER WORDS ARE   brainy   clever   intelligent   quick   smart

3 a bright smile.

OTHER WORDS ARE   cheerful   happy   radiant

The opposite is **dull**

## brilliant *adjective*
For other words, see **bright**

## brim *noun*
My cup was full to the brim.

OTHER WORDS YOU MIGHT USE ARE   **brink   edge   rim   top**

## bring *verb*
1 I helped to bring the shopping home.

OTHER VERBS YOU MIGHT USE ARE   **to carry   to fetch   to take**

2 The captain brought her team onto the field.

OTHER VERBS ARE   **to guide   to lead**

## brisk *adjective*
We set off at a brisk walk.

OTHER WORDS YOU MIGHT USE ARE   **fast   lively   quick   rapid**

## brittle *adjective*
The shell of an egg is brittle.

OTHER WORDS YOU MIGHT USE ARE   **fragile   weak**

The opposite is **strong**

## broad *adjective*
a broad area of sand.

OTHER WORDS YOU MIGHT USE ARE   **extensive   large   wide**

The opposite is **narrow**

## brook *noun*
ANOTHER WORD IS **stream**

## brother *noun*
For other members of a family, see **family**

## brush *noun*
A brush with a long handle is a **broom**.

## bubbles *noun*
OTHER WORDS YOU MIGHT USE ARE   **foam   froth   lather   suds**

## bubbly *adjective*
OTHER WORDS YOU MIGHT USE ARE   **boiling   effervescent   fizzy   foaming   sparkling**

## buffet *noun*
1 For other places where you can buy and eat food, see **café**
2 For other kinds of meal, see **meal**

---

## build *verb*
OTHER VERBS YOU MIGHT USE ARE    **to construct    to erect    to put up**

## building *noun*
VARIOUS BUILDINGS ARE

| | | | |
|---|---|---|---|
| abbey | barn | bungalow | cabin |
| castle | cathedral | chapel | church |
| cinema | cottage | factory | farmhouse |
| flats | garage | hotel | house |
| inn | lighthouse | mansion | monastery |
| mosque | museum | pagoda | palace |
| police-station | post office | power station | prison |
| pub | restaurant | shop | skyscraper |
| stable | synagogue | temple | theatre |
| tower | warehouse | windmill | |

PARTS OF BUILDINGS ARE

**balcony    doors    floors    foyer    lobby    passage
porch    rooms    staircase    veranda    walls
windows**

TOP PARTS OF A BUILDING ARE
**ceilings    chimney    dome    eaves    gable    gutters
rafters    roof    spire    steeple    tower    turret**
UNDERGROUND PARTS OF A BUILDING ARE
**basement    cellar    crypt    foundations**

For various rooms in a house, see **home**

---

## bully *verb*
I was angry with the big girl who bullied the small ones.
OTHER VERBS YOU MIGHT USE ARE    **to frighten    to persecute
to threaten    to torment**

## bump *noun*
Jo has a nasty bump on the head.
OTHER WORDS YOU MIGHT USE ARE    **bulge    hump    lump    swelling**

## bump *verb*
For other words, see **hit**

# bunch *noun*
1 a bunch of carrots.
OTHER WORDS YOU MIGHT USE ARE **clump** **cluster**
2 a bunch of flowers.
OTHER WORDS ARE **bouquet** **posy** **spray**
3 a bunch of friends.
OTHER WORDS ARE **crowd** **gathering** **group** **set**

# bundle *noun*
a bundle of papers.
OTHER WORDS YOU MIGHT USE ARE **pack** **package** **parcel** **sheaf**

# burden *noun*
a heavy burden.
OTHER WORDS YOU MIGHT USE ARE **load** **weight**

# burglar *noun*
OTHER WORDS YOU MIGHT USE ARE **intruder** **robber** **thief**
For other words, see **steal**

# burn *verb*
OTHER VERBS YOU MIGHT USE ARE **blaze** **flame** **flare** **smoulder**
WAYS YOU CAN DAMAGE THINGS BY HEAT ARE **to char** **to scald** **to scorch** **to singe**
To burn a dead person's body is **to cremate** it.
For other useful words, see **fire**

# burrow *noun*
Rabbits live in a burrow.
OTHER WORDS YOU MIGHT USE ARE **hole** **tunnel**
A place where rabbits make a lot of burrows is a **warren**.

# burst *verb*
1 He burst open the door.
OTHER VERBS YOU MIGHT USE ARE **to break** **to force open**
2 The balloon burst.
OTHER VERBS ARE **to explode** **to pop**

# bush *noun*
ANOTHER WORD IS **shrub**

## business *noun*
1 Dad's business is selling cars.
OTHER WORDS YOU MIGHT USE ARE **job** **occupation** **trade** **work**
2 I work for a computer business.
OTHER WORDS ARE **company** **firm** **industry** **organization** **shop**
3 Don't be nosey - it's none of your business!
OTHER WORDS ARE **affair** **concern**

## busy *adjective*
1 Our teacher is always busy.
OTHER WORDS YOU MIGHT USE ARE **active** **doing things** **occupied** (*informal*) **on the go**
The opposite is **idle**
2 The shops are busy during the sales.
OTHER WORDS ARE **bustling** **lively**

## buy *verb*
I bought my bike for £30.
OTHER VERBS YOU MIGHT USE ARE **to get** **to obtain** **to purchase**

# Cc

## cable *noun*
1 electric cables.
OTHER WORDS YOU MIGHT USE ARE **flex** **lead** **wire**
2 cables for tying up a ship.
OTHER WORDS ARE **cord** **line** **rope**

## café *noun*
We went into a café for a snack.
OTHER PLACES WHERE YOU MIGHT GET THINGS TO EAT ARE
**bar** **bistro** **buffet** **cafeteria** **canteen**
**fish and chip shop** **restaurant** **snack bar**
**take-away**

**cage** *noun*

> OTHER WORDS FOR PLACES TO KEEP ANIMALS IN ARE
>> **an aviary for birds**
>> **a coop for chickens**
>> **an enclosure for zoo animals**
>> **a hutch for rabbits**
>> **a kennel for a dog**
>> **a pen for sheep**

**cake** *noun*
For kinds of cake, see **food**

**call** *verb*
1 I heard someone call.
   OTHER VERBS YOU MIGHT USE ARE    **to cry out    to exclaim    to shout    to yell**
2 They called the baby Robert.
   ANOTHER VERB IS **to name**
3 Mum called us in for dinner.
   OTHER VERBS ARE    **to send for    to summon**
4 I didn't call because the phone wasn't working.
   OTHER VERBS ARE    **to phone    to ring    to telephone**

**calm** *adjective*
1 a calm sea.
   OTHER WORDS YOU MIGHT USE ARE    **even    flat    peaceful    smooth    still**
The opposite is **stormy**
2 Don't panic - keep calm!
   OTHER WORDS ARE    **cool    patient    quiet    sensible**

**camera** *noun*

> DIFFERENT KINDS OF CAMERA ARE
>> **camcorder    cine-camera    Polaroid**
> PARTS OF A CAMERA ARE
>> **flash    focus    lens    light meter    shutter    viewfinder    zoom lens**

## cancel *verb*
They cancelled the game because of the snow.
OTHER VERBS YOU MIGHT USE ARE   **to abandon**   **to give up**   **to postpone**

## cap *noun*
For things you wear on your head, see **hat**

## capacity *noun*
What is the capacity of this kettle?
OTHER WORDS YOU MIGHT USE ARE   **size**   **volume**

## captain *noun*
the captain of a team.
For words for people in charge, see **chief**

## captive *noun*
The captives were locked in a dungeon.
OTHER WORDS YOU MIGHT USE ARE   **hostage**   **prisoner**

## capture *verb*
Did they capture the thief?
OTHER VERBS YOU MIGHT USE ARE   **to arrest**   **to catch**   **to seize**

---

## car *noun*
VARIOUS KINDS OF CAR ARE
**estate**   **hatchback**   **racing car**   **saloon**   **taxi**
For other things you ride in, see **travel**

---

## card *noun*
1 CARDS YOU CAN SEND TO PEOPLE ARE
**birthday card**   **Christmas card**   **get-well card**
**invitation**   **postcard**   **Valentine**

2 IN CARD GAMES, THE SUITS ARE
**clubs**   **diamonds**   **hearts**   **spades**
THE CARDS WITH PICTURES ON ARE
**Jack**   **Joker**   **King**   **Queen**

## care *noun*

1 He hasn't a care in the world!
   OTHER WORDS YOU MIGHT USE ARE    **trouble    worry**
2 Mum drives with great care.
   OTHER WORDS ARE    **attention    caution**

**to take care**

Take care when you cross the road.
   VERBS YOU MIGHT USE ARE    **to be careful    to look out**

**to take care of**

I took care of Jo's money while she went swimming.
   PHRASES YOU MIGHT USE ARE    **to keep something safe**
   **to look after something**

## care *verb*

He doesn't care who wins.
   ANOTHER VERB IS **to mind**

**to care for**

1 We care for our pets.
   OTHER VERBS ARE    **to look after    to protect    to take care of**
2 You send a Valentine card to show that you care for someone.
For other words, see **love**

## careful *adjective*

1 Mum is a careful driver.
   OTHER WORDS YOU MIGHT USE ARE    **alert    attentive    cautious**
2 Jo's work is always careful.
   OTHER WORDS ARE    **neat    orderly    organized    thorough**
The opposite is **careless**

## careless *adjective*

1 careless driving.
   OTHER WORDS YOU MIGHT USE ARE    **negligent    reckless    thoughtless**
2 careless work.
   OTHER WORDS ARE    **disorganized    hasty    messy    untidy**
The opposite is **careful**

## cargo *noun*

The ship unloaded its cargo at the docks.
   OTHER WORDS YOU MIGHT USE ARE    **freight    goods**

## carnival *noun*

   OTHER WORDS YOU MIGHT USE ARE    **fair    festival    fête    gala    show**

## carriage *noun*
For other things you can ride in, see **travel**

## carry *verb*
1 Sam carried the food into the dining room.
OTHER VERBS YOU MIGHT USE ARE    **to bring    to lift    to move    to take    to transfer**
2 Trains can carry a lot of passengers.
OTHER VERBS ARE    **to convey    to transport**

## cart *noun*
OTHER WORDS YOU MIGHT USE ARE    **barrow    wagon    wheelbarrow**

## carve *verb*
For ways to cut things, see **cut**

## case *noun*
For other words, see **box**

## castle *noun*
OTHER WORDS YOU MIGHT USE ARE
**fort    fortress**
PARTS OF A CASTLE ARE
**battlements    courtyard    drawbridge    dungeon
keep    moat    parapet    portcullis    tower    turret**

## cat *noun*
INFORMAL WORDS ARE
**moggy    pussy    pussycat**
A young cat is a **kitten**.
A male cat is a **tomcat**.
KINDS OF CAT ARE
**Manx    marmalade cat    Persian    Siamese    tabby**

For other pets, see **pet**
'BIG CATS' OR WILD ANIMALS RELATED TO CATS ARE
**cheetah    jaguar    leopard    lion    lynx    panther
puma    tiger    wildcat**

## catalogue *noun*
1 a shopping catalogue.
ANOTHER WORD IS **brochure**
2 a catalogue of books in the library.
OTHER WORDS FOR A LIST OF NAMES OR THINGS YOU MIGHT WANT TO LOOK UP ARE
**directory    index    register**

## catch *verb*
1 to catch a ball.
OTHER VERBS YOU MIGHT USE ARE    **to grasp    to hold    to seize
to take hold of**
The opposite is **miss**
2 to catch a thief.
OTHER VERBS ARE    **to arrest    to capture    to stop**
3 to catch fish.
OTHER VERBS ARE    **to hook    to net**
4 to catch an animal.
OTHER VERBS ARE    **to snare    to trap**
5 to catch a bus.
ANOTHER VERB IS **to get**

## catching *adjective*
I hope your cold isn't catching.
ANOTHER WORD IS **infectious**

---

## cattle *noun*
ANIMALS THAT FARMERS KEEP AS CATTLE ARE
**bull    bullock    cow    ox**
Young cattle are called **calves**.

---

## cause *verb*
The storm caused terrible floods.
PHRASES YOU MIGHT USE ARE    **to bring about    to lead to
to result in**

## cautious *adjective*
For other words, see **careful**

## cave *noun*
OTHER WORDS YOU MIGHT USE ARE    **cavern    grotto    pothole**

**cease** *verb*
Cease work!
OTHER VERBS YOU MIGHT USE ARE **to break off   to end   to finish   to stop**

**cellar** *noun*
OTHER UNDERGROUND PARTS OF BUILDINGS ARE   **basement   crypt   vault**

**cemetery** *noun*
ANOTHER WORD IS **graveyard**
A graveyard round a church is a **churchyard**.

**centre** *noun*
the centre of the earth.
OTHER WORDS YOU MIGHT USE ARE   **core   heart   middle**
The centre of a wheel is the **hub**.

**cereal** *noun*
OTHER WORDS ARE   **corn   grain**
1 KINDS OF CEREAL FARMERS GROW ARE
**barley   maize** or **sweet corn   oats   rice   rye   wheat**
2 KINDS OF BREAKFAST CEREAL ARE
**bran   cornflakes   muesli   porridge**

**certain** *adjective*
Are you certain it will rain?
OTHER WORDS YOU MIGHT USE ARE   **confident   definite   positive   sure**

**chair** *noun*
For things to sit on, see **seat**

**champion** *noun*
OTHER WORDS YOU MIGHT USE ARE   **hero   winner   victor**

**chance** *noun*
1 This is your last chance.
ANOTHER WORD IS **opportunity**

2 I met him by chance.
OTHER WORDS ARE  **accident    coincidence**

3 There's a chance of rain.
OTHER WORDS ARE  **danger    possibility    risk**

## change *noun*

I need some change to pay for the bus.
OTHER WORDS YOU MIGHT USE ARE  **cash    coins**

## change *verb*

1 I changed the end of my story.
OTHER VERBS YOU MIGHT USE ARE  **to adjust    to alter    to make different    to revise    to transform**

2 I want to change this apple for an orange.
OTHER VERBS YOU MIGHT USE ARE  **to exchange    to substitute    to switch    (*informal*) to swap**

3 Tadpoles change into frogs.
OTHER VERBS YOU MIGHT USE ARE  **to become    to develop into    to turn into**

## channel *noun*

1 a channel to take water away.
OTHER WORDS YOU MIGHT USE ARE  **canal    ditch    gutter**

2 a TV channel.
ANOTHER WORD IS **station**

## chaos *noun*

There was chaos when the lights went out.
OTHER WORDS YOU MIGHT USE ARE  **confusion    a mix-up**

## character *noun*

1 My favourite character in the pantomime was Cinderella.
OTHER WORDS YOU MIGHT USE ARE  **part    role**

2 Granny has a kind character.
OTHER WORDS ARE  **manner    nature    personality**

3 Who is that character at the bus stop?
OTHER WORDS ARE  **individual    person**

## charge *noun*

Mum left me in charge of the washing-up.
OTHER WORDS YOU MIGHT USE ARE  **command    control**

## charge *verb*
1  They charge £1 for an ice cream.
   PHRASES YOU MIGHT USE ARE    **to ask    to make you pay**
2  The soldiers charged the enemy.
   OTHER VERBS ARE    **to attack    to rush at**

## charm *verb*
He charmed us with his music.
   OTHER VERBS ARE    **to bewitch    to enchant    to fascinate**

## charming *adjective*
   OTHER WORDS YOU MIGHT USE ARE    **attractive    pretty**
For other words, see **beautiful**

## chart *noun*
   OTHER WORDS YOU MIGHT USE ARE    **diagram    graph    map    plan**

## chase *verb*
The dog chased the hare for miles.
   OTHER VERBS YOU MIGHT USE ARE    **to follow    to hunt    to pursue
   to tail    to track    to trail**

## chat, chatter *verbs*
For other verbs, see **talk**

## cheap *adjective*
Jo bought a cheap coat in a sale.
   OTHER WORDS YOU MIGHT USE ARE    **cut-price    inexpensive
   reasonable**
The opposite is **expensive**

## cheat *verb*
He cheated us by keeping all the money for himself.
   OTHER VERBS YOU MIGHT USE ARE    **to deceive    to fool    to swindle
   to trick**

## check *verb*
1  Mum always checks the car before we go on a journey.
   OTHER VERBS YOU MIGHT USE ARE    **to examine    to look over    to test**
2  A traffic jam checked our progress.
   OTHER VERBS YOU MIGHT USE ARE    **to halt    to hold up    to prevent
   to slow down    to stop**

## cheeky *adjective*

My teacher hates cheeky behaviour.

OTHER WORDS YOU MIGHT USE ARE  **bold  impertinent  impolite  impudent  insolent  rude**

The opposite is **polite**

## cheer *verb*

The audience cheered.

ANOTHER VERB IS **to applaud**

**to cheer someone up**

OTHER VERBS YOU MIGHT USE ARE  **to comfort  to encourage**

## cheerful *adjective*

OTHER WORDS YOU MIGHT USE ARE  **bright  happy  jolly  laughing  light-hearted  lively  merry  pleased**

The opposite is **gloomy**

## chest *noun*

a chest full of treasure.

OTHER WORDS YOU MIGHT USE ARE  **box  case  crate**

For other words, see **container**

## chew *verb*

For other verbs, see **eat**

---

### chief *adjective*

We learned the chief spelling rules.

OTHER WORDS YOU MIGHT USE ARE

**basic  essential  important  main  major  principal**

### chief *noun*

WORDS FOR PEOPLE IN CHARGE OF VARIOUS THINGS ARE

**boss  captain  commander  director  employer  governor  head  leader  manager  president  principal  ruler**

---

## child *noun*

OTHER WORDS ARE  **baby  boy  girl  infant**  (*informal*) **kid**  (*informal*) **toddler**  (*informal*) **youngster**

**china** *noun*

When you wash up, make sure you don't chip the china.

OTHER WORDS YOU MIGHT USE ARE

crockery    porcelain    pots    pottery

THINGS MADE OF CHINA ARE

bowl    cup    dish    jug    plate    saucer    teapot

**chip** *noun*

OTHER WORDS FOR A SMALL PIECE BROKEN OFF SOMETHING ARE    flake    fragment    splinter

**chip** *verb*

I chipped one of the best plates.
For other words, see **break**

**choke** *verb*

This collar is choking me.

OTHER VERBS YOU MIGHT USE ARE    to stifle    to strangle    to suffocate

**choose** *verb*

We chose Jo as captain.

OTHER VERBS YOU MIGHT USE ARE    to decide on    to elect    to name    to pick    to select    to settle on    to vote for

**chop** *verb*

For ways to cut things, see **cut**

**chunk** *noun*

a chunk of cheese.

OTHER WORDS YOU MIGHT USE ARE    block    hunk    lump    piece    slab

**church** *noun*

For places where people worship, see **religion**

**cinema** *noun*

OTHER WORDS ARE    the pictures    the movies

**circle** *noun*

OTHER WORDS YOU MIGHT USE ARE    disc    hoop    ring
For other shapes, see **shape**

---

## circus *noun*

PEOPLE WHO PERFORM IN A CIRCUS ARE

**acrobat    clown    juggler    lion-tamer    ringmaster
trapeze artist**

---

## citizen *noun*

the citizens of a town.

OTHER WORDS YOU MIGHT USE ARE    **inhabitant    resident**

## claim *verb*

Jo claimed her lost property.

OTHER VERBS YOU MIGHT USE ARE    **to ask for    to demand    to request**

## clap *verb*

We clapped at the end of the play.

ANOTHER VERB IS **to applaud**

## class *noun*

Which class are you in?

OTHER WORDS YOU MIGHT USE ARE    **form    group    set**

## clean *adjective*

1 clean clothes.

ANOTHER WORD IS **spotless**

2 clean water.

OTHER WORDS YOU MIGHT USE ARE    **clear    fresh    pure**

3 a clean sheet of paper.

OTHER WORDS ARE    **blank    unmarked    unused**

The opposite is **dirty**

---

## clean *verb*

Sam cleaned the floor while Jo was cleaning the car.

WAYS TO CLEAN THINGS ARE

**to brush    to dust    to hoover    to mop up    to rinse
to scrub    to shampoo    to sponge down    to sweep out
to swill    to vacuum    to wash    to wipe**

---

# clear *adjective*

THIS WORD HAS MANY USES. HERE ARE SOME OF THE WAYS YOU CAN USE IT, AND SOME OTHER WORDS YOU COULD CHOOSE

1 clear water.
**clean    colourless    pure**
2 a clear sky.
**blue    bright    cloudless    starlit    sunny**
3 clear plastic.
**transparent**
4 a clear photograph.
**focused    sharp    well-defined**
5 a clear voice.
**audible    distinct**
6 a clear space.
**empty    free    open**
7 a clear case of cheating.
**obvious**
8 a clear explanation.
**plain    simple    understandable**

# clear *verb*

1 We cleared a space to play in.
OTHER VERBS YOU MIGHT USE ARE    **to empty    to free**
2 Please clear the dishes.
OTHER VERBS ARE    **to carry away    to move    to remove to take away**
3 The fog cleared.
OTHER VERBS ARE    **to disappear    to melt away    to vanish**

# clever *adjective*

1 a clever pupil.
OTHER WORDS YOU MIGHT USE ARE    (*informal*) **brainy    bright    brilliant intelligent    quick    sharp    talented    wise**
2 clever with your hands.
OTHER WORDS ARE    **expert    handy    skilful**
3 a clever trick.
OTHER WORDS ARE    **crafty    cunning**
The opposite is **stupid**

# cliff *noun*

ANOTHER WORD IS **precipice**

## climb *verb*
Take care when you climb the ladder.
OTHER VERBS YOU MIGHT USE ARE    **to ascend    to go up    to mount**

## cling *verb*
1  The ivy clings to the wall.
ANOTHER VERB IS **to stick**
2  The baby clung to her mother.
OTHER VERBS YOU MIGHT USE ARE    **to hold on    to grasp    to hug**

---

## clock *noun*
THINGS WHICH TELL THE TIME ARE
**alarm clock    digital clock    grandfather clock
hourglass    sundial    watch**

---

## clog *verb*
The leaves clogged up the drain.
OTHER VERBS YOU MIGHT USE ARE    **to block**    (*informal*) **to bung up**

## close (rhymes with dose) *adjective*
1  Our house is close to the park.
ANOTHER WORD IS **near**
2  Mum took a close look at the cut on Jo's hand.
OTHER WORDS YOU MIGHT USE ARE    **careful    thorough**

## close (rhymes with doze) *verb*
1  Please close the door.
OTHER VERBS YOU MIGHT USE ARE    **to fasten    to lock    to shut**
2  We closed the concert with some songs.
OTHER VERBS ARE    **to conclude    to end    to finish**
The opposite is **open**

---

## cloth *noun*
OTHER WORDS YOU MIGHT USE ARE    **fabric    material    textiles**
DIFFERENT KINDS OF CLOTH ARE
**canvas    corduroy    cotton    denim    felt    flannel
lace    linen    muslin    nylon    polyester    satin
silk    tartan    tweed    velvet    viscose    wool**

---

## clothes, clothing *nouns*, see opposite page

## cloudy *adjective*
1 a cloudy sky.
    OTHER WORDS YOU MIGHT USE ARE   **dull**   **grey**   **overcast**
2 cloudy water.
    OTHER WORDS ARE   **milky**   **murky**
3 a cloudy atmosphere.
    OTHER WORDS ARE   **misty**   **steamy**
The opposite is **clear**

## club *noun*
1 a football club. a chess club.
    OTHER WORDS YOU MIGHT USE ARE   **association**   **group**   **league**
    **organization**   **society**
2 The intruder tried to hit me with a club.
    OTHER WORDS ARE   **baton**   **cudgel**   **stick**   **truncheon**

## clue *noun*
Give me a clue about what we are having for dinner.
    OTHER WORDS YOU MIGHT USE ARE   **hint**   **indication**   **sign**
    **suggestion**

## clumsy *adjective*
She's clumsy and keeps dropping things.
    OTHER WORDS YOU MIGHT USE ARE   **awkward**   **blundering**

## clutch *verb*
I clutched the rope to stop myself from falling.
    OTHER VERBS YOU MIGHT USE ARE   **to cling to**   **to grab**   **to grasp**
    **to grip**   **to hold on to**   **to seize**   **to snatch**

## coach *noun*
1 We went to the seaside by coach.
For other things you travel in, see **travel**
2 Our team has got a new coach.
    ANOTHER WORD IS **trainer**

## coarse *adjective*
The coarse cloth tickled my skin.
    OTHER WORDS YOU MIGHT USE ARE   **hairy**   **rough**   **scratchy**
The opposite is **smooth**

# clothes, clothing *nouns*

OTHER WORDS YOU MIGHT USE ARE

costume     dress     garments

DIFFERENT THINGS YOU WEAR ARE

| | | | |
|---|---|---|---|
| belt | blazer | blouse | braces |
| cardigan | coat | dress | frock |
| jacket | jeans | jersey | jumper |
| kilt | leotard | miniskirt | pullover |
| rompers | sari | shawl | shorts |
| skirt | socks | stockings | suit |
| sweater | sweatshirt | tie | trousers |
| t-shirt | tunic | waistcoat | |

THINGS YOU WEAR TO KEEP CLEAN ARE

| | | | |
|---|---|---|---|
| apron | bib | dungarees | overalls |
| pinafore | | | |

CLOTHES YOU WEAR WHEN YOU GO OUT ARE

| | | | |
|---|---|---|---|
| anorak | cagoule | cloak | duffle coat |
| gloves | (*informal*) mac or mack | | mackintosh |
| mittens | muffler | overcoat | raincoat |
| scarf | | | |

CLOTHES YOU USE AT NIGHT ARE

dressing gown     night-dress     nightie     pyjamas

UNDERCLOTHES ARE

| | | | |
|---|---|---|---|
| bra | knickers | panties | pants |
| pantyhose | petticoat | slip | tights |
| underpants | vest | | |

THINGS YOU WEAR WHEN YOU GO SWIMMING ARE

bikini     swimming costume     swimsuit     trunks

For things you wear on your head, see **hat**

For things you wear on your feet, see **shoe**

## coat *noun*
For things we wear, see **clothes**

## coil *verb*
The snake coiled round a branch.

OTHER VERBS YOU MIGHT USE ARE     to curl     to entwine     to loop
to twist     to wind

## cold *adjective*

1  cold weather.

OTHER WORDS YOU MIGHT USE ARE  **Arctic  bitter  chilly  cool
freezing  fresh  frosty  icy** (*informal*) **nippy  wintry**

2  I feel cold.

OTHER WORDS ARE  **chilled  frozen  shivery**

The opposite is **hot**

## collapse *verb*

1  The shed collapsed in the storm.

PHRASES YOU MIGHT USE ARE  (*informal*) **to cave in  to fall down
to tumble down**

2  People collapsed because it was so hot.

ANOTHER VERB IS **to faint**

## collect *verb*

1  A crowd collected to watch the fire.

OTHER VERBS YOU MIGHT USE ARE  **to assemble  to gather**

2  We collected all the litter.

OTHER VERBS ARE  **to accumulate  to gather together  to heap up
to pile up**

3  Mum collected Jo from school.

OTHER VERBS ARE  **to bring  to fetch  to pick up**

## collection *noun*

Jo has a collection of toys.

OTHER WORDS YOU MIGHT USE ARE  **assortment  gathering  hoard
pile  set  stack**

For other words, see **group**

## college *noun*

For other words,  see **educate**

## collide *verb*

The car collided with a van.

OTHER PHRASES YOU MIGHT USE ARE  **to bump into  to crash into
to run into**

For other words, see **hit**

## collision *noun*

OTHER WORDS YOU MIGHT USE ARE  **accident  bump  crash  smash**

## colour *noun*
We admired the lovely colours of the sunset.

OTHER WORDS YOU MIGHT USE ARE

hue            shade            tint

DIFFERENT COLOURS ARE

| | | | |
|---|---|---|---|
| amber | black | blue | bronze |
| brown | cream | crimson | fawn |
| gold | green | grey | ivory |
| jet-black | khaki | maroon | mauve |
| navy blue | orange | pink | purple |
| red | rosy | scarlet | tan |
| turquoise | vermilion | violet | white |
| yellow | | | |

## colour *verb*
OTHER VERBS YOU MIGHT USE ARE

to dye    to paint    to stain    to tinge    to tint

## colourful *adjective*
1 colourful flowers.
OTHER WORDS YOU MIGHT USE ARE **bright   brilliant   flashy   gaudy showy**
2 a colourful description.
OTHER WORDS ARE **lively   interesting   vivid**
The opposite is **dull**

## column *noun*
The palace had stone columns in front of the door.
OTHER WORDS YOU MIGHT USE ARE **pillar   pole   post   shaft support**

## combine *verb*
1 Our class combined with Jo's class to put on a play.
OTHER VERBS YOU MIGHT USE ARE **to come together   to join   to merge to unite**
2 I combined the cake ingredients in a big bowl.
OTHER VERBS ARE **to add together   to blend   to mix to put together**

## come *verb*
1 Some dark clouds are coming.
OTHER VERBS YOU MIGHT USE ARE **to advance    to approach
to draw near**
2 Our visitors have come.
OTHER VERBS ARE **to appear    to arrive    to turn up**
The opposite is **go**

## comfort *verb*
Jo comforts baby when he cries.
OTHER VERBS YOU MIGHT USE ARE **to calm    to reassure    to soothe**

## comfortable *adjective*
a comfortable chair.
OTHER WORDS YOU MIGHT USE ARE **cosy    luxurious    relaxing
snug    soft**

## comic *adjective*
We laughed at his comic remarks.
OTHER WORDS YOU MIGHT USE ARE **amusing    comical    funny
humorous    laughable    witty**
The opposite is **serious**

## command *verb*
1 The general commanded that the fighting must stop.
OTHER VERBS YOU MIGHT USE ARE **to instruct    to order**
2 The captain commands the ship.
OTHER VERBS ARE **to be in charge of    to control    to govern
to manage    to supervise    to take over**

## comment *noun*
The teacher asked for our comments.
OTHER WORDS YOU MIGHT USE ARE **opinion    remark**

## commercial *noun*
a TV commercial.
OTHER WORDS YOU MIGHT USE ARE *(informal)* **advert
advertisement**

## commit *verb*
to commit a crime.
OTHER VERBS YOU MIGHT USE ARE **to be guilty of    to carry out**

**common** *adjective*
1  It's common for people to go to the seaside for a holiday.
  OTHER WORDS YOU MIGHT USE ARE    **customary   normal   ordinary   usual**
2  Colds are common in winter.
  OTHER WORDS ARE    **frequent   widespread**
3  'Too many cooks spoil the broth' is a common saying.
  ANOTHER WORD IS **well known**
The opposite is **rare**

---

**communication** *noun*
    Mum got a communication from school about the parents' evening.
    OTHER WORDS ARE    **message   note**
    DIFFERENT WAYS TO COMMUNICATE ARE
      **computer network   letter   newspaper   magazine   radar   radio   satellite   telephone   television**

---

**compact** *adjective*
1  a compact set of instructions.
  OTHER WORDS YOU MIGHT USE ARE    **brief   concise   short**
2  a compact typewriter.
  OTHER WORDS ARE    **neat   portable   small**

**company** *noun*
We enjoy the company of other people.
  OTHER WORDS YOU MIGHT USE ARE    **companionship   friendship**
For other words, see **crowd**

**compare** *verb*
Compare your answers with your neighbour's.
  OTHER VERBS YOU MIGHT USE ARE    **to check   to contrast**

**compartment** *noun*
The box has separate compartments for knives, forks, and spoons.
  OTHER WORDS YOU MIGHT USE ARE    **division   section   space**

**compel** *verb*
You can't compel me to go swimming in this weather!
  OTHER VERBS YOU MIGHT USE ARE    **to force   to order**

## competition *noun*
1 a sports competition.
OTHER WORDS YOU MIGHT USE ARE   **championship   contest   game   match   tournament**
2 There was fierce competition between the two teams.
ANOTHER WORD IS **rivalry**

## complain *verb*
We complained about the bad food.
OTHER VERBS YOU MIGHT USE ARE   **to grumble   to object   to protest**

## complete *adjective*
1 Did he tell you the complete story?
OTHER WORDS YOU MIGHT USE ARE   **entire   full   whole**
2 He was talking complete rubbish.
OTHER WORDS ARE   **absolute   pure   total   utter**

## complete *verb*
Can I go out when I've completed my homework?
OTHER VERBS YOU MIGHT USE ARE   **to carry out   to end   to finish**

## complicated *adjective*
The instructions were too complicated for me to understand.
OTHER WORDS YOU MIGHT USE ARE   **complex   difficult   involved**
The opposite is **simple**

---

## computer *noun*
WORDS TO DO WITH COMPUTING ARE
**cursor   data   disk drive   floppy disk   hard disk
hardware   interface   joystick   keyboard
micro-chip   micro-computer   micro-processor
monitor   mouse   PC   printer   print-out   program
screen   software   terminal   VDU   word processor**

---

## conceal *verb*
1 The bird concealed its nest.
OTHER VERBS YOU MIGHT USE ARE   **to camouflage   to disguise   to hide**
2 He tried to conceal the truth.
PHRASES ARE   **to cover up   to keep quiet about**
The opposite is **show**

## conceited *adjective*
There's no need to be conceited just because you got a prize.
OTHER WORDS YOU MIGHT USE ARE     **boastful**     (*informal*) **cocky**
**proud**
The opposite is **modest**

## concentrate *verb*
Concentrate on your work.
PHRASES YOU MIGHT USE ARE     **to attend to**     **to think about**

## concern *verb*
Road safety concerns all of us.
OTHER VERBS YOU MIGHT USE ARE     **to affect**     **to be important to**
**to involve**     **to matter to**

## concerned *adjective*
Dad is concerned about Jo's cough.
OTHER WORDS YOU MIGHT USE ARE     **anxious**     **bothered**
**worried**

## conclude *verb*
1 We concluded the concert with a song.
OTHER VERBS YOU MIGHT USE ARE     **to close**     **to end**     **to finish**
**to round off**
2 After waiting 15 minutes, I concluded that I'd missed the bus.
OTHER VERBS ARE     **to decide**     **to reach a conclusion**

## condemn *verb*
1 The head condemned the vandals who broke the window.
OTHER VERBS YOU MIGHT USE ARE     **to blame**     **to criticise**
2 The judge condemned the thief to spend a year in prison.
OTHER VERBS ARE     **to convict**     **to punish**     **to sentence**

## condition *noun*
1 Is your bike in good condition?
ANOTHER WORD IS **order**
2 Is your dog in good condition?
ANOTHER WORD IS **health**

## confess *verb*
Jo confessed that she lost her gloves.
OTHER VERBS YOU MIGHT USE ARE     **to admit**     **to own up**

## confident *adjective*

1 Sam is a confident swimmer.

OTHER WORDS YOU MIGHT USE ARE   **bold    fearless**

The opposite is **nervous**

2 Jo was confident that she knew the answer.

OTHER WORDS ARE   **certain    definite    positive    sure**

The opposite is **doubtful**

## confuse *verb*

1 Complicated sums confuse me.

OTHER VERBS YOU MIGHT USE ARE   **to bewilder    to puzzle**

2 I always confuse the names of the twins.

OTHER VERBS ARE   **to mix up    to muddle**

## congratulate *verb*

We congratulated Sam when he won.

OTHER VERBS YOU MIGHT USE ARE   **to compliment    to praise**

## connect *verb*

Dad connected a loudspeaker to the TV set.

OTHER VERBS YOU MIGHT USE ARE   **to attach    to join    to link**

## conquer *verb*

We easily conquered the opposition.

OTHER VERBS YOU MIGHT USE ARE   **to beat    to defeat    to overcome**   (*informal*) **to thrash    to win against**

## conscious *adjective*

In spite of the knock on the head, he remained conscious.

OTHER WORDS YOU MIGHT USE ARE   **alert    awake**

The opposite is **unconscious**

## consent *verb*

We can go on the trip if Mum and Dad consent.

OTHER VERBS YOU MIGHT USE ARE   **to agree    to allow it    to approve    to permit it**

## consider *verb*

We considered the problem.

OTHER VERBS YOU MIGHT USE ARE   **to study    to think about**

## considerate *adjective*
It was considerate of you to lend me your umbrella.
OTHER WORDS YOU MIGHT USE ARE     **friendly     helpful     kind     thoughtful     unselfish**
The opposite is **selfish**

## construct *verb*
We constructed a model aeroplane.
OTHER VERBS YOU MIGHT USE ARE     **to assemble     to build     to make     to put together**

## consume *verb*
The hungry dog consumed the food.
For other words, see **eat**

## contain *verb*
1 What does this box contain?
ANOTHER VERB IS **to hold**
2 What does this stew contain?
A PHRASE IS **to consist of**

---

## container *noun*
THINGS THAT CONTAIN WATER OR LIQUID ARE
**barrel     basin     bath     bin     bottle     bucket     can     cask     casserole     cauldron     churn     cup     dish     flask     glass     goblet     jar     jug     kettle     mug     pail     pan     pot     saucepan     tank     teapot     tub     tumbler     vase     watering can**

CONTAINERS FOR OTHER THINGS ARE
**bag     basket     box     carton     case     casket     chest     dustbin     envelope     handbag     haversack     holdall     knapsack     money box     pouch     purse     rucksack     sack     satchel     suitcase     tin     trunk     wallet**

---

## contented *adjective*
The cat looks very contented.
OTHER WORDS YOU MIGHT USE ARE     **happy     relaxed     satisfied**

## contest *noun*
For other words, see **competition** or **fight**

**continent** *noun*

THE SEVEN CONTINENTS ARE

Africa    Antarctica    Asia    Australasia    Europe
North America    South America

# continual *adjective*

Continual chatter annoys the teacher.

OTHER WORDS YOU MIGHT USE ARE    ceaseless    constant    continuous    endless    everlasting    incessant    non-stop    persistent    repeated    unending

# continue *verb*

1   How long will this rain continue?

OTHER VERBS YOU MIGHT USE ARE    to go on    to keep on    to last    to persist

2   Please continue with your work.

OTHER VERBS ARE    to carry on    to keep going    to persevere

# continuous *adjective*

For other words, see **continual**

# contrast *noun*

OTHER WORDS YOU MIGHT USE ARE    comparison    difference

# contribute *verb*

I contributed £1 to the collection.

OTHER VERBS YOU MIGHT USE ARE    to donate    to give

# control *verb*

She couldn't control the horse.

OTHER VERBS YOU MIGHT USE ARE    to command    to deal with    to handle    to manage    to restrain

# convenient *adjective*

1   There's a convenient shop just round the corner.

OTHER WORDS YOU MIGHT USE ARE    handy    useful

2   It isn't convenient for Granny to visit us today.

OTHER WORDS ARE    appropriate    easy    suitable

The opposite is **inconvenient**

## conversation *noun*
Jo and Sam had a long conversation about their holiday.
OTHER WORDS ARE  (*informal*) **chat**  **discussion**  **talk**

---

## cook *noun*
The chief cook in a big restaurant or hotel is the **chef**.

## cook *verb*
WAYS TO COOK THINGS ARE
**to bake**  **to barbecue**  **to boil**  **to fry**  **to grill**
**to poach**  **to roast**  **to steam**  **to stew**  **to toast**

---

## cool *adjective*
1 a cool wind.
OTHER WORDS YOU MIGHT USE ARE  **chilly**  **cold**
The opposite is **warm**
2 Don't panic – keep cool!
ANOTHER WORD IS **calm**

## copy *noun*
The painting was not genuine: it was a copy.
OTHER WORDS YOU MIGHT USE ARE  **counterfeit**  **fake**  **forgery**

## copy *verb*
1 The budgie copies Jo's voice.
OTHER VERBS YOU MIGHT USE ARE  **to imitate**  **to impersonate**
2 Our teacher copied our poems so that everyone could read them.
OTHER VERBS ARE  **to duplicate**  **to photocopy**  **to reproduce**

## corn *noun*
ANOTHER WORD IS **cereal**
KINDS OF CORN ARE  **barley**  **maize** or **sweet corn**  **oats**  **rye**
**wheat**

## corner *noun*
1 a corner between two walls.
ANOTHER WORD IS **angle**
2 the corner of the road.
OTHER WORDS ARE  **bend**  **crossroads**  **junction**

**correct** *adjective*
Is that the correct time?
OTHER WORDS YOU MIGHT USE ARE    **accurate    exact    precise    right true**
The opposite is **wrong**

**corridor** *noun*
ANOTHER WORD IS **passage**

**costly** *adjective*
costly jewels.
OTHER WORDS YOU MIGHT USE ARE    **expensive    precious    valuable**
The opposite is **cheap**

**costume** *noun*
costumes for a play.
OTHER WORDS YOU MIGHT USE ARE    **clothes    clothing    disguise fancy dress**

**cosy** *adjective*
For other words, see **comfortable**

---

**council** *noun*
GROUPS OF PEOPLE WHO DISCUSS THINGS AND MAKE DECISIONS ARE
**assembly    committee    conference    parliament**

---

**count** *verb*
Jo counted her pocket money.
OTHER VERBS YOU MIGHT USE ARE    **to add up    to calculate    to total to work out**

**country** *noun*
1  I like to visit other countries.
OTHER WORDS YOU MIGHT USE ARE    **land    nation    state**
2  There's some lovely country near here.
OTHER WORDS ARE    **countryside    landscape    scenery**

**courage** *noun*
The firemen showed great courage.
OTHER WORDS ARE    **bravery    daring    heroism**

**cover** *noun*

DIFFERENT KINDS OF COVER ARE

cap   coat   covering   envelope   folder   hat   lid
roof   top   wrapper

**cover** *verb*

DIFFERENT WAYS TO COVER THINGS ARE

to bury   to camouflage   to clothe   to conceal
to hide   to mask   to screen

# crack *noun*

a crack in the wall.

OTHER WORDS YOU MIGHT USE ARE   **break   crevice   gap   opening
split**

# crafty *adjective*

People say that the fox is a crafty animal.

OTHER WORDS YOU MIGHT USE ARE   **clever   cunning   sly   wily**

# crash *noun*

1 a crash on the motorway.

OTHER WORDS YOU MIGHT USE ARE   **accident   collision**

For other words, see **hit**

2 There was a loud crash when Sam dropped the plates.

For other words, see **sound**

# crazy *adjective*

1 The poor dog went crazy when she was stung by a wasp.

OTHER WORDS YOU MIGHT USE ARE   **berserk   frantic   wild**

2 It was a crazy idea to go for a walk in the rain.

OTHER WORDS ARE   **absurd   mad   ridiculous   silly
stupid**

The opposite is **sensible**

# crease *verb*

Don't crease the paper.

OTHER VERBS YOU MIGHT USE ARE   **to crumple   to fold   to wrinkle**

## create *verb*
Mum created a new kind of cake.
OTHER VERBS YOU MIGHT USE ARE **to invent   to make   to produce   to think up**
For other words, see **make**

---

### creator *noun*
ANOTHER WORD IS **maker**
The creator of a new way to do something is an **inventor**.
The creator of a book is an **author** or **poet** or **writer**.
The creator of a piece of music is a **composer**.
The creator of a painting or a statue is an **artist**.

---

## creature *noun*
For names of different creatures, see **animal** and **bird**

## creep *verb*
For other ways to move, see **move**

---

### crime *noun*
OTHER WORDS YOU MIGHT USE ARE
**dishonesty   offence   wrongdoing**

SOME CRIMES ARE
**arson   blackmail   burglary   forgery   hijacking
joy-riding   kidnapping   manslaughter   murder
poaching   robbery   shoplifting   smuggling
stealing**

### criminal *noun*
OTHER WORDS YOU MIGHT USE ARE
(*informal*) **crook   culprit   delinquent   offender
wrongdoer**

DIFFERENT KINDS OF CRIMINAL ARE
**blackmailer   burglar   gangster   hijacker
kidnapper   mugger   murderer   poacher   robber
shoplifter   smuggler   terrorist   vandal**

## crippled *adjective*
She has been crippled since her road accident.
OTHER WORDS YOU MIGHT USE ARE  **disabled  handicapped  lame**

## crisp *adjective*
I like biscuits if they are crisp.
OTHER WORDS TO DESCRIBE THINGS WHICH BREAK EASILY ARE  **brittle  crackly  fragile**
The opposite is **soft**

## crooked *adjective*
a crooked path.
OTHER WORDS YOU MIGHT USE ARE  **bent  twisting  winding  zigzag**
The opposite is **straight**

## cross *adjective*
For other words, see **angry**

## cross *verb*
Take care when you cross the road.
A PHRASE YOU MIGHT USE IS **to go across**
**to cross something out**
OTHER VERBS ARE  **to cancel  to delete  to erase**

## crossroads *noun*
OTHER WORDS ARE  **intersection  junction**

## crouch *verb*
We had to crouch to go through the small opening.
OTHER VERBS YOU MIGHT USE ARE  **to bend  to stoop**

## crowd *noun*
a crowd of people.
OTHER WORDS YOU MIGHT USE ARE  **company  group  horde**
A noisy, violent crowd is a **mob**.
Another word for the crowd at a football match is **spectators**.
For other words, see **group**

## cruel *adjective*
I think it's cruel to hunt foxes.
OTHER WORDS YOU MIGHT USE ARE  **bloodthirsty  brutal  cold-hearted
heartless  merciless  pitiless  ruthless  unkind  vicious**
The opposite is **kind**

**crumb** *noun*
a crumb of bread.
OTHER WORDS YOU MIGHT USE ARE  **bit    fragment    scrap**

**crumple** *verb*
Don't crumple the clothes I've just ironed!
OTHER VERBS YOU MIGHT USE ARE  **to crease    to crush    to fold    to wrinkle**

**crush** *verb*
I crushed my finger in the door.
OTHER VERBS YOU MIGHT USE ARE  **to smash    to squash    to squeeze**

**cry** *verb*
Baby cries when she's tired.
OTHER VERBS YOU MIGHT USE ARE  **to grizzle    to shed tears    to sob    to wail    to weep**
**to cry out**
OTHER VERBS ARE  **to call    to shout    to yell**

**cuddle** *verb*
Sam loves to cuddle the baby.
OTHER VERBS YOU MIGHT USE ARE  **to embrace    to hug**

**cunning** *adjective*
We had a cunning plan to trick our friends.
OTHER WORDS YOU MIGHT USE ARE  **clever    crafty    ingenious    skilful    sly    wily**

**cup** *noun*
THINGS YOU CAN DRINK FROM ARE
**beaker    glass    goblet    mug    tumbler**

**cure** *noun*
Have you got a cure for a cold?
OTHER WORDS YOU MIGHT USE ARE  **medicine    remedy    treatment**

**cure** *verb*
Will this medicine cure me?
ANOTHER VERB IS **to heal**

## curious *adjective*

1 Jo is curious about what she will get for Christmas.
   OTHER WORDS YOU MIGHT USE ARE   **inquisitive   interested**
2 Sam thought there was a curious smell in the pantry.
   OTHER WORDS ARE   **funny   odd   peculiar   queer   strange
   unusual**

## curl *verb*

I curl my hair round my fingers.
   OTHER VERBS YOU MIGHT USE ARE   **to bend   to coil   to loop   to twist
   to wind**

## curse *verb*

He cursed when he hit his finger with the hammer.
   ANOTHER VERB IS **to swear**

## curtain *noun*

   OTHER WORDS YOU MIGHT USE ARE   **blind   drape   screen**

---

### curve *noun*

The driver slowed down as she approached the curve in the road.
   OTHER WORDS YOU MIGHT USE ARE   **bend   turn   twist**
   THINGS THAT MAKE THE SHAPE OF A CURVE ARE   **arch   bow   curl
   hook   horse shoe   loop   rainbow   semi-circle
   wave**

### curved *adjective*

   OTHER WORDS YOU MIGHT USE ARE   **arched   bent   bowed
   concave   convex   crescent-shaped   curled
   rounded   twisted**

---

## custom *noun*

It's a custom to give presents on a person's birthday.
   OTHER WORDS YOU MIGHT USE ARE   **convention   habit   tradition**

---

### cut *noun*

a cut on your finger.
   OTHER WORDS ARE   **gash   injury   nick   wound**

## cut *verb*

There are a lot of verbs which mean 'to cut'.

You **carve** meat, or an artist can **carve** a statue.

You can **chisel** wood.

You **chop** things with an axe.

You **clip** the hedge with shears.

You **mince** meat into tiny pieces.

You **mow** the lawn.

You can **prune** branches off a tree.

You **saw** wood.

You **shave** with a razor.

You **slice** bread with a breadknife.

You can **slit** open an envelope.

You **snip** things with scissors.

You **stab** with a dagger.

You **trim** your hair to make it tidy.

To **cut** prices is to lower or reduce them.

## cutlery *noun*

ITEMS OF CUTLERY ARE

**breadknife**    **carving knife**    **dessertspoon**    **fork**
**knife**    **spoon**    **tablespoon**    **teaspoon**

## cycle *noun*

A cycle with two wheels is a **bicycle** or **bike**.

A cycle with three wheels is a **tricycle**.

A cycle with an engine is a **moped** or **motorbike**.

# Dd

**damage** *noun*

The storm caused a lot of damage.

OTHER WORDS YOU MIGHT USE ARE　**destruction　havoc**

**damage** *verb*

OTHER VERBS YOU MIGHT USE ARE　**to harm　to hurt　to injure　to spoil**

WAYS YOU CAN DAMAGE THINGS ARE　**to break　to chip　to dent　to scratch　to smash　to wound**

**damp** *adjective*

Don't sit on the damp grass.

OTHER WORDS YOU MIGHT USE ARE　**moist　rather wet**

The opposite is **dry**

---

**dance** *noun*

Sam and Jo went to a dance on St Valentine's Day.
A very formal dance is a **ball**.
A dance where music is played on records is a **disco**.
A dance you see in a theatre or on TV which tells a story is a **ballet**.

---

**dance** *verb*

OTHER VERBS YOU MIGHT USE ARE　**to jump about　to leap about　to prance　to skip**

**danger** *noun*

1　The rocks are a danger to ships.

ANOTHER WORD IS **peril**

2　In summer there's a danger of getting sunburnt.

OTHER WORDS YOU MIGHT USE ARE　**chance　possibility　risk　threat**

## dangerous *adjective*

1 a dangerous adventure.

OTHER WORDS YOU MIGHT USE ARE     **hazardous     perilous     risky     unsafe**

2 a dangerous criminal.

OTHER WORDS ARE     **desperate     treacherous     violent**

3 a dangerous poison.

OTHER WORDS ARE     **deadly     harmful     lethal**

The opposite is **safe**

## daring *adjective*

Sam thought Jo was very daring to climb up the big rock.

OTHER WORDS YOU MIGHT USE ARE     **adventurous     bold     brave     fearless**

The opposite is **cowardly**

## dark *adjective*

1 a dark night.

OTHER WORDS YOU MIGHT USE ARE     **black     starless**

2 a dark place.

OTHER WORDS YOU MIGHT USE ARE     **gloomy     shadowy     shady     sunless     unlit**

The opposite is **bright**

## darling *noun*

OTHER WORDS YOU MIGHT USE ARE     **beloved     dear     love     sweetheart**

## dawdle *verb*

Don't dawdle: we're late!

OTHER VERBS YOU MIGHT USE ARE     **to be slow     to hang about     to linger**

The opposite is **hurry**

## day *noun*

THE DAYS OF THE WEEK ARE

**Monday     Tuesday     Wednesday     Thursday     Friday
Saturday     Sunday**

For times of the day and special days of the year, see **time**

## dead *adjective*

OTHER WORDS YOU MIGHT USE ARE     **deceased     killed     lifeless**

The opposite is **alive**

## deal *verb*
I dealt the cards.
OTHER VERBS YOU MIGHT USE ARE    **to distribute    to give out    to share out**
**to deal with**
Jo can deal with the problem.
OTHER VERBS ARE    **to attend to    to handle    to manage    to sort out**

## dear *adjective*
1 a dear friend.
OTHER WORDS YOU MIGHT USE ARE    **beloved    loved    precious**
2 Mum didn't buy any shoes because they were too dear.
OTHER WORDS ARE    **costly    expensive    (*informal*) pricey**

## decay *verb*
Meat smells nasty when it decays.
OTHER VERBS YOU MIGHT USE ARE    **to decompose    to go bad    to rot**

## deceitful *adjective*
We knew he was often deceitful, so we didn't believe him.
OTHER WORDS YOU MIGHT USE ARE    **dishonest    insincere    lying    untrustworthy**
The opposite is **honest**

## deceive *verb*
He tried to deceive us, but we discovered the truth.
OTHER VERBS YOU MIGHT USE ARE    **to cheat    to mislead    to swindle    to trick**

## decorate *verb*
1 I decorated the room with flowers.
ANOTHER VERB YOU MIGHT USE IS **to adorn**
2 Dad decorated Sam's bedroom.
OTHER VERBS ARE    **to paint    to paper**

## decrease *verb*
1 They decreased my pocket money!
OTHER VERBS YOU MIGHT USE ARE    **to cut    to reduce**
2 The number of children in Jo's class decreased this term.
OTHER VERBS ARE    **to get smaller    to go down    to lessen**
The opposite is **increase**

## deep *adjective*
deep water. a deep hole.
The opposite is **shallow**

## defeat *verb*
Our team defeated them 8–0.
OTHER VERBS YOU MIGHT USE ARE **to beat**   **to conquer**
(*informal*) **to thrash**

## defend *verb*
1 The mother bird defended her babies.
OTHER VERBS YOU MIGHT USE ARE **to guard**   **to keep safe**
**to protect**
The opposite is **attack**

## definite *adjective*
1 Is it definite that I can go?
OTHER WORDS YOU MIGHT USE ARE **certain**   **positive**   **settled**
2 He gave a definite signal.
OTHER WORDS ARE **clear**   **noticeable**   **obvious**   **sure**
The opposite is **vague**

## delay *verb*
1 A traffic jam delayed us.
OTHER VERBS YOU MIGHT USE ARE **to hinder**   **to hold up**   **to slow down**
2 They had to delay the start of the match.
OTHER VERBS ARE **to postpone**   **to put off**
3 Don't delay - do it now!
OTHER VERBS ARE **to hang about**   **to hesitate**   **to wait**

## deliberate *adjective*
a deliberate mistake.
OTHER WORDS YOU MIGHT USE ARE **intentional**   **planned**
The opposite is **accidental**

## delicate *adjective*
1 delicate material.
OTHER WORDS YOU MIGHT USE ARE **dainty**   **fine**   **flimsy**   **fragile**
**soft**
2 a delicate child.
OTHER WORDS ARE **sickly**   **unhealthy**   **weak**
The opposite is **strong**

**delicious** *adjective*
a delicious dinner.
OTHER WORDS YOU MIGHT USE ARE    **appetizing    tasty**
For other words, see **taste**

**delighted** *adjective*
I was delighted with your gift.
ANOTHER WORD IS **pleased**
For other words, see **happy**

**deliver** *verb*
The postman delivers letters.
PHRASES YOU MIGHT USE ARE    **to hand over    to take round**

**demand** *verb*
When the new TV didn't work, Mum demanded to have her money back.
OTHER VERBS YOU MIGHT USE ARE    **to ask    to beg    to request**

**demolish** *verb*
They had to demolish some houses when they built the new road.
OTHER VERBS YOU MIGHT USE ARE    **to destroy    to dismantle    to knock down**

**demonstration** *noun*
1  We gave a PE demonstration.
OTHER WORDS YOU MIGHT USE ARE    **display    exhibition    show**
2  There was a big demonstration against the new motorway.
OTHER WORDS YOU MIGHT USE ARE    (*informal*) **demo    march    protest**

**dense** *adjective*
1  dense fog. a dense crowd.
ANOTHER WORD IS **thick**
2  a dense pupil.
For other words, see **stupid**

**deny** *verb*
He denied that he had cheated.
PHRASES YOU MIGHT USE ARE    **to refuse to agree    to reject the idea**

**depart** *verb*
She departed without saying where she was going.
OTHER VERBS YOU MIGHT USE ARE    **to go away    to go out    to leave    to set off    to set out**

## depend *verb*
We can depend on Jo to do her best.
> OTHER VERBS YOU MIGHT USE ARE    **to count on    to rely on    to trust**

## depress *verb*
His dog's death depressed him.
> OTHER VERBS YOU MIGHT USE ARE    **to sadden    to upset**

**depressed**, **depressing** *adjectives*, see **sad**

## describe *verb*
Can you describe what happened?
> OTHER VERBS YOU MIGHT USE ARE    **to explain    to tell**

## deserted *adjective*
a deserted house.
> OTHER WORDS YOU MIGHT USE ARE    **abandoned    empty    forsaken**

## design *verb*
When we moved into our new house, we helped Mum design the garden.
> OTHER VERBS YOU MIGHT USE ARE    **to draw    to plan    to sketch**

## desire *verb*
The fairy promised he could have what he desired.
> OTHER VERBS YOU MIGHT USE ARE    **to fancy    to long for    to want
> to wish for**

## desperate *adjective*
The situation was desperate.
> OTHER WORDS YOU MIGHT USE ARE    **hopeless    serious**

## destroy *verb*
1  The explosion destroyed the building.
> OTHER VERBS YOU MIGHT USE ARE    **to demolish    to knock down    to ruin
> to wreck**

2  Dad used a special powder to destroy the ants in the garden.
> OTHER VERBS YOU MIGHT USE ARE    **to exterminate**    (*informal*) **to finish off
> to kill    to wipe out**

## detest *verb*
Jo detests the smell of onions.
> OTHER VERBS YOU MIGHT USE ARE    **to dislike    to hate    to loathe**

The opposite is **love**

## develop *verb*

1 Jo's swimming is developing.
    OTHER VERBS YOU MIGHT USE ARE     **to get better**     **to improve**
    **to progress**
2 You must water plants if you want them to develop.
    OTHER VERBS YOU MIGHT USE ARE     **to get bigger**     **to grow**

## device *noun*

Our new tin-opener is a clever device.
    OTHER WORDS YOU MIGHT USE ARE     **contraption**     **gadget**     **implement**
    **instrument**     **tool**

## diagram *noun*

We drew a diagram to show how the machine worked.
    OTHER WORDS YOU MIGHT USE ARE     **chart**     **graph**     **plan**     **sketch**

## die *verb*

    OTHER VERBS YOU MIGHT USE ARE     **to pass away**     **to perish**

## difference *noun*

1 Will it make any difference to our plans if it rains?
    OTHER WORDS YOU MIGHT USE ARE     **alteration**     **change**
2 Can you see any difference between these two colours?
    OTHER WORDS YOU MIGHT USE ARE     **contrast**     **distinction**

## different *adjective*

1 The sweets are different flavours.
    OTHER WORDS YOU MIGHT USE ARE     **assorted**     **mixed**     **various**
2 Jo and Sam often have different ideas about things.
    OTHER WORDS YOU MIGHT USE ARE     **contradictory**     **contrasting**
    **dissimilar**     **opposite**
The opposite is **the same**

## difficult *adjective*

a difficult problem.
    OTHER WORDS YOU MIGHT USE ARE     **complex**     **complicated**     **hard**
    **tough**     (*informal*) **tricky**
The opposite is **easy**

## difficulty *noun*

The explorers met many difficulties before they reached home.
    OTHER WORDS YOU MIGHT USE ARE     **complication**     **hardship**     **obstacle**
    **problem**     **snag**     **trouble**

**dig** *verb*
    OTHER VERBS ARE    **to burrow**    **to excavate**    **to hollow out** **to scoop**    **to tunnel**

**dignified** *adjective*
    Please behave in a dignified way.
    OTHER WORDS YOU MIGHT USE ARE    **calm**    **formal**    **proper**    **serious** **sober**    **solemn**    **stately**

**dilute** *verb*
    You dilute squash with water.
    PHRASES YOU MIGHT USE ARE    **to make weaker**    **to water down**

**dim** *adjective*
    We saw a dim outline in the mist.
    OTHER WORDS YOU MIGHT USE ARE    **dark**    **faint**    **gloomy**    **indistinct** **shadowy**
    The opposite is **clear**

**din** *noun*
    OTHER WORDS YOU MIGHT USE ARE    **noise**    (*informal*) **racket** (*informal*) **row**    **uproar**
    For other words, see **sound**

**direct** *verb*
    1  Please direct me to the bus stop.
       OTHER VERBS YOU MIGHT USE ARE    **to guide**    **to point**    **to show**
    2  The officer directed the soldiers to stand in a line.
       OTHER VERBS YOU MIGHT USE ARE    **to command**    **to instruct**    **to order** **to tell**

**dirt** *noun*
    OTHER WORDS YOU MIGHT USE ARE    **dust**    **filth**    **grime**    **muck**    **mud** **pollution**

**dirty** *adjective*
    OTHER WORDS YOU MIGHT USE ARE    **dusty**    **filthy**    **foul**    **grimy** **grubby**    **mucky**    **muddy**    **polluted**    **soiled**    **stained**
    The opposite is **clean**

**disagree** *verb*
    OTHER VERBS YOU MIGHT USE ARE    **to argue**    **to differ**    **to quarrel**
    The opposite is **agree**

## disappear *verb*
OTHER VERBS YOU MIGHT USE ARE    **to fade    to melt away    to vanish**
The opposite is **appear**

## disapprove *verb*
We disapprove of cruelty to pets.
OTHER VERBS YOU MIGHT USE ARE    **to condemn    to criticize    to dislike**

## disaster *noun*
Many people died in the disaster.
OTHER WORDS YOU MIGHT USE ARE    **accident    calamity    catastrophe**

## discipline *noun*
Our teacher likes to have discipline in the classroom.
OTHER WORDS YOU MIGHT USE ARE    **control    obedience    order**

## discover *verb*
1  I discovered a lot about dinosaurs in the library.
OTHER VERBS YOU MIGHT USE ARE    **to find    to learn    to research    to track down**
2  Dad discovered an old coin in the garden.
OTHER VERBS YOU MIGHT USE ARE    **to come across    to uncover    to unearth**
The opposite is **hide**

## discuss *verb*
Let's discuss the problem.
OTHER VERBS YOU MIGHT USE ARE    **to argue about    to consider    to talk about**

## disease *noun*
OTHER WORDS YOU MIGHT USE ARE    **ailment    illness    sickness**
For other words, see **health**

## disguise *verb*
1  Dad disguised himself as Father Christmas.
PHRASES ARE    **to dress up as    to pretend to be**
2  We disguised our hiding-place.
OTHER VERBS ARE    **to camouflage    to conceal    to cover up    to hide**

## disgust *verb*
The dirty kitchen disgusted us.
OTHER VERBS YOU MIGHT USE ARE    **to offend    to revolt    to sicken**
**disgusting** *adjective*, see **nasty**

## dishonest *adjective*
1  It is dishonest to tell lies.
OTHER WORDS YOU MIGHT USE ARE    **deceitful    insincere**
2  It is dishonest to steal.
OTHER WORDS YOU MIGHT USE ARE    **cheating    criminal    unfair**
The opposite is **honest**

## dislike *verb*
OTHER VERBS YOU MIGHT USE ARE    **to detest    to loathe    to hate**
The opposite is **like**

## dismiss *verb*
1  The teacher dismissed the class.
OTHER VERBS YOU MIGHT USE ARE    **to let go    to release    to send away**
2  The boss dismissed her from her job.
OTHER VERBS ARE    **to fire    to sack**

## disorder *noun*
Jo and Sam cleared up the disorder after the party.
OTHER WORDS YOU MIGHT USE ARE    **chaos    confusion    mess    muddle**

## display *noun*
We put up a display of our work.
OTHER WORDS YOU MIGHT USE ARE    **exhibition    presentation    show**

## display *verb*
We display our work when parents come to school.
OTHER VERBS YOU MIGHT USE ARE    **to exhibit    to present    to show**

## distance *noun*
What's the distance between the goal posts?
OTHER WORDS YOU MIGHT USE ARE    **gap    space**
For more words, see **measurement**

## distant *adjective*
distant places.
OTHER WORDS YOU MIGHT USE ARE    **far-away    remote**
The opposite is **near**

## distinct *adjective*
1  I heard a distinct echo.
   OTHER WORDS YOU MIGHT USE ARE    **audible    clear**
2  The footprints in the mud were quite distinct.
   OTHER WORDS ARE    **definite    obvious    plain    visible**
3  The twins wear distinct colours.
   OTHER WORDS ARE    **contrasting    different**

## distressed *adjective*
The mother blackbird was very distressed when she saw the cat.
   OTHER WORDS YOU MIGHT USE ARE    **anxious    frightened    upset    worried**

## distribute *verb*
Jo distributed the pencils and paper.
   OTHER VERBS YOU MIGHT USE ARE    **to deal out    to give out    to hand out    to share out**

## district *noun*
We live in a hilly district.
   OTHER WORDS YOU MIGHT USE ARE    **area    locality    region    zone**

## disturb *verb*
1  Don't disturb me while I'm working.
   OTHER VERBS YOU MIGHT USE ARE    **to bother    to interrupt    to trouble    to worry**
2  A fox disturbed the chickens.
   OTHER VERBS ARE    **to alarm    to excite    to frighten    to upset**

## dive *verb*
We watched the sea birds diving into the water.
   OTHER VERBS YOU MIGHT USE ARE    **to drop    to plunge    to swoop**

## divide *verb*
1  Divide the sweets between you.
   OTHER VERBS YOU MIGHT USE ARE    **to deal out    to distribute    to share**
2  At the next junction the road divides.
   OTHER VERBS YOU MIGHT USE ARE    **to branch    to fork    to separate    to split**

## dizzy *adjective*
I feel dizzy if I stand up quickly.
   OTHER WORDS YOU MIGHT USE ARE    **faint    giddy    unsteady**

**do** *verb*

THIS VERB HAS MANY USES. HERE ARE SOME OF THE WAYS YOU CAN USE IT, AND SOME OTHER VERBS YOU COULD CHOOSE.

1  I have done my work.
   **to carry out    to complete    to finish    to perform**
2  Sam is going to do the dinner.
   **to attend to    to deal with    to handle    to make
   to manage    to prepare**
3  Will four big potatoes do?
   **to be enough    to be sufficient    to be suitable**

**doctor** *noun*
For other people who look after our health, see **health**

**dog** *noun*
A female dog is a **bitch**.
A young dog is a **pup** or **puppy**.
VARIOUS BREEDS OF DOG ARE

| | | | |
|---|---|---|---|
| **Alsatian** | **bloodhound** | **bulldog** | **collie** |
| **dachshund** | **Dalmatian** | **greyhound** | **Labrador** |
| **Pekingese** | **poodle** | **retriever** | **Rotweiller** |
| **sheepdog** | **spaniel** | **terrier** | **whippet** |

A dog of mixed breed is a **mongrel**.

**dot** *noun*
OTHER WORDS YOU MIGHT USE ARE    **mark    point    speck    spot**

**doubt** *noun*
There's some doubt about whether Sam is well enough to play.
OTHER WORDS YOU MIGHT USE ARE    **anxiety    hesitation    question
uncertainty    worry**

**doubtful** *adjective*
The rain made us doubtful about our picnic.
OTHER WORDS YOU MIGHT USE ARE    **uncertain    unsure
worried**
The opposite is **certain**

## drag *verb*
The tractor was dragging a load of logs.
>OTHER VERBS YOU MIGHT USE ARE **to draw    to haul    to pull    to tow    to tug**

## drama *noun*
1 Drama is one of Sam's favourite lessons.
>OTHER WORDS YOU MIGHT USE ARE **acting    improvisation    plays**
2 We had some drama today when the fire engines came.
>ANOTHER WORD IS **excitement**

## draw *verb*
1 Jo drew a picture with a pencil.
>ANOTHER VERB IS **to sketch**
2 The pony was drawing a cart.
>OTHER VERBS YOU MIGHT USE ARE **to haul    to pull    to tow**
3 The match drew a large crowd.
>OTHER VERBS ARE **to attract    to bring in    to pull in**
4 We drew 1–1 on Saturday.
>OTHER VERBS ARE **to be equal    to tie**

## dreadful *adjective*
a dreadful storm.
>OTHER WORDS YOU MIGHT USE ARE **alarming    awful    fearful    frightening    horrifying    terrible**
The opposite is **wonderful**

## dream *noun*
A nasty dream is a **nightmare**.
>SOMETHING LIKE A DREAM WHICH YOU HAVE WHILE YOU ARE AWAKE IS A **daydream    fantasy    illusion    vision**

## dream *verb*
>OTHER VERBS YOU MIGHT USE ARE **to fancy    to imagine**

## dress *noun*
>A DRESS FOR A SPECIAL OCCASION IS **evening dress    gown    party dress**
For things you wear, see **clothes**

## dribble *verb*

When I cut my knee, blood dribbled down my leg.

OTHER VERBS YOU MIGHT USE ARE     **to drip     to flow     to ooze     to run     to trickle**

---

## drink *verb*

To drink greedily is **to gulp** or **to guzzle** or **to swig**.
To drink a tiny bit at a time is **to sip**.
To drink with your tongue like a cat is **to lap**.

DIFFERENT COLD DRINKS ARE
**juice     lemonade     milk     mineral water     orangeade     squash     water**

SOME ALCOHOLIC DRINKS ARE
**beer     champagne     cider     lager     whisky     wine**

SOME HOT DRINKS ARE
**cocoa     coffee     tea**

---

## drip *verb*

Don't let paint drip on to the carpet!

OTHER VERBS YOU MIGHT USE ARE     **to dribble     to drop     to leak     to trickle**

## drive *verb*

1  Is it easy to drive a car?

OTHER VERBS YOU MIGHT USE ARE     **to control     to steer**

2  I drove the cow into the field.

OTHER VERBS ARE     **to force     to push     to urge**

## droop *verb*

The weather was so dry that the flowers began to droop.

OTHER VERBS YOU MIGHT USE ARE     **to flop     to go limp     to sag     to wilt**

## drop *noun*

drops of water.

OTHER WORDS YOU MIGHT USE ARE     **bead     drip     tear**

## drop *verb*

1  A lorry dropped its load on the motorway.

OTHER VERBS YOU MIGHT USE ARE     **to dump     to shed**

2 The waterfall drops from a high cliff.
OTHER VERBS ARE    **to cascade     to fall     to plunge**
3 The temperature drops at night.
OTHER VERBS ARE    **to decrease     to fall     to go down**

## dry *adjective*
1 Is the washing dry?
The opposite is **wet**
2 I feel dry: can I have a drink?
OTHER WORDS YOU MIGHT USE ARE    **parched     thirsty**

## duck *noun*
A male duck is a **drake**.
A young duck is a **duckling**.

## dull *adjective*
1 dull colours.
OTHER WORDS YOU MIGHT USE ARE    **dingy     drab     gloomy**
2 a dull day.
OTHER WORDS ARE    **cloudy     grey     overcast**
3 a dull pupil.
OTHER WORDS ARE    **dim     slow     stupid**
The opposite is **bright**
4 a dull film.
OTHER WORDS ARE    **boring     uninteresting**
The opposite is **interesting**

## dumb *adjective*
She was dumb with amazement.
OTHER WORDS YOU MIGHT USE ARE    **mute     silent     speechless**

## dump *verb*
1 I hate people who dump rubbish by the side of the road.
OTHER VERBS YOU MIGHT USE ARE    **to abandon     to discard
to throw away**
2 I dumped my things on the table.
OTHER VERBS ARE    **to drop     to leave     to unload**

## duty *noun*
1 If you see a crime, it's your duty to tell the police.
ANOTHER WORD IS **responsibility**
2 We can go to play when we've finished our duties.
OTHER WORDS ARE    **job     task**

# Ee

**eager** *adjective*
We were eager to start the game.
OTHER WORDS YOU MIGHT USE ARE   **enthusiastic   impatient   keen**

**earn** *verb*
How much does Sam earn when he washes the car?
OTHER VERBS YOU MIGHT USE ARE   **to deserve   to get   to make**

**earth** *noun*
1  We live on the planet Earth.
OTHER WORDS YOU MIGHT USE ARE   **the globe   the world**
2  Plants grow in the earth.
OTHER WORDS ARE   **ground   land   soil**

**easy** *adjective*
1  Jo finished her work quickly because the sums were easy.
OTHER WORDS YOU MIGHT USE ARE   **simple   straightforward
uncomplicated**
The opposite is **difficult**
2  The cat has an easy life.
OTHER WORDS ARE   **carefree   comfortable   relaxing   restful**

---

**eat** *verb*
The dog ate our dinner!
OTHER VERBS YOU MIGHT USE ARE
**to consume   to feed on   to swallow   to tuck into**
DIFFERENT WAYS TO EAT THINGS ARE
**to bite   to chew   to munch**
IF YOU EAT FOOD GREEDILY, OTHER VERBS ARE
**to bolt   to devour   to gobble   to gulp   to guzzle**
If you eat a tiny bit at a time, you **nibble**.
A cow **grazes** on grass.
A chicken **pecks** at its food.
A dog will **gnaw** at a bone.

## edge *noun*

THIS WORD HAS MANY USES. HERE ARE SOME OF THE WAYS YOU CAN USE IT, AND SOME OTHER WORDS YOU CAN CHOOSE

1 The edge of a picture.
   **border     frame**
2 The edge of a cricket field.
   **boundary     perimeter**
3 The edge of the road.
   **side     verge**
4 The edge of a curtain.
   **frill     fringe     hem**
5 The edge of a cup.
   **brim     rim**
6 The edge of a circle.
   **circumference**

The space down the edge of a piece of paper you have written on is the **margin**.

## educate *verb*

Our parents and teachers educate us.

OTHER VERBS YOU MIGHT USE ARE

**to bring up     to instruct     to teach     to train**

PLACES WHERE PEOPLE GO TO BE EDUCATED ARE

**college     playgroup     school     university**

DIFFERENT KINDS OF SCHOOL ARE

**boarding school     comprehensive school     infant school
junior school     kindergarten     nursery school
playgroup     primary school     secondary school**

## effort *noun*

1 You deserve a rest after all that effort.
   OTHER WORDS YOU MIGHT USE ARE     **labour     toil     trouble     work**
2 I made an effort to be good.
   OTHER WORDS ARE     **attempt     try**

## elect *verb*
We elected Jo as captain of the rounders team.
OTHER VERBS YOU MIGHT USE ARE **to choose** **to pick** **to select** **to vote for**

## election *noun*
We had an election to choose the captain of the team.
OTHER WORDS YOU MIGHT USE ARE **ballot** **vote**

## embarrassed *adjective*
1 Jo was embarrassed when she forgot her words in the play.
OTHER WORDS YOU MIGHT USE ARE **ashamed** **upset**
2 He was too embarrassed to ask for a second helping.
ANOTHER WORD IS **shy**

## emergency *noun*
We knew there was an emergency when we heard the fire engine.
ANOTHER WORD IS **crisis**

## empty *adjective*
1 an empty cup.
ANOTHER WORD IS **unfilled**
The opposite is **full**
2 an empty space.
ANOTHER WORD IS **hollow**
The opposite is **solid**
3 an empty house.
OTHER WORDS YOU MIGHT USE ARE **deserted** **uninhabited** **unoccupied** **vacant**
The opposite is **occupied**

## encourage *verb*
We shouted to encourage our team.
OTHER VERBS YOU MIGHT USE ARE **to support** **to urge on**

## end *noun*
1 We didn't stay for the end of the film.
OTHER WORDS YOU MIGHT USE ARE **conclusion** **ending** **finish**
2 We walked to the end of the train.
OTHER WORDS ARE **back** **rear** **tail**
3 He poked me with the end of a stick.
OTHER WORDS ARE **point** **tip**

## end *verb*

1 We waited for the storm to end.
> OTHER VERBS YOU MIGHT USE ARE **to cease   to finish   to stop**
The opposite is **begin**
2 It would be wonderful if we could end all wars.
> ANOTHER VERB IS **to abolish**

## enemy *noun*

> OTHER WORDS YOU MIGHT USE ARE **attacker   foe   opponent**
Opposites are **ally, friend**

## energetic *adjective*

Mum says that we are so energetic that she can't keep up with us.
> OTHER WORDS YOU MIGHT USE ARE **active   enthusiastic   lively   vigorous**
The opposite is **lazy**

## energy *noun*

You use up a lot of energy playing rounders.
> OTHER WORDS YOU MIGHT USE ARE **power   strength**

---

## engine *noun*

Cars, ships, and aeroplanes have engines to keep them going.
> DIFFERENT KINDS OF ENGINE ARE
> **diesel engine   electric motor   jet engine
> petrol engine   steam engine**

A railway engine is a **locomotive**.

---

## enjoy *verb*

The things Jo enjoys most are ice-skating and reading.
> OTHER VERBS YOU MIGHT USE ARE **to appreciate   to like   to love**
The opposite is **dislike**

## enough *adjective*

Have you had enough food?
> OTHER WORDS YOU MIGHT USE ARE **adequate   sufficient**

## enter *verb*

Don't enter the classroom until the teacher tells you to.
> PHRASES YOU MIGHT USE ARE **to come in   to go in**

## entertain *verb*
A conjuror entertained us at Jo's party.
ANOTHER VERB IS **to amuse**

---

## entertainment *noun*
OTHER WORDS YOU MIGHT USE ARE
amusement   enjoyment   fun

ENTERTAINMENTS YOU GO OUT TO ENJOY INCLUDE
ballet   cinema   circus   concert   dance   disco
drama   fair   opera   pantomime   play   waxworks
zoo

ENTERTAINMENTS YOU ENJOY AT HOME INCLUDE
computer games   music   radio   television   video

PEOPLE WHO ENTERTAIN US IN THE THEATRE OR ON RADIO AND TV ARE
actor   actress   broadcaster   comedian   comic
conjuror   dancer   DJ   magician   musician   singer
ventriloquist

PEOPLE WHO ENTERTAIN US IN A CIRCUS ARE
acrobat   clown   juggler   lion tamer   trapeze artist

---

## enthusiastic *adjective*
Sam is an enthusiastic member of the football team.
OTHER WORDS YOU MIGHT USE ARE   **eager   interested   keen**

## entrance *noun*
Pay your money at the entrance.
OTHER WORDS YOU MIGHT USE ARE   **door   entry   way in**
The opposite is **exit**

## envious *adjective*
Jo was a bit envious when she saw what Sam got for his birthday.
ANOTHER WORD IS **jealous**

## equal *adjective*
At half time the scores were equal.
OTHER WORDS YOU MIGHT USE ARE   **even   identical   level   the same**
The opposite is **different**

## equipment noun
We keep the games equipment in a shed in the playground.
OTHER WORDS YOU MIGHT USE ARE     **apparatus**     (*informal*) **gear     tackle**

## error noun
Our teacher corrects the errors in our work.
OTHER WORDS YOU MIGHT USE ARE     **fault     mistake**     (*informal*) **slip**

## escape verb
The cat chased the mouse, but it escaped.
PHRASES YOU MIGHT USE ARE     **to get away     to run away**

## essential adjective
It's essential to start early if you want to avoid traffic jams.
OTHER WORDS YOU MIGHT USE ARE     **important     necessary     vital**
The opposite is **unnecessary**

## estimate verb
Jo estimated how many sandwiches everyone would eat at her party.
OTHER VERBS YOU MIGHT USE ARE     **to calculate     to guess     to work out**

## even adjective
1  You need an even field for playing rounders.
OTHER WORDS ARE     **flat     level     smooth**
The opposite is **bumpy**
2  At half time the scores were even.
OTHER WORDS YOU MIGHT USE ARE     **equal     level     the same**
The opposite is **different**
3  Even numbers are numbers you can divide by two, such as 2, 8, 20.
The opposite is **odd**

## evening noun
VARIOUS TIMES OF THE EVENING ARE     **dusk     sunset     twilight**

## event noun
The fathers' sack race was the funniest event on sports day.
OTHER WORDS YOU MIGHT USE ARE     **happening     incident     occasion**

## evidence noun
The police had evidence that he was guilty.
OTHER WORDS YOU MIGHT USE ARE     **information     proof**

**evil** *adjective*

Murder is an evil thing.

OTHER WORDS YOU MIGHT USE ARE   **hateful   immoral   sinful   wicked   wrong**

The opposite is **good**

**exact** *adjective*

Have you got the exact time?

OTHER WORDS YOU MIGHT USE ARE   **accurate   correct   precise   right   true**

**examination** *noun*

1 Sam had a music examination at the end of term.

OTHER WORDS YOU MIGHT USE ARE   (*informal*) **exam   test**

2 When I was ill, I went to the doctor's for an examination.

ANOTHER WORD IS (*informal*) **check-up**

**examine** *verb*

1 We examined the strange insect carefully.

OTHER VERBS YOU MIGHT USE ARE   **to inspect   to study**

2 The police examined the suspect.

OTHER VERBS ARE   **to interrogate   to question**

**example** *noun*

When the parents come to school, we display examples of our work.

OTHER WORDS YOU MIGHT USE ARE   **sample   specimen**

**excellent** *adjective*

OTHER WORDS YOU MIGHT USE ARE   (*informal*) **brilliant** (*informal*) **fantastic   marvellous   outstanding** (*informal*) **tremendous   wonderful**

For other words, see **good**

**exchange** *verb*

Sam exchanged his old bike for some roller skates.

OTHER VERBS YOU MIGHT USE ARE   **to substitute** (*informal*) **to swop   to trade in**

**excite** *verb*

The amazing goal excited the crowd.

OTHER VERBS YOU MIGHT USE ARE   **to arouse   to provoke   to rouse   to stimulate   to stir up   to thrill**

## excited *adjective*
We were excited on the morning before we had the party.
OTHER WORDS YOU MIGHT USE ARE     **boisterous     lively     worked up**

## excitement *noun*
The game was full of excitement.
OTHER WORDS YOU MIGHT USE ARE     **action     drama     suspense     thrills**

## exclaim *verb*
OTHER VERBS YOU MIGHT USE ARE     **to call out     to shout     to yell**

## excuse *verb*
1  Please excuse our dog's bad behaviour.
OTHER VERBS YOU MIGHT USE ARE     **to forgive     to overlook     to pardon**
2  I was excused from swimming because I had a cold.
A PHRASE IS **to let off**

## exhausted *adjective*
I was exhausted after my long walk.
OTHER WORDS YOU MIGHT USE ARE     **tired     weary     worn out**

## exhibition *noun*
We had an exhibition of our work.
OTHER WORDS YOU MIGHT USE ARE     **display     show**

## exist *verb*
Plants can't exist without water.
OTHER VERBS YOU MIGHT USE ARE     **to keep going     to live     to survive**

## exit *noun*
OTHER WORDS YOU MIGHT USE ARE     **door     way out**
The opposite is **entrance**

## expect *verb*
I expect it will rain later.
ANOTHER VERB IS **to     forecast**

## expedition *noun*
On Saturday, Mum and Jo went on an expedition to the shops.
OTHER WORDS YOU MIGHT USE ARE     **journey     outing     trip**

## expel *verb*
The dog was expelled from the shop because he was a nuisance.
OTHER VERBS YOU MIGHT USE ARE    (*informal*) **to kick out    to throw out**
TO EXPEL SOMEONE FROM A COUNTRY    **to banish    to deport    to exile**
TO EXPEL SOMEONE FROM THEIR HOME **to evict**

## expensive *adjective*
Mum didn't buy me any new jeans because they were too expensive.
OTHER WORDS YOU MIGHT USE ARE    **costly    dear**    (*informal*) **pricey**
The opposite is **cheap**

## explain *verb*
Mum explained how computers work.
OTHER VERBS YOU MIGHT USE ARE    **to make clear    to show**

## explode *verb*
The firework exploded.
OTHER VERBS YOU MIGHT USE ARE    **to blow up    to burst    to go off**

## explore *verb*
Sam went off with his friends to explore the caves.
OTHER VERBS YOU MIGHT USE ARE    **to investigate    to look round**

---

## expression *noun*
I noticed Jo's unhappy expression.
OTHER WORDS YOU MIGHT USE ARE    **face    look**
DIFFERENT EXPRESSIONS YOU SEE ON PEOPLE'S FACES ARE
**frown    glare    grin    laugh    scowl    smile    sneer
yawn**

---

## extra *adjective*
Do you want some extra milk in your tea?
OTHER WORDS YOU MIGHT USE ARE    **additional    more**

## extraordinary *adjective*
I didn't believe his extraordinary story about a space ship.
OTHER WORDS YOU MIGHT USE ARE    **amazing    incredible    odd
peculiar    queer    remarkable    strange    unbelievable
uncommon    unusual**
The opposite is **ordinary**

## extravagant *adjective*

Mum says it's extravagant to cook more food than you can eat.

OTHER WORDS YOU MIGHT USE ARE     **expensive     wasteful**

## extreme *adjective*

1 extreme cold.

OTHER WORDS YOU MIGHT USE ARE     **exceptional     great     intense     severe**

2 the extreme corner of the playground.

OTHER WORDS ARE     **farthest     furthest**

# Ff

## face *noun*

1 He made a funny face.

For other words, see **expression**

2 Each face of a dice has a different number of dots.

OTHER WORDS YOU MIGHT USE ARE     **side     surface**

## facts *noun*

You find lots of facts in an encyclopaedia.

OTHER WORDS YOU MIGHT USE ARE     **data     evidence     information**

## fade *verb*

1 The sun faded the curtains.

OTHER VERBS YOU MIGHT USE ARE     **to bleach     to discolour     to whiten**

2 In the evening, the light fades and the stars begin to shine.

OTHER VERBS ARE     **to disappear     to dwindle     to melt away**

## fail *verb*

1 He failed to stop at the red light.

OTHER VERBS YOU MIGHT USE ARE     **to neglect     to omit**

2 He failed his driving test.

A PHRASE IS **to be unsuccessful**

The opposite is **pass**

## faint *adjective*

1  I saw a faint shape in the mist.
> OTHER WORDS YOU MIGHT USE ARE    **blurred    dim    hazy    misty    pale    unclear**

The opposite is **clear**

2  We heard faint cries for help.
> OTHER WORDS ARE    **distant    low    muffled    weak**

The opposite is **loud**

3  Sam felt faint because he stood up too quickly.
> OTHER WORDS ARE    **dizzy    giddy    unsteady**

## faint *verb*

It was so hot that he fainted.
> OTHER VERBS ARE    **to become unconscious    to collapse**

## fair *adjective*

1  fair hair.
> OTHER WORDS YOU MIGHT USE ARE    **blond    light    pale**

The opposite is **dark**

2  It's not fair if she gets more than me.
> OTHER WORDS ARE    **just    proper    right**

The opposite is **unfair**

3  Was the referee fair?
> OTHER WORDS YOU MIGHT USE ARE    **honest    unbiased**

The opposite is **biased**

4  I had a fair chance of winning.
> OTHER WORDS ARE    **moderate    reasonable**

## faithful *adjective*

The dog is his faithful companion.
> OTHER WORDS YOU MIGHT USE ARE    **devoted    loyal    reliable    trustworthy**

The opposite is **treacherous**

## fall *verb*

1  The dog was so excited that he fell in the river.
> OTHER VERBS YOU MIGHT USE ARE    **to drop    to plunge    to slip    to topple    to tumble**

2  The burning tower fell to the ground.
> OTHER VERBS YOU MIGHT USE ARE    **to collapse    to crash**

3  The temperature falls at night.
> OTHER VERBS ARE    **to decrease    to go down**

The opposite is **rise**

## false *adjective*

1 He gave us false information.

OTHER WORDS YOU MIGHT USE ARE    **inaccurate    incorrect    made-up    misleading    wrong**

The opposite is **correct**

2 Father Christmas wore a false beard.

OTHER WORDS ARE    **artificial    fake    imitation**

The opposite is **real**

## familiar *adjective*

I like to be back in my familiar surroundings after a holiday.

OTHER WORDS YOU MIGHT USE ARE    **normal    regular    usual    well-known**

The opposite is **strange**

---

## family *noun*

The members of your family are your **relations** or **relatives**.

MEMBERS OF YOUR IMMEDIATE FAMILY ARE

**brother    daughter    father    husband    mother    sister    son    stepfather    stepmother    wife**

OTHER RELATIONS YOU MIGHT HAVE ARE

**aunt    cousins    grandfather    grandmother    nephew    niece    uncle**

Members of your family who lived in the past are your **ancestors**.

---

## famous *adjective*

a famous TV actor.

ANOTHER WORD IS **well-known**

## fan *noun*

Sam is a fan of our football team.

OTHER WORDS YOU MIGHT USE ARE    **admirer    follower    supporter**

## fancy *verb*

1 What do you fancy to eat?

OTHER VERBS YOU MIGHT USE ARE    **to feel like    to long for    to want    to wish for**

2 I fancied I saw a ghost.

OTHER VERBS ARE    **to dream    to imagine    to think**

## fantastic *adjective*

1  We heard a fantastic story about dragons and wizards.
OTHER WORDS YOU MIGHT USE ARE    **amazing    extraordinary**
**incredible    strange    weird**
2  (*informal*) We had a fantastic time at the party.
For other words, see **good**

---

## farm *noun*

Another word for a small farm is **smallholding**.
A word for a small farm in Scotland is a **croft**.
A word for a cattle farm in North America is a **ranch**.

BUILDINGS YOU SEE ON A FARM ARE
**barn    cow-shed    farmhouse    granary    pigsty
stable**

MACHINES AND EQUIPMENT YOU SEE ON A FARM ARE
**combine harvester    cultivator    drill    harrow
milking-machine    mower    plough    tractor
wagon**

OTHER THINGS YOU MIGHT SEE ON A FARM ARE
**battery cages    farmyard    hayrick** or **haystack    silo**

Farmers grow various crops.
KINDS OF CORN OR CEREALS ARE
**barley    maize** or **sweetcorn    oats    rye    wheat**

OTHER CROPS ARE
**potatoes    sugarbeet    vegetables**

ANIMALS THAT FARMERS KEEP ARE
**bull    calf    cow    goat    horse    lamb    pig
sheep**
Bulls and cows are called **cattle**.

BIRDS THAT YOU SEE ON A FARM ARE
**chicken    duck    goose    hen    turkey**
These birds are called **poultry**.

---

## fashion *noun*

Sam knows about the latest fashion in music.
OTHER WORDS YOU MIGHT USE ARE    **craze    style    trend**

## **fast** *adjective*

1 We started off at a fast pace.
OTHER WORDS YOU MIGHT USE ARE     **brisk     hurried     quick     rapid
smart     speedy     swift**

2 Granny caught a fast train to London.
OTHER WORDS ARE     **express     high-speed**
The opposite is **slow**

## **fat** *adjective*

1 a fat person.
OTHER WORDS YOU MIGHT USE ARE     **chubby     overweight     plump**
(*informal*) **podgy     stout**     (*informal*) **tubby**

2 a fat book.
ANOTHER WORD IS **thick**
The opposite is **thin**

---

## **fat** *noun*

KINDS OF FAT YOU MIGHT EAT OR USE IN COOKING ARE
**butter     cooking oil     dripping     lard     margarine
suet**

---

## **fault** *noun*

The teacher pointed out the faults in my work.
OTHER WORDS YOU MIGHT USE ARE     **error     flaw     mistake**
(*informal*) **slip     weakness**

## **favour** *noun*

She did me a favour and lent me her umbrella.
OTHER WORDS YOU MIGHT USE ARE     **good deed     kindness**

## **fear** *noun*

Fear spread through the town when the earthquake started.
OTHER WORDS YOU MIGHT USE ARE     **alarm     dread     fright     horror
panic     terror**

## **feeble** *adjective*

I felt feeble after I was ill.
OTHER WORDS YOU MIGHT USE ARE     **delicate     frail     weak**
The opposite is **strong**

**feel** *verb*

1 Feel the cat's soft fur.

OTHER VERBS YOU MIGHT USE ARE  **to finger**  **to stroke**  **to touch**

2 Granny feels the cold more than I do.

OTHER VERBS YOU MIGHT USE ARE  **to notice**  **to suffer from**

**feeling** *noun*

My feeling is that it will be fine tomorrow.

OTHER WORDS YOU MIGHT USE ARE  **guess**  **instinct**  **intuition**  **opinion**

**feelings**

1 When you are very sad, it's hard not to show your feelings.

ANOTHER WORD IS **emotions**

2 Vegetarians often have strong feelings about killing animals.

OTHER WORDS ARE  **beliefs**  **opinions**

---

**female** *noun*

OTHER WORDS YOU MIGHT USE

A female human being is a **woman**.

A female dog is a **bitch**.

A female deer or rabbit is a **doe**.

A female sheep is a **ewe**.

A female bird is a **hen**.

A female lion is a **lioness**.

A female horse is a **mare**.

A female goat is a **nanny goat**.

A female pig is a **sow**.

A female fox is a **vixen**.

---

**fence** *noun*

OTHER THINGS USED TO MARK THE EDGE OF A PIECE OF LAND ARE  **barrier**  **hedge**  **railings**  **wall**

**fetch** *verb*

Jo's dog fetched the newspaper.

OTHER VERBS YOU MIGHT USE ARE  **to bring**  **to carry**  **to collect**  **to get**

**fidget** *verb*

Please don't fidget!

OTHER VERBS YOU MIGHT USE ARE  **to be restless**  **to fiddle**

## field *noun*

OTHER WORDS YOU MIGHT USE ARE

a field of grass:    **meadow**    **pasture**

a small field for horses: **paddock**

## fierce *adjective*

a fierce dog.

OTHER WORDS YOU MIGHT USE ARE    **ferocious**    **savage**    **vicious**

The opposite is **gentle**

---

## fight *noun*

OTHER WORDS YOU MIGHT USE ARE

**combat**    **conflict**    **contest**    **quarrel**    (*informal*) **row**

WORDS FOR DIFFERENT KINDS OF FIGHTING ARE

a fight between armies

**battle**    **war**

a fight betwen two people

**duel**

a fight between two families or gangs

**feud**

a fight in the street

**brawl**    **riot**    **scuffle**

a fight to entertain people

**bout**    **boxing match**    **wrestling match**

a fight between knights in old times

**joust**

a friendly or unimportant fight

(*informal*) **scrap**    **squabble**    **tussle**

WORDS FOR FIGHTER ARE

**soldier**    **warrior**

An archer used to fight with a **bow** and **arrow**.
A boxer fights with **fists**.
A gladiator used to fight to **entertain** people.
A gunman fights with **guns**.
Knights used to fight on **horses**.
A wrestler fights with **hands** and **arms**.

For other words, see **soldier**

## figure *noun*
1 Jo added up the figures.
OTHER WORDS YOU MIGHT USE ARE  **digit**  **number**
2 Sam has a slim figure.
ANOTHER WORD IS **shape**

## file *noun*
We lined up in a single file.
OTHER WORDS YOU MIGHT USE ARE  **column**  **line**  **queue**  **row**

## fill *verb*
I filled the box with sweets.
OTHER VERBS YOU MIGHT USE ARE  **to cram**  **to load**  **to pack**

## film *noun*
I watched a good film on TV.
ANOTHER WORD IS **movie**
DIFFERENT KINDS OF FILM ARE
**adventure**  **cartoon**  **comedy**  **documentary**  **horror**
**science fiction**  **western**

## filthy *adjective*
Put those filthy jeans in the washing machine!
OTHER WORDS YOU MIGHT USE ARE  **dirty**  **foul**  (*informal*) **grubby**
**messy**  (*informal*) **mucky**  **muddy**
The opposite is **clean**

## final *adjective*
They scored in the final moments of the game.
OTHER WORDS YOU MIGHT USE ARE  **closing**  **concluding**  **last**
The opposite is **first**

## find *verb*
1 Did you find the money you lost?
OTHER VERBS YOU MIGHT USE ARE  **to come across**  **to discover**
**to get back**  **to recover**
The opposite is **lose**
2 Did the police find the thief?
OTHER VERBS ARE  **to trace**  **to track down**
3 I found the information I need.
ANOTHER VERB IS **to discover**

## fine *adjective*

1 fine thread.
   OTHER WORDS YOU MIGHT USE ARE       **slender**    **thin**
The opposite is **thick**
2 fine sand.
   ANOTHER WORD IS **powdery**
The opposite is **coarse**
3 fine weather.
   OTHER WORDS ARE       **bright**    **dry**    **sunny**
The opposite is **wet**
4 a fine piece of work.
   OTHER WORDS ARE       **good**    **great**    **excellent**
The opposite is **bad**

## finish *verb*

1 Finish your work now.
   OTHER VERBS YOU MIGHT USE ARE       **to complete**    **to round off**
   **to stop**
2 The film finished with an exciting car chase.
   OTHER VERBS ARE       **to conclude**    **to end**
3 Did you finish those sweets?
   OTHER WORDS ARE       **to consume**    **to use up**
The opposite is **start**

---

### fire *noun*

We watched the firemen put out the fire.
   OTHER WORDS YOU MIGHT USE ARE
      **blaze**    **flames**    **inferno**

   FIRES USED FOR HEAT OR COOKING ARE
      **barbecue**    **boiler**    **camp fire**    **central heating**
      **coal fire**    **electric fire**    **furnace**    **gas fire**    **gas ring**
      **grill**    **hot plate**    **immersion heater**    **oven**    **stove**

   FIRES WHICH BURN THINGS WE DON'T WANT ARE
      **bonfire**    **incinerator**

---

## fire *verb*

to fire a gun.
   OTHER VERBS YOU MIGHT USE ARE       **to let off**    **to shoot**

## firm *adjective*

1　Make sure the rock is firm before you step on it.
OTHER WORDS YOU MIGHT USE ARE　**fixed　secure　steady**
2　Mum whisked the cream until it was firm.
OTHER WORDS ARE　**set　solid　stiff**

## first *adjective*

1　Jo was the first to arrive at the party.
OTHER WORDS YOU MIGHT USE ARE　**earliest　soonest**
2　Who was the first man in space?
ANOTHER WORD IS **original**
The opposite is **last**

---

### fish *noun*

SOME DIFFERENT KINDS OF FISH ARE
**carp　cod　eel　goldfish　haddock　herring
jellyfish　mackerel　minnow　octopus　perch
pike　pilchard　plaice　salmon　sardine　shark
sole　stickleback　trout**

ANIMALS WHICH LIVE IN WATER BUT ARE NOT REAL FISH ARE
**dolphin　octopus　porpoise　whale**

---

## fisherman *noun*

A person who fishes with a rod is an **angler**.
A person who goes to sea in a boat to catch fish is a **trawlerman**.

## fit *adjective*

1　You have to be fit to play football.
OTHER WORDS YOU MIGHT USE ARE　**healthy　strong　well**
2　Is the old house fit to live in?
ANOTHER WORD IS **suitable**

## fit *verb*

Jo helped Sam fit the pieces of his model aeroplane together.
OTHER VERBS YOU MIGHT USE ARE　**to assemble　to put together**

## fix *verb*

Dad fixed a shelf to the wall.
OTHER VERBS YOU MIGHT USE ARE　**to attach　to secure**
For other verbs, see **fasten**

**fizzy** *adjective*
fizzy drinks.
OTHER WORDS YOU MIGHT USE ARE    **bubbly    effervescent
sparkling**

**flame** *noun*
For other words, see **fire**

**flap** *verb*
The flags flapped in the wind.
OTHER VERBS YOU MIGHT USE ARE    **to flutter    to wave**

**flat** *adjective*
A games field must be flat.
OTHER WORDS YOU MIGHT USE ARE    **even    level    smooth**

**flavour** *noun*
I like the flavour of this drink.
ANOTHER WORD IS **taste**

**fling** *verb*
I flung a pebble into the water.
OTHER VERBS YOU MIGHT USE ARE    (*informal*) **to chuck    to throw
to toss**

**float** *verb*
1  Will this toy boat float?
A PHRASE IS **to stay up**
The opposite is **sink**
2  The smoke from the bonfire floated in the air.
OTHER VERBS YOU MIGHT USE ARE    **to drift    to hover**

**flock** *noun*
For other words, see **group**

**floor** *noun*
THINGS USED TO COVER A FLOOR ARE
**carpet    lino    mat    rug    tiles**

## flow *verb*

Water flowed from the broken pipe.

OTHER VERBS YOU MIGHT USE ARE

to flow fast    **to gush    to pour    to run    to spurt    to squirt    to stream**

to flow slowly    **to dribble    to drip    to leak    to ooze    to trickle**

to flow over the edge    **to overflow    to spill**

---

## flower *noun*

OTHER WORDS YOU MIGHT USE ARE

**bloom    blossom**

WORDS FOR A BUNCH OF FLOWERS ARE

**arrangement    bouquet    posy**

FLOWERS YOU SEE IN GARDENS ARE

**carnation    chrysanthemum    crocus    daffodil    daisy    forget-me-not    geranium    hollyhock    hyacinth    lily    lupin    marigold    pansy    rose    snowdrop    sunflower    tulip    wallflower**

FLOWERS THAT OFTEN GROW WILD ARE

**bluebell    buttercup    dandelion    foxglove    poppy    primrose    violet**

---

## fluffy *adjective*

OTHER WORDS YOU MIGHT USE ARE    **feathery    furry    soft    woolly**

## fly *verb*

Birds, bats, and aeroplanes fly.

OTHER VERBS YOU MIGHT USE ARE    **to glide    to hover    to rise    to soar    to swoop**

## fog *noun*

I couldn't see because of the fog.

OTHER WORDS YOU MIGHT USE ARE    **haze    mist**

## fold *verb*

The paper will go in the envelope if you fold it.

OTHER VERBS YOU MIGHT USE ARE    **to bend over    to crease    to double over**

## follow *verb*

1 A dog followed me.
    OTHER VERBS YOU MIGHT USE ARE    **to chase**    **to come after**    **to pursue**
    **to tail**    **to track**
2 Follow this road.
    OTHER VERBS ARE    **to go along**    **to take**
3 Did you follow what she said?
    ANOTHER VERB IS **to understand**

## food *noun*, see next page

## foolish *adjective*

It's foolish to run across the main road.
    OTHER WORDS YOU MIGHT USE ARE    (*informal*) **daft**    **idiotic**    **mad**
    **silly**    **stupid**    **unwise**
The opposite is **sensible**

## foot *noun*

An animal's foot is a **hoof** or **paw**.
A bird has **toes** or **claws**.
For other parts of the body, see **body**

## forbid *verb*

The head forbids eating in class.
    OTHER VERBS YOU MIGHT USE ARE    **to ban**    **to prohibit**
The opposite is **allow**

## force *noun*

We had to use force to open the door.
    OTHER WORDS YOU MIGHT USE ARE    **might**    **power**    **strength**    **violence**

## force *verb*

They can't force me to play.
    OTHER VERBS YOU MIGHT USE ARE    **to compel**    **to make**    **to order**

## forest *noun*

Don't get lost in the forest!
    OTHER WORDS YOU MIGHT USE ARE    **jungle**    **wood**

## forgery *noun*

The shopkeeper checked to see if the £10 note was a forgery.
    OTHER WORDS YOU MIGHT USE ARE    **copy**    **fake**    **imitation**

# food *noun*

OTHER WORDS YOU MIGHT USE ARE

> diet    nourishment    provisions    refreshments

Food for farm animals is **fodder**.

BASIC INGREDIENTS OF FOOD ARE

> carbohydrate    fat    fibre    protein    starch
> vitamins

CEREALS ARE

> barley    maize or sweetcorn    oats    rice    rye    wheat

FOOD MADE FROM CEREALS:

> bran    cornflakes    cornflour    flour
> muesli    oatmeal    porridge

KINDS OF BREAD:

> bagel    brown bread    chapatti    crusty bread
> French bread    nan    rye bread    white bread
> wholemeal bread

OTHER FOODS MADE FROM FLOUR:

> biscuits    cake    dumplings    noodles
> pasta    pastry    pizza

SOME KINDS OF CAKE ARE

> bun    doughnut or donut    flan
> fruitcake    gingerbread    meringue    muffin
> scone    shortbread    spongecake    tart

KINDS OF PASTA:

> lasagne    macaroni    spaghetti

THINGS MADE WITH PASTRY:

> pasty    pie    mince pies    quiche    sausage rolls

FOOD MADE WITH MILK:

> blancmange    butter    cheese    cream
> custard    milk pudding    yogurt

KINDS OF MEAT ARE

> bacon    beef    chicken    ham
> lamb    pork    turkey    veal
> venison

FOOD USUALLY MADE WITH MEAT:

> burgers    chop suey    curry    fritters
> goulash    hash    hot-pot    meat pie
> mince    paté    rissole    sausage
> stew

Food which doesn't contain any meat is **vegetarian** food.

FOOD MADE WITH EGGS:

omelette        pancakes        soufflé

FISH WHICH PEOPLE EAT ARE

| | | | |
|---|---|---|---|
| cod | haddock | herring | kipper |
| mackerel | pilchard | plaice | salmon |
| sardine | scampi | shellfish | sole |
| trout | tuna | | |

A mixture of fish and shellfish is **seafood**.
Caviare is a very expensive food from a fish called **sturgeon**.

FRUIT WHICH YOU CAN EAT ARE

| | | | |
|---|---|---|---|
| apple | apricot | banana | blackberry |
| blackcurrant | cherry | coconut | damson |
| date | fig | gooseberry | grape |
| grapefruit | kiwi fruit | lemon | lime |
| melon | orange | peach | pear |
| pineapple | plum | raspberry | strawberry |
| tangerine | tomato | | |

VEGETABLES PEOPLE EAT INCLUDE

| | | | |
|---|---|---|---|
| asparagus | beans | Brussels sprouts | |
| cabbage | carrot | cauliflower | greens |
| leek | marrow | nuts | onion |
| parsnip | pea | potato | pumpkin |
| spinach | swede | turnip | |

VEGETABLES WE EAT IN SALAD ARE

| | | | |
|---|---|---|---|
| beetroot | celery | cress | cucumber |
| lettuce | mustard and cress | | onion |
| potato | radish | tomato | watercress |

SOME SWEET FOODS:

| | | | |
|---|---|---|---|
| honey | ice cream | icing | jam |
| jelly | marmalade | mousse | pudding |
| syrup | tart | treacle | trifle |

THINGS USED TO ADD FLAVOUR TO FOOD

| | | | |
|---|---|---|---|
| chutney | dressing | garlic | gravy |
| herbs | ketchup | mayonnaise | mustard |
| pepper | pickle | salt | sauce |
| seasoning | spice | sugar | vanilla |
| vinegar | | | |

## forget *verb*
I forgot my money.
> OTHER VERBS YOU MIGHT USE ARE **to leave behind    to overlook**

The opposite is **remember**

## forgetful *adjective*
He was so forgetful that he left his money behind.
> OTHER WORDS YOU MIGHT USE ARE **absent-minded    careless    scatterbrained    thoughtless**

## forgive *verb*
Sam forgave Jo for forgetting his birthday.
> OTHER VERBS YOU MIGHT USE ARE **to excuse    to pardon**

## form *noun*
The wizard could change his form.
> OTHER WORDS YOU MIGHT USE ARE **appearance    shape**

## fortunate *adjective*
It's fortunate that it didn't rain.
> ANOTHER WORD IS **lucky**

The opposite is **unlucky**

## foul *adjective*
foul slime. foul weather.
> OTHER WORDS YOU MIGHT USE ARE **dirty    disgusting    filthy    horrible    nasty    revolting**

The opposite is **nice**

## fragile *adjective*
Take care with the best china because it is fragile.
> OTHER WORDS YOU MIGHT USE ARE **brittle    delicate    thin**

The opposite is **strong**

## fragment *noun*
When Jo broke the tea-pot, Mum made her sweep up the fragments.
> OTHER WORDS YOU MIGHT USE ARE **bit    chip    piece    scrap**

## frail *adjective*
I felt frail after my illness.
> OTHER WORDS YOU MIGHT USE ARE **delicate    feeble    weak**

The opposite is **strong**

## free *adjective*

1 The cat is free to wander about.
A PHRASE YOU MIGHT USE IS **at liberty**
2 Is the bathroom free?
OTHER WORDS ARE     **available     unoccupied     vacant**

## free *verb*

The prisoner asked the guards when they were going to free him.
OTHER VERBS YOU MIGHT USE ARE     **to let out     to liberate     to release**
The opposite is **capture**

## frequent *adjective*

Our picnic was spoiled by frequent showers.
OTHER WORDS YOU MIGHT USE ARE     **many     numerous     repeated**

## fresh *adjective*

1 fresh bread.
ANOTHER WORD IS **new**
The opposite is **stale**
2 fresh air.
OTHER WORDS YOU MIGHT USE ARE     **clean     cool     pure**
3 fresh after a rest.
OTHER WORDS ARE     **lively     rested**
4 a fresh page.
OTHER WORDS ARE     **different     new     unused**

## friend *noun*

An informal word is **mate**.
A friend who fights on your side is an **ally**.
A friend who works with you is a **partner**.
Someone you don't know very well is an **acquaintance**.
The opposite is **enemy**

## friendly *adjective*

a friendly smile.     **affectionate     kind     loving**
The opposite is **unfriendly**

## frighten *verb*

Don't frighten the animals.
OTHER VERBS YOU MIGHT USE ARE     **to alarm     to scare     to startle**
**to terrify**
**frightened** *adjective*, see **afraid**
**frightening** *adjective*, see **terrible**

**froth** *noun*
The soap leaves froth in the bowl.
OTHER WORDS YOU MIGHT USE ARE   **bubbles   foam   lather   scum**

**frown** *verb*
Dad frowns when he is angry.
OTHER VERBS YOU MIGHT USE ARE   **to look stern   to scowl**

**fruit** *noun*
For fruit you can eat, see **food**

**fuel** *noun*
THINGS WE USE AS FUEL ARE
**coal   electricity   gas   oil   petrol   wood**

**full** *adjective*
1  The bus was full.
OTHER WORDS YOU MIGHT USE ARE   **crowded   jammed   packed**
2  My cup is full.
ANOTHER WORD IS **overflowing**
The opposite is **empty**

**fun** *noun*
We had lots of fun at Jo's party.
OTHER WORDS YOU MIGHT USE ARE   **amusement   enjoyment   games   jokes   laughing   pleasure**

**funeral** *noun*
KINDS OF FUNERAL ARE   **burial   cremation**

**funny** *adjective*
1  funny jokes.
OTHER WORDS YOU MIGHT USE ARE   **amusing   comic   comical   humorous   laughable   ridiculous   witty**
The opposite is **serious**
2  The ice cream has a funny taste.
For other words, see **peculiar**

**furious** *adjective*
For other words, see **angry**

## furniture *noun*

KINDS OF FURNITURE YOU PUT THINGS IN OR ON ARE

**bookcase     bureau     cabinet     chest of drawers
coffee table     cupboard     desk     dresser     sideboard
table     wardrobe**

KINDS OF FURNITURE YOU SIT ON ARE

**armchair     chair     pouffe     rocking chair     settee
sofa     stool**

KINDS OF FURNITURE YOU CAN SLEEP ON ARE

**bed     cot     couch     divan**

## furry *adjective*

furry animals.

OTHER WORDS YOU MIGHT USE ARE     **fluffy     hairy     woolly**

## fuss *noun*

There was a lot of fuss when a lion escaped from the zoo.

OTHER WORDS YOU MIGHT USE ARE     **bother     commotion     excitement
trouble     uproar**

## fussy *adjective*

Our cat is fussy about her food.

OTHER WORDS YOU MIGHT USE ARE     **choosy     particular**

# Gg

## gain *verb*

Sam gained first prize for swimming.

OTHER VERBS YOU MIGHT USE ARE     **to earn     to get     to obtain
to receive     to win**

**game** *noun*

1 What's your favourite game?
OTHER WORDS YOU MIGHT USE ARE
amusement   entertainment   pastime   sport

2 Let's have a game of chess.
OTHER WORDS ARE   competition   match   tournament
VARIOUS GAMES ARE
bingo   cards   charades   chess   darts   dominoes
draughts   hide-and-seek   hopscotch   ludo   marbles
skittles   snooker   table tennis   tiddlywinks

For other games, see **sport**

**gang** *noun*
For other words, see **group**

**gaol** *noun*
Some people spell this word as 'jail'
OTHER WORDS ARE   dungeon   prison

**gap** *noun*

1 a gap in the fence.
OTHER WORDS YOU MIGHT USE ARE   break   hole   space

2 a gap between lessons.
OTHER WORDS ARE   break   interval   pause   rest

**garden** *noun*

THINGS YOU GROW IN A GARDEN ARE
flowers   fruit   shrubs   trees   vegetables

PARTS OF A GARDEN ARE
border   compost heap   flower bed   greenhouse
hedge   lawn   orchard   path   patio   pond
rockery   shed   shrubbery

TOOLS YOU USE IN THE GARDEN ARE
broom   fork   hoe   lawn-mower   rake   shears
spade   trowel   watering can

OTHER THINGS YOU USE IN THE GARDEN ARE
compost   fertilizer   manure   peat   weedkiller

## garment *noun*
For other words, see **clothes**

## gasp *verb*
The smoke made us gasp.
OTHER VERBS YOU MIGHT USE ARE   **to choke**   **to pant**   **to puff**   **to wheeze**

## gather *verb*
1 People gathered to watch the fire.
OTHER VERBS YOU MIGHT USE ARE   **to assemble**   **to crowd round**   **to meet**
2 We gathered information for our project.
OTHER VERBS ARE   **to collect**   **to put together**

## general *adjective*
1 The general opinion is that our team is the best.
OTHER WORDS YOU MIGHT USE ARE   **common**   **usual**   **widespread**
2 He only gave us a general idea of what he wanted.
OTHER WORDS ARE   **broad**   **vague**

## generous *adjective*
1 It was generous of Jo to share her sweets.
OTHER WORDS YOU MIGHT USE ARE   **kind**   **unselfish**
The opposite is **mean**
2 Mum gave us generous helpings of pudding.
OTHER WORDS ARE   **big**   **large**   **sizeable**
The opposite is **small**

## gentle *adjective*
1 a gentle kiss.
OTHER WORDS YOU MIGHT USE ARE   **kind**   **soft-hearted**   **tender**
2 a gentle breeze.
OTHER WORDS ARE   **pleasant**   **slight**
The opposite is **rough**
3 gentle music.
OTHER WORDS ARE   **quiet**   **relaxing**   **restful**   **soft**
The opposite is **noisy**

## genuine *adjective*
genuine gold.
ANOTHER WORD IS **real**
The opposite is **false**

**get** *verb*

THIS WORD HAS MANY USES. HERE ARE SOME OF THE WAYS YOU CAN USE IT, AND SOME OTHER WORDS YOU COULD CHOOSE

1 What did you get at the shop?
**to buy    to obtain    to purchase**
2 Sam got a nice present from Jo.
**to be given    to receive**
3 Jo got first prize for swimming.
**to earn    to win**
4 Did the thief get anything valuable?
**to steal    to take**
5 Tell the dog to get the ball.
**to bring    to fetch    to retrieve**
6 I got cold waiting for the bus.
**to become    to grow    to turn**

**ghost** *noun*

Sam doesn't believe in ghosts.
OTHER WORDS YOU MIGHT USE ARE    **phantom    spectre    spirit**
(*informal*) **spook**

**gift** *noun*

1 a birthday gift.
ANOTHER WORD IS **present**
2 a gift to charity.
OTHER WORDS YOU MIGHT USE ARE    **contribution    donation    offering**

**girl** *noun*

OLD-FASHIONED WORDS ARE    **damsel    maid    maiden    virgin**

**give** *verb*

1 I gave some sweets to Sam.
OTHER VERBS YOU MIGHT USE ARE    **to hand over    to offer    to pass
to present**
2 Dad gives money to charity.
OTHER VERBS ARE    **to contribute    to donate**
3 Our teacher gave us pencils to write with.
OTHER VERBS ARE    **to provide with    to supply with**
4 Jo gave out the books.
OTHER VERBS ARE    **to deal out    to distribute    to hand out**

## glad *adjective*
For other words, see **happy**

---

## glass *noun*
A sheet of glass in a window is a **pane**.
A glass you drink out of is a **tumbler**.
Glasses you wear to help you see better are **spectacles**.
GLASSES YOU LOOK THROUGH TO MAKE DISTANT OBJECTS SEEM NEARER ARE
**binoculars**   **field glasses**

---

## gloomy *adjective*
1  a gloomy room.
OTHER WORDS YOU MIGHT USE ARE   **cheerless**   **dark**   **depressing**
**dismal**
2  a gloomy face.
OTHER WORDS ARE   **depressed**   **glum**   **miserable**   **sad**
**unhappy**
The opposite is **cheerful**

## glow *verb*
The ashes of the bonfire glowed in the dark.
OTHER VERBS YOU MIGHT USE ARE   **to gleam**   **to shine**

## glue *noun*
OTHER SUBSTANCES YOU STICK THINGS WITH ARE   **adhesive**   **cement**   **gum**
**paste**

## go *verb*
1  Jo has gone to the shops.
OTHER VERBS YOU MIGHT USE ARE   **to travel**   **to walk**
For more verbs, see **move**
2  What time does the train go?
OTHER VERBS ARE   **to depart**   **to leave**   **to set out**
**to start**
3  This road goes into the town.
OTHER VERBS ARE   **to continue**   **to lead**
4  My watch doesn't go.
OTHER VERBS ARE   **to function**   **to operate**   **to work**
5  She went quiet when she heard the bad news.
OTHER VERBS ARE   **to become**   **to grow**   **to turn**

**good** *adjective*

SOME WORDS WHICH MEAN GOOD IN A GENERAL WAY ARE

**lovely   marvellous   nice   wonderful**

SOME INFORMAL WORDS ARE

**brilliant   fabulous   great**

THESE ARE SOME PARTICULAR WAYS WE USE THE WORD, AND SOME OF THE OTHER WORDS YOU MIGHT USE

1 good work.
   **correct   faultless   perfect   thorough**
2 a good friend.
   **caring   considerate   faithful   generous   helpful honest   kind   loving   loyal   reliable   thoughtful true**
3 a good dog.
   **obedient   well-behaved**
4 a good footballer.
   **clever   skilful   skilled   talented**
5 a good film.
   **entertaining   exciting   interesting**

The opposite is **bad**

**govern** *verb*

At election time, we choose people to govern the country.

OTHER VERBS YOU MIGHT USE ARE   **to be in charge of   to control to look after   to manage   to rule   to run**

**government** *noun*

The person in charge of the government is the **prime minister**.
The people who help the prime minister run the government are the **cabinet**.
Decisions about how to govern the country are discussed in **parliament**.

**grab** *verb*

For other verbs, see **seize**

## graceful *adjective*
graceful movements.
OTHER WORDS YOU MIGHT USE ARE    **attractive    elegant    flowing**
The opposite is **clumsy**

## gradual *adjective*
There was a gradual improvement in the weather.
OTHER WORDS YOU MIGHT USE ARE    **slow    steady**
The opposite is **sudden**

## grand *adjective*
The wedding was a grand occasion.
For other words, see **great**

## grant *verb*
The fairy granted Cinderella what she wanted.
OTHER VERBS YOU MIGHT USE ARE    **to allow    to give**

## grass *noun*
An area of grass in a garden is a **lawn**.
An area of grass on a farm is a **field** or **meadow** or **pasture**.
An area of grass in a village is a **green**.
A large area of grass in North America is a **prairie**.
A large area of grass in South Africa is **veld** or **veldt**.

## grateful *adjective*
I was grateful for her help.
OTHER WORDS YOU MIGHT USE ARE    **appreciative    thankful**
The opposite is **ungrateful**

## grave *adjective*
Mum looked grave when she heard the bad news.
OTHER WORDS YOU MIGHT USE ARE    **gloomy    serious    solemn
thoughtful**
The opposite is **cheerful**

## greasy *adjective*
I don't like greasy chips.
OTHER WORDS YOU MIGHT USE ARE    **fatty    oily**

## great *adjective*

1 a great storm.
    OTHER WORDS YOU MIGHT USE ARE    **huge**    **tremendous**
For more words, see **big**

2 a great occasion.
    OTHER WORDS ARE    **grand**    **important**    **impressive**    **magnificent**
    **spectacular**    **splendid**

3 a great piece of music.
    OTHER WORDS ARE    **classic**    **famous**    **well-known**

4 We had a great time.
    OTHER WORDS ARE    **excellent**    **marvellous**    **wonderful**
For more words, see **good**

## greedy *adjective*

It was greedy to eat all the cake.
    OTHER WORDS YOU MIGHT USE ARE    (*informal*) **piggish**    **selfish**

## greet *verb*

I greeted our guests at the door.
    ANOTHER VERB IS **to welcome**

## grief *noun*

I sympathized with Jo's grief when the dog died.
    OTHER WORDS YOU MIGHT USE ARE    **misery**    **sadness**    **sorrow**
    **unhappiness**

## grim *adjective*

a grim look on someone's face.
    OTHER WORDS YOU MIGHT USE ARE    **bad-tempered**    **gloomy**    **serious**
    **severe**    **stern**    **unfriendly**
The opposite is **happy**

## grin *verb*

For other verbs, see **laugh**

## groan *verb*

The injured man groaned because of the pain.
    OTHER VERBS YOU MIGHT USE ARE    **to moan**    **to wail**

## grope *verb*

I groped about to find the light switch.
    OTHER VERBS YOU MIGHT USE ARE    **to feel**    **to fumble**

## ground *noun*

1 Potatoes grow in the ground.
OTHER WORDS YOU MIGHT USE ARE

**earth    soil**

2 We play football on a piece of ground behind the school.
ANOTHER WORD IS **land**
PLACES WHERE YOU CAN PLAY GAMES ARE

**playground    playing field    pitch    recreation ground stadium**

Ground where you build something is a **plot** or **site**.
A big area of ground owned by one person or used for a special purpose is an **estate**.
The grounds of a big school or college are called a **campus**.

## group *noun*, see next page

## grow *verb*

1 Jo grows flowers in the garden.
OTHER VERBS YOU MIGHT USE ARE     **to cultivate    to plant    to raise**
2 The seeds only grow when the weather is warm.
OTHER VERBS ARE     **to germinate    to spring up    to sprout**
3 Jo looks to see how much her vegetables have grown.
OTHER VERBS ARE     **to develop    to fill out    to get bigger to get taller    to increase**

## grown-up *adjective*

OTHER WORDS YOU MIGHT USE ARE     **adult    mature**

## gruesome *adjective*

I didn't like the gruesome picture of the accident.
OTHER WORDS YOU MIGHT USE ARE     **disgusting    gory    horrible    nasty sickening**

## gruff *adjective*

a gruff voice.
OTHER WORDS YOU MIGHT USE ARE     **deep    harsh    hoarse    rough**

## grumble *verb*

Mum doesn't like it when Sam grumbles about the food.
OTHER VERBS YOU MIGHT USE ARE     **to complain**    (*informal*) **to moan**

**group** *noun*

OTHER WORDS YOU MIGHT USE ARE

a group of things:
**assortment**     **collection**     **set**

a group of people:
**assembly**     **company**     **crowd**     **gang**     **gathering**
**mob**     **throng**

an organized group of people:
**alliance**     **army**     **association**     **club**     **force**     **society**
**team**

a group of musicians:
**band**     **choir**     **chorus**     **orchestra**

OTHER GROUPS ARE:

An **army** of ants.
A **brood** of chicks.
A **bunch** of flowers.
A **class** of children.
A **clump** of trees.
A **clutch** of eggs.
A **colony** of ants.
A **congregation** in church.
A **constellation** or **galaxy** of stars.
A **convoy** or **fleet** of ships.
A **covey** of partridges.
A **crew** of sailors.
A **flock** of birds.
A **flock** of sheep.
A **gaggle** of geese.
A **gang** of robbers.
A **herd** of cows.
A **herd** of elephants.
A **leap** of leopards.
A **litter** of puppies.
A **pack** of wolves.
A **pride** of lions.
A **school** of whales.
A **shoal** of fish.
A **swarm** of bees.
A **troop** of soldiers.

## guard *verb*

The farmer's dog guards the sheep.

OTHER VERBS YOU MIGHT USE ARE    **to care for    to defend    to look after    to protect    to shield    to tend    to watch over**

## guess *verb*

1 I guess you are hungry.

OTHER VERBS YOU MIGHT USE ARE    **to assume    to suppose**

2 Jo tried to guess how many sweets there were in the jar.

ANOTHER VERB IS **to estimate**

## guide *verb*

I wish someone would guide us out of this maze!

OTHER VERBS YOU MIGHT USE ARE    **to direct    to escort    to lead    to steer**

## guilty *adjective*

He was guilty of stealing.
The opposite is **innocent**

---

## gun *noun*

KINDS OF GUN ARE

**airgun    cannon    machine-gun    pistol    revolver    rifle    shotgun**

---

# Hh

## habit *noun*

1 It's our habit to send people a card when they have a birthday.

OTHER WORDS YOU MIGHT USE ARE    **custom    practice    tradition**

2 Smoking is a bad habit.

ANOTHER WORD IS **addiction**

## hair *noun*

DIFFERENT WAYS PEOPLE DO THEIR HAIR ARE

**in curls     with a fringe     permed     in a pigtail
in plaits     in a ponytail**

WORDS TO DESCRIBE THE COLOUR OF PEOPLE'S HAIR ARE

**auburn     black     blond     brown     fair     ginger     grey
red     silver     white**

WORDS FOR HAIR ON AN ANIMAL ARE

**bristles     fur**

## hairy *adjective*

OTHER WORDS YOU MIGHT USE ARE     **bristly     furry     fuzzy     shaggy
woolly**

## halt *verb*

You must halt if the light is red.

OTHER VERBS YOU MIGHT USE ARE     **to draw up     to pull up
to stop**

## hand *noun*

For other parts of the body, see **body**

## handicap *noun*

When you run for the bus, it's a handicap to have lots of shopping.

OTHER WORDS YOU MIGHT USE ARE

**disadvantage     drawback     hindrance     inconvenience**

## handicapped *adjective*

It's hard for you to do some things if you are handicapped.

WAYS YOU CAN BE HANDICAPPED ARE

**blind     deaf     disabled     dumb     lame     limbless
paralysed**

# handle *verb*
1  Handle the kittens carefully.
   OTHER VERBS YOU MIGHT USE ARE
   **to feel    to stroke    to touch**
2  The rider handled the frightened horse well.
   OTHER VERBS ARE
   **to control    to deal with    to look after    to manage**

# handsome *adjective*
a handsome man.
   OTHER WORDS YOU MIGHT USE ARE    **attractive    good-looking**
The opposite is **ugly**

# hang *verb*
**to hang on to something**
Hang on to the rope!
   OTHER VERBS YOU MIGHT USE ARE    **to cling on to    to grasp    to hold
   to seize**
**to hang about**
Don't hang about after school.
   OTHER VERBS ARE    **to be slow    to dawdle    to delay    to loiter**

# happen *verb*
Did anything interesting happen?
   OTHER VERBS YOU MIGHT USE ARE    **to occur    to take place**

# happy *adjective*
Jo is happy when the sun shines.
   OTHER WORDS YOU MIGHT USE ARE    **cheerful    contented    delighted
   glad    good-humoured    joyful    light-hearted    merry
   pleased**
The opposite is **sad**

---

# harbour *noun*
   PLACES WHERE SHIPS UNLOAD GOODS ARE
   **docks    port**

   A place where you see lots of **pleasure boats** is a **marina**.
   PLACES WHERE SHIPS TIE UP ARE
   **jetty    landing stage    mooring    pier    quay    wharf**

## hard *adjective*
1 hard concrete.
OTHER WORDS YOU MIGHT USE ARE  **firm   rigid   solid**
The opposite is **soft**
2 hard work.
OTHER WORDS ARE  **exhausting   tiring   tough**
The opposite is **easy**
3 a hard problem.
OTHER WORDS ARE  **complex   complicated   difficult   puzzling**
The opposite is **simple**
4 a hard punishment.
OTHER WORDS ARE  **cruel   harsh   merciless   severe**
The opposite is **merciful**

## hardly *adverb*
I'm so tired I can hardly walk.
OTHER WORDS YOU MIGHT USE ARE  **barely   only just   scarcely**

## harm *verb*
1 Jo would never harm an animal.
OTHER VERBS YOU MIGHT USE ARE  **to hurt   to injure   to wound**
2 Did the accident harm the car?
OTHER VERBS ARE  **to damage   to spoil**

## harmful *adjective*
It can be harmful to take too much medicine.
OTHER WORDS YOU MIGHT USE ARE  **bad   damaging   dangerous**

## harsh *adjective*
1 The teacher's harsh voice showed that she was angry.
OTHER WORDS YOU MIGHT USE ARE  **grating   rough   shrill**
2 We blinked in the harsh light.
OTHER WORDS ARE  **brilliant   dazzling   glaring**
3 We thought the decision to send the player off was harsh.
OTHER WORDS ARE  **cruel   hard   merciless   severe**
The opposite is **gentle**

## hasty *adjective*
The teacher said we were too hasty doing our work.
OTHER WORDS YOU MIGHT USE ARE  **careless   hurried   impetuous   quick   (*informal*) slapdash   thoughtless**

**hat** *noun*

DIFFERENT THINGS PEOPLE WEAR ON THEIR HEADS ARE

beret    bonnet    cap    crash helmet    crown    helmet
hood    turban

**hate** *verb*

Sam can't understand why some people hate cabbage.

OTHER VERBS YOU MIGHT USE ARE    **to detest    to dislike    to loathe**

The opposite is **like**

**haul** *verb*

We hauled our sledge to the top of the hill.

OTHER VERBS YOU MIGHT USE ARE    **to drag    to draw    to pull    to tow
to tug**

**have** *verb*

THIS VERB HAS MANY USES. HERE ARE SOME OF THE WAYS YOU CAN USE IT, AND SOME
OTHER VERBS YOU COULD CHOOSE.

1 Jo has a new kitten.
   **to own    to possess**
2 Jo's class has thirty pupils.
   **to consist of    to contain    to include**
3 I was having a good time, but Sam had a cold.
   **to enjoy    to experience    to suffer**
4 I had some nice presents on my birthday.
   **to be given    to get    to obtain    to receive**

**hazy** *adjective*

The view from the top of the hill was hazy.

OTHER WORDS YOU MIGHT USE ARE    **blurred    foggy    misty**

The opposite is **clear**

**head** *noun*

For other parts of your body, see **body**

**heal** *verb*

The ointment helps to heal spots.

OTHER VERBS YOU MIGHT USE ARE    **to cure    to make better    to remedy**

**health** *noun*, see opposite page

**healthy** *adjective*
We all want to be healthy.
OTHER WORDS YOU MIGHT USE ARE    **fit    sound    strong    well**
The opposite is **ill**

**heap** *noun*
Sam left his clothes in a heap.
OTHER WORDS ARE    **mound    pile    stack**

**hear** *verb*
Did you hear the weather forecast?
ANOTHER VERB IS **to listen to**

**heart** *noun*
The explorers were lost in the heart of the jungle.
OTHER WORDS YOU MIGHT USE ARE    **centre    core    middle**

**heat** *noun*
The cat loves the heat from the fire.
OTHER WORDS YOU MIGHT USE ARE    **glow    warmth**

**heat** *verb*
VARIOUS WAYS TO HEAT THINGS ARE    **to boil    to burn    to melt    to scald
to scorch**
For other verbs, see **cook**

**heater** *noun*
VARIOUS KINDS OF HEATER ARE
**central heating    coal fire    convector
electric fire    gas fire    immersion heater
radiator    stove**

**heavy** *adjective*
a heavy load.
ANOTHER WORD IS **weighty**
The opposite is **light**

# health *noun*

We all want to have good health.

OTHER WORDS YOU MIGHT USE ARE

**fitness    strength**

PEOPLE WHO LOOK AFTER OUR HEALTH ARE

**doctor    health visitor    nurse**

A **paediatrician** is a specialist in children's health.

A **midwife** helps to deliver babies.

A **surgeon** does operations.

A **dentist** looks after your teeth.

An **optician** looks at your eyes.

A **physiotherapist** helps people recover from injuries.

A **pharmacist** makes up medicines.

A person who looks after the health of animals is a **vet** or **veterinary surgeon**.

PLACES WHERE WE CAN GET HELP WITH OUR HEALTH ARE

**clinic    health centre    hospital    nursing home surgery**

We can get medicines at a chemist's or a pharmacy.

OTHER WORDS FOR MEDICINE ARE

**cure    remedy    treatment**

Medicine you get with a note from the doctor is a **prescription**.

SOME MEDICINES YOU MIGHT TAKE ARE

**antibiotic    aspirin    capsule    drug    gargle    linctus lotion    ointment    pill    tablet    tonic**

ILLNESSES PEOPLE CAN HAVE ARE

| | | | |
|---|---|---|---|
| allergy | appendicitis | arthritis | asthma |
| bilious attack | bronchitis | cancer | catarrh |
| chickenpox | chill | cholera | cold |
| constipation | cough | diabetes | diarrhoea |
| diphtheria | dysentery | earache | epilepsy |
| fever | flu | hay fever | headache |
| indigestion | influenza | jaundice | leprosy |
| leukaemia | malaria | measles | migraine |
| mumps | paralysis | plague | pneumonia |
| polio | rabies | rheumatism | scarlet fever |
| seasickness | smallpox | spina bifida | stroke |
| sunstroke | tonsillitis | toothache | tuberculosis |
| typhoid | typhus | whooping cough | |

COMPLAINTS YOU CAN GET ON YOUR SKIN ARE

| | | | |
|---|---|---|---|
| abscess | blister | boil | chilblains |
| corns | dermatitis | sty | ulcer |
| verruca | wart | | |

## help *noun*
The policeman radioed for help.
> OTHER WORDS YOU MIGHT USE ARE **assistance   backing   back-up   support**

## help *verb*
1 I help Dad with the washing up.
> OTHER VERBS YOU MIGHT USE ARE **to assist   to support**
2 I couldn't help laughing.
> ANOTHER VERB IS **to stop**

## helpful *adjective*
1 Our neighbours are very helpful.
> OTHER WORDS YOU MIGHT USE ARE **considerate   kind   willing**
2 She gave me some helpful advice.
> OTHER WORDS ARE **useful   valuable**

## helping *noun*
I had a big helping of pudding.
> OTHER WORDS YOU MIGHT USE ARE **portion   serving**

## herd *noun*
a herd of cows.
For other words, see **group**

## hesitate *verb*
Jo hesitated before diving in.
> OTHER VERBS YOU MIGHT USE ARE **to delay   to pause   to wait   to waver**

## hide *verb*
He hid his money under the carpet.
> OTHER VERBS YOU MIGHT USE ARE **to conceal   to cover   to put away**

## high *adjective*
1 a high building.
> OTHER WORDS YOU MIGHT USE ARE **lofty   tall**
2 high prices.
> ANOTHER WORD IS **expensive**
The opposite is **low**

## hill *noun*

1  We climbed a hill to see the view.
   OTHER WORDS YOU MIGHT USE ARE    **mountain    peak**
2  It's hard cycling up that hill.
   OTHER WORDS ARE    **incline    rise    slope**

## hinder *verb*

The firemen were angry because the people watching the fire hindered them.
   OTHER VERBS YOU MIGHT USE ARE    **to check    to delay**
   **to get in the way of    to hamper**

## hint *noun*

1  I can't guess the answer - give me a hint.
   ANOTHER WORD IS **clue**
2  The expert gave us some hints on playing chess.
   OTHER WORDS ARE    **suggestion    tip**

---

### hit *verb*

VARIOUS WAYS TO HIT THINGS ARE

**to bang**    (*informal*) **to bash**    **to batter**    **to beat**
**to bump into**    **to collide with**    **to hammer**    **to knock**
**to rap**    **to smash**    **to strike**    **to tap**    **to thump**
(*informal*) **to wallop**    (*informal*) **to whack**    **to whip**

A goat may **butt** you with horns.
Teachers used to **cane** pupils as a punishment.
You can **flog** someone with a whip.
You **jog** someone with your elbow.
You **kick** with your foot.
You **lash** or **thrash** someone with a whip.
You **poke** or **prod** with a stick.
You **punch** with your fist.
You can **ram** a vehicle into something.
You **slap** or **smack** or **spank** someone with your hand.
You **stub** your toe on something.
You **swat** a fly.

---

## hoarse *adjective*

Dad's voice was hoarse because he had a cold.
   OTHER WORDS YOU MIGHT USE ARE    **croaking    deep    husky    rough**

## hobby *noun*
My hobbies are skating and chess.
OTHER WORDS YOU MIGHT USE ARE     **interest     pastime**

## hold *verb*
1  I held the ladder while Dad climbed up.
OTHER VERBS YOU MIGHT USE ARE     **to grasp     to grip     to hang on to     to seize     to support**
2  Sam held the baby carefully.
OTHER VERBS ARE     **to carry     to embrace     to hug**
3  The box holds all Jo's toys.
ANOTHER VERB IS **to contain**

## hole *noun*
1  a hole in the ground.
OTHER WORDS YOU MIGHT USE ARE     **burrow     cave     crater     pit     pothole     tunnel**
2  a hole in the fence.
OTHER WORDS ARE     **break     chink     crack     gap     opening**
3  a hole in your jacket.
OTHER WORDS ARE     **slit     split     tear**
4  a hole in a tyre.
OTHER WORDS ARE     **leak     puncture**

## holiday *noun*
VARIOUS KINDS OF HOLIDAY ARE
**adventure holiday     activity holiday     camping holiday     cruise     honeymoon     package holiday     safari     seaside holiday     touring holiday**

PLACES PEOPLE STAY ON HOLIDAY ARE
**bed and breakfast     camp site     guest house     hotel     motel     self-catering accommodation     youth hostel**

## hollow *noun*
a hollow in the ground.
OTHER WORDS YOU MIGHT USE ARE     **depression     dip     hole     valley**

## holy *adjective*
The temple is a holy place.
OTHER WORDS YOU MIGHT USE ARE     **religious     sacred**

## home *noun*

PLACES WHERE PEOPLE LIVE ARE

apartment    bungalow    caravan    chalet    cottage
council house    detached house    farmhouse    flat
maisonette    manor house    mansion    mobile home
semi-detached house    terrace house    thatched cottage

DIFFERENT ROOMS IN A HOME ARE

attic    bathroom    bedroom    cellar    cloakroom
conservatory    dining room    drawing room    hall
kitchen    landing    larder    lavatory    living room
loft    lounge    pantry    parlour    passage    porch
scullery    sitting room    study    toilet    WC

## honest *adjective*

Mum believed Sam because he is always honest.
OTHER WORDS YOU MIGHT USE ARE    **sincere    trustworthy    truthful**
The opposite is **dishonest**

## hop *verb*

Dad hopped up and down when he dropped the hammer on his foot.
OTHER VERBS YOU MIGHT USE ARE    **to jump    to leap    to spring**

## hopeful *adjective*

I'm hopeful that my cold will be better tomorrow.
OTHER WORDS YOU MIGHT USE ARE    **confident    optimistic**

## hopeless *adjective*

Sam's friend is hopeless at games.
OTHER WORDS YOU MIGHT USE ARE    **no good    useless**

## horizontal *adjective*

A snooker table must be perfectly horizontal.
OTHER WORDS YOU MIGHT USE ARE    **flat    level**
The opposite is **vertical**

## horrible *adjective*

1 a horrible taste.
OTHER WORDS YOU MIGHT USE ARE    **horrid    nasty    unpleasant**
2 a horrible shock.
OTHER WORDS ARE    **dreadful    frightening    terrible**

## horror *noun*
We were filled with horror when the huge beast ran towards us.
OTHER WORDS YOU MIGHT USE ARE   **dread   fear   terror**

---

## horse *noun*
VARIOUS WORDS FOR HORSE ARE
**carthorse   nag   piebald   pony   racehorse
shire-horse   steed**

A female horse is a **mare**.
A male horse is a **stallion**.
A young horse is a **colt** or **foal**.

---

## hospital *noun*
For other places where you can go if you are ill, see **health**

## hostile *adjective*
I didn't like the opposing team's hostile comments.
OTHER WORDS YOU MIGHT USE ARE   **aggressive   threatening
unfriendly**
The opposite is **friendly**

## hot *adjective*
1 a hot fire.
OTHER WORDS YOU MIGHT USE ARE   **blazing   glowing   red-hot
roasting   scorching   sizzling**
2 hot weather.
ANOTHER WORD IS **sweltering**
3 hot water.
OTHER WORDS ARE   **boiling   scalding**
For other words, see **warm**
The opposite is **cold**
4 hot-tasting food.
OTHER WORDS ARE   **peppery   spicy**

## hotel *noun*
For other places where people stay, see **holiday**

## house *noun*
For places where people live, see **home**

**hug** *verb*

Granny hugged us and said goodbye.
OTHER VERBS YOU MIGHT USE ARE    **to cuddle    to embrace    to hold**

**huge** *adjective*

For other words, see **big**

**human** *noun*

For other words, see **person**

**humble** *adjective*

Sam was humble about winning a prize.
ANOTHER WORD IS **modest**
The opposite is **proud**

**humorous** *adjective*

We laughed at her humorous remark.
OTHER WORDS YOU MIGHT USE ARE    **amusing    comic    funny    witty**
The opposite is **serious**

**hump** *noun*

They put humps in the road to make cars go slower.
OTHER WORDS YOU MIGHT USE ARE    **bulge    bump    lump**

**hunger** *noun*

1  Will a sandwich satisfy your hunger?
ANOTHER WORD IS **appetite**
2  In some countries many people die of hunger.
OTHER WORDS ARE    **famine    starvation**

**hungry** *adjective*

I was hungry after my long walk.
OTHER WORDS YOU MIGHT USE ARE    **famished**    (*informal*) **peckish**
**ravenous    starved    starving**
If you eat more food than you need you are **greedy**.

**hunt** *verb*

1  I think it's cruel to hunt foxes.
OTHER VERBS YOU MIGHT USE ARE    **to chase    to pursue    to stalk
to track down**
2  We hunted for Mum's lost purse.
OTHER VERBS ARE    **to look for    to search for    to seek**

## hurry *verb*

I hurried home from school.

> OTHER VERBS YOU MIGHT USE ARE  **to dash**    **to hasten**    **to hurtle**
> **to race**    **to run**    **to rush**    **to speed**

The opposite is **dawdle**

## hurt *verb*

1 The cut on my hand hurts.

> OTHER VERBS YOU MIGHT USE ARE  **to ache**    **to be painful**    **to smart**
> **to sting**    **to throb**

2 Don't hurt the kittens!

> OTHER VERBS ARE  **to damage**    **to harm**    **to injure**    **to torment**
> **to wound**

# I i

---

### ice *noun*

A river of ice is a **glacier**.

A large lump of ice floating in the sea is an **iceberg**.

A finger of ice hanging down is an **icicle**.

Dangerous ice on the road is **black ice**.

---

## idea *noun*

1 I've got an idea!

> OTHER WORDS YOU MIGHT USE ARE  (*informal*) **brainwave**    **plan**
> **suggestion**    **thought**

2 I have an idea that you are tired.

> OTHER WORDS ARE  **belief**    **feeling**    **impression**    **opinion**

## ideal *adjective*

The weather was ideal for a picnic.

> OTHER WORDS YOU MIGHT USE ARE  **excellent**    **just right**    **perfect**
> **suitable**

## idle *adjective*

Jo is never idle, even in the holidays.
> OTHER WORDS YOU MIGHT USE ARE **doing nothing   inactive   lazy   unemployed   unoccupied**

The opposite is **busy**

## ignorant *adjective*

1 ignorant of the truth.
> ANOTHER WORD IS **unaware**

The opposite is **aware**

2 an ignorant fool.
> OTHER WORDS ARE **foolish   stupid   unintelligent**

The opposite is **clever**

## ignore *verb*

You get into trouble if you ignore what the teacher says.
> OTHER VERBS YOU MIGHT USE ARE **to disobey   to disregard   to neglect   to overlook   to take no notice of**

## ill *adjective*

Sam stayed away from school because he was ill.
> OTHER WORDS YOU MIGHT USE ARE **indisposed   in poor health   (**informal**) poorly   sick   unwell**

The opposite is **healthy**
For other words, see **health**

## illegal *adjective*

Stealing is illegal.
> OTHER WORDS YOU MIGHT USE ARE **banned   criminal   forbidden   unlawful**

The opposite is **legal**

## illness *noun*

> OTHER WORDS YOU MIGHT USE ARE **ailment   (**informal**) bug   complaint   disease   infection   malady   sickness**

For other words, see **health**

## imaginary *adjective*

Unicorns are imaginary animals.
> OTHER WORDS YOU MIGHT USE ARE **fictitious   invented   made-up   non-existent   unreal**

The opposite is **real**

## imagine *verb*
You didn't really see a ghost: you only imagined it.
> OTHER VERBS YOU MIGHT USE ARE   **to dream   to invent   to make up   to picture   to think**

## imitate *verb*
The budgie can imitate Jo's voice.
> OTHER VERBS YOU MIGHT USE ARE   **to copy   to impersonate   to reproduce**

## imitation *noun*
It isn't real – it's an imitation.
> OTHER WORDS YOU MIGHT USE ARE   **copy   counterfeit   fake   forgery   likeness   reproduction**

## immediate *adjective*
Granny wants an immediate answer to her invitation.
> OTHER WORDS YOU MIGHT USE ARE   **instant   prompt**
For more words, see **quick**

## impatient *adjective*
We were impatient to begin.
> OTHER WORDS YOU MIGHT USE ARE   **anxious   eager**
The opposite is **patient**

## impertinent *adjective*
Teachers don't like impertinent comments from the children.
> OTHER WORDS YOU MIGHT USE ARE   **cheeky   impolite   improper   impudent   insolent   rude**
The opposite is **polite**

## important *adjective*
1 The important thing in swimming is to breathe properly.
> OTHER WORDS YOU MIGHT USE ARE   **basic   chief   essential   main   necessary**
2 an important person.
> OTHER WORDS ARE   **famous   great   notable   powerful   respected   well-known**
3 an important message.
> OTHER WORDS ARE   **serious   urgent**
4 an important event.
> OTHER WORDS ARE   **big   major   significant   special**
The opposite is **unimportant**

# impression *noun*
I have the impression that you are bored.
OTHER WORDS YOU MIGHT USE ARE   **feeling   idea   opinion**

# impressive *adjective*
an impressive occasion.
OTHER WORDS YOU MIGHT USE ARE   **grand   great   magnificent
memorable   spectacular   splendid   wonderful**

# improve *verb*
1 Jo's swimming has improved.
OTHER VERBS YOU MIGHT USE ARE   **to develop   to get better   to progress**
2 Go over your work and try to improve it.
OTHER VERBS ARE   **to make better   to revise**

# improvise *verb*
We improvised some music.
OTHER VERBS YOU MIGHT USE ARE   **to invent   to make up**

# include *verb*
The packet includes everything you need to make a cake.
OTHER VERBS YOU MIGHT USE ARE   **to consist of   to contain**

# inconvenient *adjective*
It is inconvenient to visit auntie today.
OTHER WORDS YOU MIGHT USE ARE   **awkward   troublesome**
The opposite is **convenient**

# incorrect *adjective*
an incorrect answer.
OTHER WORDS YOU MIGHT USE ARE   **false   inaccurate   mistaken
untrue   wrong**
The opposite is **correct**

# increase *verb*
1 They increased the number of children in our class.
OTHER VERBS YOU MIGHT USE ARE   **to add to   to make bigger   to raise**
2 The noise increased as the train got nearer.
OTHER VERBS ARE   **to get louder   to rise**
**to increase in size**
OTHER VERBS YOU MIGHT USE ARE   **to get bigger   to expand   to swell**
The opposite is **decrease**

## incredible *adjective*

His story about dinosaurs was incredible.

OTHER WORDS YOU MIGHT USE ARE    **far-fetched    unbelievable    unconvincing    unlikely**

## infant *noun*

For other words, see **child**

## infectious *adjective*

an infectious disease.

ANOTHER WORD IS **catching**

## inflate *verb*

to inflate a tyre.

OTHER VERBS YOU MIGHT USE ARE    **to blow up    to pump up**

## influence *verb*

1  Does the weather influence the way you behave?

ANOTHER VERB IS **to affect**

2  Don't try to influence the referee!

OTHER VERBS YOU MIGHT USE ARE    **to bribe    to persuade**

## inform *verb*

The teacher informed my mother that I was ill.

OTHER VERBS YOU MIGHT USE ARE    **to notify    to tell**

## informal *adjective*

1  informal clothes.

OTHER WORDS YOU MIGHT USE ARE    **casual    comfortable**

2  an informal party.

OTHER WORDS ARE    **easygoing    friendly    relaxed**

The opposite is **formal**

## information *noun*

1  We rang up to get some information about the accident.

OTHER WORDS YOU MIGHT USE ARE    **facts    knowledge    news**

2  We put the information into the computer.

ANOTHER WORD IS **data**

## injure *verb*

Did you injure yourself when you fell over?

OTHER VERBS YOU MIGHT USE ARE    **to damage    to harm    to hurt**

## injury *noun*
For other words, see **wound**

## innocent *adjective*
The judge declared that the accused man was innocent.
OTHER WORDS YOU MIGHT USE ARE   **blameless   guiltless**
The opposite is **guilty**

## inquisitive *adjective*
It's rude to be inquisitive about other people's affairs.
OTHER WORDS YOU MIGHT USE ARE   **curious   nosy   prying**

---

## insect *noun*
VARIOUS INSECTS ARE
**ant   bee   beetle   bluebottle   bumble-bee
butterfly   cockroach   cricket   daddy-long-legs
dragonfly   earwig   fly   glow-worm   gnat
grasshopper   hornet   ladybird   locust   mosquito
moth   nit   wasp**
OTHER CRAWLING CREATURES (WHICH ARE NOT PROPER INSECTS) ARE
**centipede   slug   spider   worm**

---

## insolent *adjective*
It is insolent to answer back to a teacher.
OTHER WORDS YOU MIGHT USE ARE   **cheeky   impertinent   impolite
improper   impudent   rude**
The opposite is **polite**

## inspect *verb*
The man at the garage inspected the damage to the car.
OTHER VERBS YOU MIGHT USE ARE   **to check   to examine   to look at**

## instant *adjective*
He didn't keep us waiting, but gave us an instant reply.
OTHER WORDS YOU MIGHT USE ARE   **immediate   prompt   quick**

## instruct *verb*
1 The policeman instructed us to stay where we were.
OTHER VERBS YOU MIGHT USE ARE   **to command   to direct   to order**
2 Our teacher instructed us in how to use the PE equipment.
OTHER VERBS ARE   **to coach   to teach   to train**

## instrument *noun*
The dentist has an interesting instrument for drilling teeth.
OTHER WORDS YOU MIGHT USE ARE **apparatus   device   gadget   implement   machine   tool**
For musical instruments, see **music**

## insult *verb*
He insulted me by walking away without speaking.
OTHER VERBS YOU MIGHT USE ARE **to be rude to   to offend   to snub**

## intelligent *adjective*
Our dog is so intelligent that she understands what we say.
OTHER WORDS YOU MIGHT USE ARE **brainy   bright   clever**
The opposite is **stupid**

## intend *verb*
Jo intends to learn the piano next year.
OTHER VERBS YOU MIGHT USE ARE **to aim   to plan   to propose**

## intense *adjective*
intense heat. intense pain.
OTHER WORDS YOU MIGHT USE ARE **extreme   great   severe   strong**

## intentional *adjective*
The player was sent off the field for an intentional foul.
OTHER WORDS YOU MIGHT USE ARE **deliberate   intended**
The opposite is **accidental**

## interest *verb*
Dad's stories always interest us.
OTHER VERBS YOU MIGHT USE ARE **to appeal to   to attract   to fascinate**
The opposite is **bore**

## interested *adjective*
OTHER WORDS YOU MIGHT USE ARE **attentive   curious   keen**
IF YOU ARE TOO INTERESTED, YOU ARE **inquisitive   nosy**
The opposite is **bored**

## interfere *verb*
Don't interfere in my business!
OTHER VERBS YOU MIGHT USE ARE **to intrude   to meddle   to pry**
(*informal*) **to snoop**

# interrupt *verb*
It's rude to interrupt when someone is talking.
OTHER VERBS YOU MIGHT USE ARE     (*informal*) **to butt in**     **to interfere**

# interval *noun*
1 When we went to the pictures, we had ice cream in the interval.
OTHER WORDS YOU MIGHT USE ARE     **break**     **intermission**
2 There is an interval between the lightning and the thunder.
OTHER WORDS ARE     **gap**     **pause**     **rest**     **space**

# introduce *verb*
Jo introduced me to her friend.
OTHER VERBS YOU MIGHT USE ARE     **to make known**     **to present**

# introduction *noun*
1 an introduction to a book.
OTHER WORDS YOU MIGHT USE ARE     **preface**     **prologue**
2 an introduction to a ballet.
OTHER WORDS ARE     **overture**     **prelude**

# invade *verb*
to invade a foreign country.
OTHER VERBS YOU MIGHT USE ARE     **to attack**     **to march into**     **to occupy**
**to overrun**     **to raid**

# invent *verb*
Who invented the first computer?
OTHER VERBS YOU MIGHT USE ARE     **to create**     **to devise**     **to plan**
**to put together**     **to think up**

# investigate *verb*
The police spent many weeks investigating the crime.
OTHER VERBS YOU MIGHT USE ARE     **to examine**     **to explore**
**to inquire into**     **to study**

# invisible *adjective*
The door into the secret garden was invisible.
OTHER WORDS YOU MIGHT USE ARE     **concealed**     **hidden**     **undetectable**
The opposite is **visible**

# invite *verb*
Jo invited me to her party.
ANOTHER VERB IS **to ask**

## irritable *adjective*

Dad gets irritable if we chatter while the football is on.

OTHER WORDS YOU MIGHT USE ARE **annoyed   bad-tempered   grumpy   short-tempered   snappy   touchy**

For other words, see **angry**

## irritate *verb*

The flies irritated the horse.

OTHER VERBS YOU MIGHT USE ARE **to anger   to annoy   to bother   to upset   to worry**

## issue *verb*

The teacher issued one pencil to each child.

OTHER VERBS YOU MIGHT USE ARE **to distribute   to give out   to pass round**

## item *noun*

Have you got any items for the jumble sale?

OTHER WORDS YOU MIGHT USE ARE **article   object   thing**

# Jj

## jab *verb*

He jabbed me with his finger.

OTHER VERBS YOU MIGHT USE ARE **to poke   to prod   to stab**

## jagged *adjective*

The broken plank had a jagged edge.

OTHER WORDS YOU MIGHT USE ARE **rough   sharp   uneven**

The opposite is **smooth**

## jail *noun*

see **gaol**

## jam *verb*

1  I jammed my things into a box.
OTHER VERBS YOU MIGHT USE ARE    **to cram    to crush    to squeeze**
2  Cars jammed the street.
OTHER VERBS ARE    **to block    to fill**
3  Our back door keeps jamming.
ANOTHER VERB IS **to stick**

## jar *noun*

For other things to put things in, see **container**

## jealous *adjective*

Jo was a bit jealous when Sam got a lot of money for his birthday.
OTHER WORDS YOU MIGHT USE ARE    **bitter    envious    resentful**

## jeans *noun*

For things to wear, see **clothes**

## jeer *verb*

The crowd jeered at the player who argued with the referee.
OTHER VERBS YOU MIGHT USE ARE    **to laugh at    to mock    to sneer at    to taunt**

## jet *noun*

a jet of water.
OTHER WORDS YOU MIGHT USE ARE    **fountain    spray    spurt    squirt**

## jewel *noun*

OTHER WORDS YOU MIGHT USE ARE
**gem    precious stone**

STONES USED IN MAKING JEWELLERY ARE
**amber    diamond    emerald    jet    opal    pearl    ruby    sapphire**

METALS USED TO MAKE JEWELLERY ARE
**gold    platinum    silver**

VARIOUS KINDS OF JEWELLERY ARE
**bangle    beads    bracelet    brooch    chain    clasp    earrings    locket    necklace    pendant    ring**

# job *noun*

1 I have some jobs to do for Mum before I come out to play.
OTHER WORDS YOU MIGHT USE ARE
**chore    errand    task**
2 Sam's cousin has left school and is looking for a job.
OTHER WORDS ARE
**employment    occupation    profession    trade    work**
SOME OF THE JOBS PEOPLE DO TO EARN THEIR LIVING ARE
**accountant    actor    air hostess    architect    artist
barber    builder    caretaker    carpenter    chef
chemist    cleaner    clergyman    clerk    cook
decorator    dentist    designer    detective    driver
doctor    dustman    electrician    engineer    entertainer
farmer    fireman    gardener    hairdresser    journalist
lawyer    lecturer    librarian    mechanic    midwife
milkman    model    musician    nurse    optician
photographer    pilot    plumber    policewoman
postman    receptionist    reporter    scientist
secretary    shopkeeper    social worker    teacher
traffic warden    typist    vet    waiter    writer**

# join *verb*

1 to join one thing to another.
OTHER VERBS YOU MIGHT USE ARE    **to attach    to connect    to fasten
to fix    to link**
For other verbs, see **fasten**
2 Two motorways join in a mile.
OTHER VERBS ARE    **to come together    to meet    to merge**

# joint *noun*

JOINTS IN YOUR BODY ARE
**ankle    elbow    hip    knee    knuckle    shoulder
wrist**

# jolt *verb*

The car jolted along the rough road.
OTHER VERBS YOU MIGHT USE ARE    **to bounce    to bump    to jerk
to shake**

## journey *noun*

KINDS OF JOURNEY ARE

**excursion    expedition    outing    tour    trip**

A journey in a ship is a **cruise** or a **sail** or a **voyage**.
A journey in a car is a **drive**.
A journey in a plane is a **flight**.
A journey on a horse or bicycle is a **ride**.
A journey on foot is a
   **hike    ramble    trek    walk.**
A journey with a special purpose is a **mission**.
For other words, see **travel**

## judge *verb*

1  The criminal was judged in a court of law.
   OTHER VERBS YOU MIGHT USE ARE    **to condemn    to convict    to punish to sentence**

2  The referee judged that the player was off-side.
   OTHER VERBS ARE    **to consider    to decide    to rule**

## jumble *noun*

Dad wanted to know why there was a jumble of clothes on the floor.
   OTHER WORDS YOU MIGHT USE ARE    **assortment    chaos    clutter confusion    mess    muddle**

## jump *verb*

1  We jumped over the fence.
   OTHER VERBS YOU MIGHT USE ARE    **to bound    to hop    to leap    to skip to vault**

2  The cat jumped on the mouse.
   OTHER VERBS ARE    **to spring    to pounce**

## just *adjective*

The referee's decision was just.
   OTHER WORDS YOU MIGHT USE ARE    **fair    honest    lawful    proper right    unbiased**
The opposite is **unfair**

# Kk

**keen** *adjective*

Jo is keen to learn the piano.

OTHER WORDS YOU MIGHT USE ARE   **anxious   eager   enthusiastic**

**keep** *verb*

1  I'll keep some sweets for later.

OTHER VERBS YOU MIGHT USE ARE   **to save   to store**

2  If you can't do it straight away, keep trying!

OTHER VERBS ARE   **to carry on   to continue   to persist**

3  Please keep still.

OTHER VERBS ARE   **to remain   to stay**

4  Mum says it's expensive to keep a family.

OTHER VERBS ARE   **to care for   to feed   to look after   to mind   to provide for   to support   to tend**

---

**kill** *verb*

OTHER VERBS YOU MIGHT USE ARE

(*informal*) **to finish off   to slay**

to kill a famous person

**to assassinate**

to kill a criminal

**to execute** or **put to death**

to kill a person

**to murder**

to kill a lot of people

**to massacre**

to kill pests

**to exterminate**

to kill an animal that is old or ill

**to put to sleep**

to kill an animal for food

**to slaughter**

WAYS TO KILL A PERSON ARE

**to behead   to choke   to crucify   to drown   to electrocute   to gas   to hang   to knife   to poison   to shoot   to stab   to strangle   to suffocate   to throttle**

## kind *adjective*
We are lucky to have kind neighbours.
> OTHER WORDS YOU MIGHT USE ARE **considerate   friendly   good-natured   helpful   kind-hearted   loving   neighbourly   sympathetic   thoughtful   unselfish**

The opposite is **unkind**

## kind *noun*
1  A terrier is a kind of dog.
> OTHER WORDS YOU MIGHT USE ARE **breed   sort   species   type**

2  What kind of butter do you buy?
> OTHER WORDS ARE **brand   make   variety**

---

## kitchen *noun*

THINGS YOU USE IN A KITCHEN TO HEAT OR COOK FOOD ARE
**cooker   electric plate   gas ring   grill   hotplate   kettle   microwave   oven   stove   toaster**

OTHER THINGS YOU USE IN A KITCHEN ARE
**baking tin   blender   bowl   breadboard   breadknife   carving knife   casserole   chip pan   crockery   cutlery   dishes   dish rack   dishwasher   draining board   jug   mincer   mixer   pans   percolator   pots   rolling pin   salt cellar   saucepan   scales   sink   tea towel   teapot   tin-opener   tray   whisk**

PLACES WHERE YOU KEEP FOOD ARE
**freezer   fridge** or **refrigerator   larder   pantry**

---

## kneel *verb*
I kneeled down to tie my shoe.
> OTHER VERBS YOU MIGHT USE ARE **to bend   to crouch   to stoop**

## knife *noun*
> OTHER WORDS YOU MIGHT USE ARE **carving knife   dagger   penknife**

## knob *noun*
1  the knob on the door.
> ANOTHER WORD IS **handle**

2  a knob of butter.
> ANOTHER WORD IS **lump**

## knock *verb*
I knocked on the door.
> OTHER VERBS YOU MIGHT USE ARE   **to rap    to tap**

For other verbs, see **hit**

## know *verb*
1 Sam knows the names of all the kings and queens of England.
> OTHER VERBS YOU MIGHT USE ARE   **to recognize    to remember**
2 Mum knows a bit of French.
> ANOTHER VERB IS **to understand**

## knowledge *noun*
1 You get a lot of knowledge from an encyclopaedia.
> OTHER WORDS YOU MIGHT USE ARE   **facts    information**
2 Farmers have a great knowledge of the countryside.
> OTHER WORDS ARE   **experience    understanding**

# Ll

## lag *verb*
If we lag behind we'll miss the bus.
> OTHER VERBS YOU MIGHT USE ARE   **to dawdle**    (*informal*) **to hang about**
> **to linger    to loiter    to straggle**

## lake *noun*
For other words, see **water**

## lame *adjective*
The lame man used a walking stick.
> OTHER WORDS YOU MIGHT USE ARE   **crippled    disabled    limping**

## land *noun*
1 foreign lands.
> OTHER WORDS YOU MIGHT USE ARE   **country    nation**
2 land to grow crops on.
> OTHER WORDS ARE   **earth    ground    soil**

# land *verb*
1  The plane landed at the airport.
> OTHER VERBS YOU MIGHT USE ARE  **to arrive**  **to come down**  **to touch down**
2  The sailors landed on an island.
> OTHER VERBS ARE  **to come ashore**  **to disembark**

# large *adjective*
> OTHER WORDS YOU MIGHT USE ARE  **big**  **broad**  **fat**  **grand**  **great**  **long**  **roomy**  **spacious**  **tall**  **wide**
> WORDS FOR VERY LARGE THINGS ARE  **colossal**  **enormous**  **giant**  **gigantic**  **huge**  **immense**  **infinite**  **massive**  **mighty**  **monstrous**  **tremendous**  **vast**

The opposite is **small**

# last *adjective*
Our song was the last item in the concert.
> OTHER WORDS YOU MIGHT USE ARE  **concluding**  **final**

The opposite is **first**

# last *verb*
The fine weather lasted all week.
> OTHER VERBS YOU MIGHT USE ARE  **to continue**  **to go on**  **to keep on**  **to persist**  **to remain**  **to stay**

# late *adjective*
The bus is late.
> OTHER WORDS YOU MIGHT USE ARE  **delayed**  **overdue**

Opposites are **early** or **punctual**

# lately *adverb*
> ANOTHER WORD IS **recently**

# laugh *verb*
> VARIOUS WAYS WE LAUGH ARE  **to chuckle**  **to giggle**  **to grin**  **to smile**  **to titter**
> TO LAUGH UNKINDLY AT SOMEONE IS  **to jeer**  **to sneer**  **to snigger**

For other verbs, see **mock**

# law *noun*
We obey the laws of the country.
> OTHER WORDS YOU MIGHT USE ARE  **regulation**  **rule**

## lay *verb*
I laid the papers on the desk.
OTHER VERBS YOU MIGHT USE ARE    **to leave    to place    to put    to set down    to spread**

## layer *noun*
There was a layer of ice over the playground.
OTHER WORDS YOU MIGHT USE ARE    **coating    film    sheet    skin    thickness**

## lazy *adjective*
That cat leads a lazy life!
ANOTHER WORD IS **idle**
The opposite is **busy**

## lead *verb*
1  The teacher led the children back to the classroom.
OTHER VERBS YOU MIGHT USE ARE    **to conduct    to guide    to take**
2  The captain led her team with great skill.
OTHER VERBS ARE    **to command    to direct    to manage**

## leak *verb*
Water leaked out of the bucket.
OTHER VERBS YOU MIGHT USE ARE    **to drip    to escape    to ooze    to seep    to trickle**

## lean *verb*
The sinking ship leaned to one side.
OTHER VERBS YOU MIGHT USE ARE    **to heel over    to list    to slant    to slope    to tilt**

## leap *verb*
Sam leaped over the fence.
OTHER VERBS YOU MIGHT USE ARE    **to bound    to jump    to spring    to vault**

## learn *verb*
1  We learned a lot about history when we went to the castle.
OTHER VERBS YOU MIGHT USE ARE    **to discover    to find out**
2  We learned the song by heart.
ANOTHER VERB IS **to memorize**

## leave *verb*

1 Don't leave your pets when you go on holiday.
   OTHER VERBS YOU MIGHT USE ARE  **to abandon  to desert  to forsake**
2 The guard blew a whistle to show that the train was ready to leave.
   OTHER VERBS ARE  **to depart  to go  to set off**
3 Leave the empty milk bottles outside the front door.
   OTHER VERBS ARE  **to deposit  to place  to put down  to set down**

## lecture *noun*

A policewoman gave us a lecture on road safety.
   OTHER WORDS YOU MIGHT USE ARE  **lesson  speech  talk**

## leg *noun*

For parts of the body, see **body**

## legal *adjective*

Is it legal to park on this road?
   OTHER WORDS YOU MIGHT USE ARE  **allowed  lawful  permitted**
The opposite is **illegal**

## lend *verb*

Can you lend me a pen?
   ANOTHER VERB IS **to loan**
If you give something to someone to use for a short time, you **lend** it.
If someone gives something to you to use, you **borrow** it.

## length *noun*

   OTHER WORDS YOU MIGHT USE ARE  **distance  measurement**

## let *verb*

1 Sam let Jo ride his bike.
   OTHER VERBS YOU MIGHT USE ARE  **to allow  to permit**
2 Aunt Jean lets her caravan to holidaymakers in the summer.
   OTHER VERBS ARE  **to hire  to rent**

## level *adjective*

1 You need a level field for playing rounders.
   OTHER WORDS YOU MIGHT USE ARE  **even  flat  horizontal  smooth**
2 At half time the scores were level.
   ANOTHER WORD IS **equal**

## licence *noun*
You need a licence to go fishing.
ANOTHER WORD IS **permit**

## lid *noun*
Put the lid back on the jam.
OTHER WORDS YOU MIGHT USE ARE **cap** **cover** **top**

## lie *noun*
Don't tell lies!
OTHER WORDS YOU MIGHT USE ARE **falsehood** (*informal*) **fib**

## lie *verb*
1 Don't believe her - I think she's lying.
OTHER VERBS YOU MIGHT USE ARE **to bluff** (*informal*) **to fib**
2 Sam lay on the sofa.
OTHER VERBS ARE **to lean back** **to recline** **to sprawl**

## life *noun*
Our dog is full of life.
OTHER WORDS YOU MIGHT USE ARE **energy** **liveliness** **vitality**

## lifelike *adjective*
The wax models were very lifelike.
OTHER WORDS YOU MIGHT USE ARE **natural** **realistic**

## lift *verb*
1 Lift the box onto the shelf.
OTHER VERBS YOU MIGHT USE ARE **to hoist** **to raise**
2 Jo lifted baby out of her pram.
ANOTHER VERB IS **to pick up**

## light *adjective*
1 a light suitcase.
The opposite is **heavy**
2 a light room.
OTHER WORDS YOU MIGHT USE ARE **bright** **well-lit**
The opposite is **dark**
3 light colours.
OTHER WORDS ARE **faint** **pale**
The opposite is **strong**

## light *noun*

THINGS WHICH GIVE LIGHT ARE

**bulb    candle    electric light    floodlight    headlight    lamp    lantern    searchlight    spotlight    streetlight    torch**

LIGHTS USED FOR DECORATION ARE

**fairy lights    illuminations**

NATURAL LIGHT IS

**daylight    moonlight    starlight    sunlight**

DIFFERENT WAYS LIGHT SHINES ARE

**blaze    burn    dazzle    flash    flicker    glare    gleam    glimmer    glint    glisten    glitter    glow    shine    spark    sparkle    twinkle**

## light *verb*

1  At Christmas we lit the church with candles.
   OTHER VERBS YOU MIGHT USE ARE    **to brighten    to illuminate    to lighten**
2  We tried to light the bonfire.
   OTHER VERBS ARE    **to ignite    to kindle    to set fire to**

## like *verb*

1  We like our neighbours.
   OTHER VERBS YOU MIGHT USE ARE    **to approve of    to be fond of    to respect**
For other verbs, see **love**
2  I would like a drink, please.
   OTHER VERBS ARE    **to enjoy    to fancy    to want    to wish for**
The opposite is **hate**

## likely *adjective*

1  Rain is likely today.
   ANOTHER WORD IS **probable**
2  Sam is a likely person to be captain of the team.
   OTHER WORDS ARE    **appropriate    suitable**

## limp *adjective*

1 limp covers on a book.
    OTHER WORDS YOU MIGHT USE ARE    **flexible**    **soft**
The opposite is **stiff**
2 limp lettuce.
    OTHER WORDS ARE    **drooping**    **floppy**
The opposite is **crisp**

## limp *verb*

Jo limped because her shoe hurt.
    ANOTHER VERB IS **to hobble**
For other verbs, see **lame**

## line *noun*

1 lines on the road.
    OTHER WORDS YOU MIGHT USE ARE    **dash**    **mark**    **streak**    **stripe**
2 lines on someone's face.
    OTHER WORDS ARE    **crease**    **furrow**    **wrinkle**
3 a railway line.
    OTHER WORDS ARE    **rails**    **route**    **track**
4 We waited in a line.
    OTHER WORDS ARE    **column**    **file**    **queue**    **rank**    **row**

## linger *verb*

Don't linger in the playground.
    OTHER VERBS YOU MIGHT USE ARE    **to dawdle**    **to delay**
    (*informal*) **to hang about**    **to loiter**    **to remain**    **to stay**
    **to wait about**

## link *verb*

Sam can link his keyboard to a computer.
    OTHER VERBS YOU MIGHT USE ARE    **to attach**    **to connect**    **to join**

## litter *noun*

We get into trouble if we leave litter round the school.
    OTHER WORDS YOU MIGHT USE ARE    **clutter**    **junk**    **rubbish**

## little *adjective*

1 Sam's got a little radio that he can put in his pocket.
    OTHER WORDS YOU MIGHT USE ARE    **compact**    **miniature**    **minute**
    **small**    **tiny**
2 We had a little chat.
    OTHER WORDS ARE    **brief**    **short**

3  She gave us little helpings.
> OTHER WORDS ARE    **mean**    (*informal*) **measly**    **stingy**

4  They had a little argument.
> OTHER WORDS ARE    **minor**    **slight**    **trivial**    **unimportant**

The opposite is **big**

# live *adjective*
There aren't any live dinosaurs.
> OTHER WORDS YOU MIGHT USE ARE    **existing**    **living**

# live *verb*
1  Plants can't live without water.
> OTHER VERBS YOU MIGHT USE ARE    **to exist**    **to remain alive**    **to survive**

2  Jo's Granny lives in a flat.
> OTHER VERBS ARE    **to dwell in**    **to inhabit**    **to occupy**

# lively *adjective*
Those puppies are lively!
> OTHER WORDS YOU MIGHT USE ARE    **active**    **energetic**    **frisky**

The opposite is **lazy**

# load *noun*
Can you carry that heavy load?
> OTHER WORDS YOU MIGHT USE ARE    **burden**    **weight**

# load *verb*
We loaded the trolley with food.
> OTHER VERBS YOU MIGHT USE ARE    **to fill**    **to pack**

# lock *noun*
Mum fitted a lock to the door.
> OTHER WORDS YOU MIGHT USE ARE    **bolt**    **catch**    **latch**    **padlock**

# lock *verb*
Did you lock the door?
> OTHER VERBS YOU MIGHT USE ARE    **to fasten**    **to secure**

# logical *adjective*
a logical argument.
> OTHER WORDS YOU MIGHT USE ARE    **intelligent**    **reasonable**    **sensible**

## lonely *adjective*

1  Jo felt lonely when Sam went away.
   OTHER WORDS YOU MIGHT USE ARE  **alone**  **forsaken**  **friendless**  **neglected**  **solitary**
2  We heard a ghost story about a lonely farmhouse.
   OTHER WORDS ARE  **isolated**  **remote**  **secluded**

## long *adjective*

It seemed a long journey.
   OTHER WORDS YOU MIGHT USE ARE  **endless**  **lengthy**
The opposite is **short**

## long *verb*

I longed for a drink.
   OTHER VERBS YOU MIGHT USE ARE  **to fancy**  **to hanker after**  **to want**  **to wish for**  **to yearn for**

## look *verb*

1  We looked at the things we had collected on our walk.
   OTHER VERBS YOU MIGHT USE ARE  **to examine**  **to study**  **to survey**  **to view**
   TO LOOK AT SOMETHING QUICKLY  **to glance**  **to peep**
   TO LOOK FOR A LONG TIME  **to gaze**  **to stare**  **to watch**
2  The dog looked friendly.
   OTHER VERBS ARE  **to appear**  **to seem**
3  I helped Mum look for her purse.
   OTHER VERBS ARE  **to hunt**  **to search for**  **to seek**

## loose *adjective*

1  My tooth is loose.
   OTHER WORDS YOU MIGHT USE ARE  **shaky**  **unsteady**  **wobbly**
2  The animals were all loose.
   OTHER WORDS ARE  **at liberty**  **free**

## lorry *noun*

For other words, see **travel**

## lose *verb*

1  Sam was upset when he lost his watch.
   ANOTHER VERB IS **to mislay**
2  Our team lost on Saturday.
   A PHRASE IS **to be defeated**

## loud *adjective*
The neighbours complained about the loud music.
> OTHER WORDS YOU MIGHT USE ARE    **deafening    noisy    shrill**
The opposite is **quiet**

## lounge *noun*
> OTHER WORDS YOU MIGHT USE ARE    **drawing room    living room    sitting room**

## love *verb*
> OTHER VERBS YOU MIGHT USE ARE    **to adore    to be fond of    to be in love with    to care for    to idolize    to like    to treasure    to worship**

## lovely *adjective*
For other words, see **beautiful**

## low *adjective*
The opposite is **high**

## loyal *adjective*
Sam is a loyal supporter of his local team.
> OTHER WORDS YOU MIGHT USE ARE    **devoted    faithful    reliable    trustworthy**

## luck *noun*
Sam found his lost watch by luck.
> OTHER WORDS YOU MIGHT USE ARE    **accident    chance    coincidence**

## lucky *adjective*
I was lucky to find what I wanted.
> ANOTHER WORD IS **fortunate**
The opposite is **unlucky**

---

## luggage *noun*
The driver put our luggage in the back of the car.
> DIFFERENT ITEMS OF LUGGAGE MIGHT BE
> **bag    box    case    holdall    suitcase    trunk**

## lump *noun*

1 Uncle gave Jo a lump of chocolate.
OTHER WORDS YOU MIGHT USE ARE    **bar    block    chunk    hunk    piece    slab**

2 Dad got a lump on the head where he hit himself.
OTHER WORDS YOU MIGHT USE ARE    **bulge    bump    hump    knob    swelling**

## luxury *noun*

That cat lives a life of luxury!
OTHER WORDS YOU MIGHT USE ARE    **comfort    ease    pleasure    relaxation**

# Mm

## machine *noun*

The workshop had a machine for doing woodwork.
OTHER WORDS YOU MIGHT USE ARE    **apparatus    instrument    tool**
A word you might use for machines in general is **machinery**

## mad *adjective*

1 He behaved so strangely that people said he was mad.
OTHER WORDS YOU MIGHT USE ARE    (*informal*) **crazy    insane    mentally ill    unbalanced**

2 He's mad to go out in this rain!
For other words, see **silly**

## magic *noun*

1 Can witches really do magic?
OTHER WORDS YOU MIGHT USE ARE    **charms    enchantments    sorcery    spells    witchcraft**

2 The conjuror did some magic.
A PHRASE YOU MIGHT USE IS **conjuring tricks**

## magician *noun*

OTHER WORDS YOU MIGHT USE ARE    **conjuror    sorcerer    wizard**

## magnificent *adjective*

a magnificent palace.

OTHER WORDS YOU MIGHT USE ARE  **grand    impressive    majestic    noble    splendid    stately**

## mail *noun*

For other words, see **post**

## main *adjective*

The main ingredient of bread is flour.

OTHER WORDS YOU MIGHT USE ARE  **basic    chief    essential    important    principal**

## make *verb*, see next page

---

## make-up *noun*

KINDS OF MAKE-UP ARE

**blusher    eye-liner    eye-shadow    face cream    face powder    lipstick    nail varnish**

THINGS PEOPLE USE TO MAKE THEMSELVES SMELL NICER ARE

**aftershave    deodorant    perfume    scent    talc** or **talcum powder**

---

## male *noun*

There are special words for male and female human beings and some animals.

A male human being is a **boy** or **man.**

A male bird is a **cock.**
A male cat is a **tom-cat.**
A male chicken is a **cockerel.**
A male deer is a **buck** or **stag.**
A male duck is a **drake.**
A male goat is a **billy goat.**

A male goose is a **gander.**
A male horse is a **stallion.**
A male pig is a **hog.**
A male rabbit is a **buck.**
A male sheep is a **ram.**
A male swan is a **cob.**

For words for females, see **female**

## make *verb*

THIS VERB HAS MANY USES. HERE ARE SOME OF THE WAYS YOU CAN USE IT, AND SOME OTHER VERBS YOU COULD CHOOSE

1  I made a plan.
   **to form    to invent    to produce    to think up**

2  We made a den in the garden.
   **to build    to construct    to create    to erect**

3  They make cars in that factory.
   **to assemble    to manufacture**

4  Don't make trouble.
   **to bring about    to cause    to provoke**

5  You can't make me do it.
   **to compel    to force    to oblige    to order**

6  The head made a speech.
   **to deliver    to give**

7  It's easy to make a P into a B.
   **to alter    to change    to convert    to transform
   to turn**

8  How can I make some money?
   **to earn    to get    to obtain    to receive**

9  You'll make a good player if you practise.
   **to become    to change into    to grow into    to turn into**

10  Will our team make the final?
   **to get to    to reach**

11  2 and 2 make 4.
   **to add up to    to come to**

12  Mum made an appointment at the doctor's.
   **to arrange    to fix**

13  I can't make out what happened.
   **to follow    to hear    to see    to understand**

14  She made up an excuse.
   **to invent    to plan    to think up**

## man *noun*

OTHER WORDS YOU MIGHT USE ARE

a polite word
**gentleman**

a married man
**husband**

a man who is not married
**bachelor**

a man whose wife has died
**widower**

a man who has children
**father**

a young man
**boy**     **youth**

## manage *verb*

1 The head manages the school.
OTHER VERBS YOU MIGHT USE ARE     **to be in charge of**     **to control**
**to look after**     **to run**
2 Can you manage a big helping?
OTHER VERBS YOU MIGHT USE ARE     **to cope with**     **to deal with**
**to handle**
3 Could you manage to help us on Saturday?
ANOTHER VERB IS **to arrange**

## manner *noun*

He spoke in a friendly manner.
OTHER WORDS YOU MIGHT USE ARE     **fashion**     **style**     **way**

## map *noun*

A simple map is a **diagram** or **plan**.
A map used by sailors is a **chart**.
A book of maps is an **atlas**.

**mark** *noun*

There's a mark on my new dress.

OTHER WORDS YOU MIGHT USE ARE **smear** **smudge** **spot** **stain**

---

**market** *noun*

DIFFERENT KINDS OF MARKET ARE

**auction** **bazaar** **car boot sale** **fair**
**street market**

---

**marsh** *noun*

We began to sink into the marsh.

OTHER WORDS YOU MIGHT USE ARE **bog** **swamp**

**marvellous** *adjective*

I had a marvellous holiday.

OTHER WORDS YOU MIGHT USE ARE **excellent** (*informal*) **fabulous**
**splendid** **wonderful**

**mash** *verb*

We mashed the baby's dinner until it was soft.

OTHER VERBS YOU MIGHT USE ARE **to crush** **to pulp** **to purée**
**to smash** **to squash**

**mass** *noun*

There was a mass of rubbish to clear away.

OTHER WORDS YOU MIGHT USE ARE **heap** **mound** **pile** **quantity**
**stack**

**match** *noun*

a boxing match.

OTHER WORDS YOU MIGHT USE ARE **competition** **contest**
**game**

**material** *noun*

1 building materials.

OTHER WORDS YOU MIGHT USE ARE **stuff** **substances** **things**

2 material to make curtains.

For other words, see **cloth**

# mathematics *noun*

A short word for mathematics is **maths**.
Working with numbers is also called **arithmetic**.

WORDS FOR THINGS YOU DO IN MATHEMATICS ARE
**addition** or **adding**     **calculation** or **calculating**
**counting**     **division** or **dividing**     **investigating**
**measuring**     **multiplication** or **multiplying**
**subtraction** or **subtracting** or **taking away**     **sums**

VERBS YOU MIGHT USE IN MATHS ARE
**to add     to add up     to calculate     to count     to divide
to investigate     to measure     to multiply     to subtract
to take away     to work out**

OTHER WORDS YOU MIGHT USE IN MATHS ARE
**angle     answer     area     capacity     diagonal
difference     digit     figure     fraction     graph
measurement     minus     number     pattern     plus
problem     shape     sum     symmetry     times     total
unit     volume**

THINGS YOU MIGHT USE TO HELP YOU IN MATHEMATICS ARE
**calculator     compasses     computer     ruler     set square**

For words you might use when you measure things, see **measurement**
For names of different shapes, see **shape**

# matter *noun*

1 We have some matters to discuss.
OTHER WORDS YOU MIGHT USE ARE     **business     subject     topic**
2 What's the matter?
OTHER WORDS ARE     **difficulty     problem     trouble**

# meal *noun*

DIFFERENT MEALS ARE
**breakfast     dinner     high tea     lunch     supper     tea**

A very splendid meal is a **banquet** or **feast**.
A meal where you help yourself is a **buffet**.
A small meal is a **snack**.
A meal you eat out of doors is a **picnic**.
A meal you cook out of doors is a **barbecue**.

**mean** *adjective*
He's mean with his money.
OTHER WORDS YOU MIGHT USE ARE　**miserly**　(*informal*) **stingy**
The opposite is **generous**

**mean** *verb*
1　What does this word mean?
OTHER VERBS YOU MIGHT USE ARE　**to convey**　**to indicate**　**to say**
**to stand for**
2　What do you mean to do?
OTHER VERBS ARE　**to aim**　**to intend**　**to plan**　**to propose**

---

**measurement** *noun*
ANOTHER WORD IS **size**
OTHER WORDS YOU MIGHT USE ARE
how long something is: **length**
how wide something is: **breadth** or **width**
how tall something is: **height**
UNITS TO MEASURE LENGTH, BREADTH, OR HEIGHT ARE
**centimetres**　**metres**　**kilometres**
OLD UNITS ARE
**inches**　**feet**　**yards**　**miles**

how big a surface is: **area**
UNITS TO MEASURE AREA ARE
**square metres**　**hectares**
OLD UNITS ARE
**square feet**　**square yards**　**acres**

how much something holds: **volume**
UNITS TO MEASURE VOLUME ARE
**cubic centimetres** or **litres**
OLD UNITS ARE
**pints** or **gallons**

how heavy something is: **weight**
UNITS TO MEASURE WEIGHT ARE
**grams**　**kilograms**　**tonnes**
OLD UNITS ARE
**ounces**　**pounds**　**tons**

**meat** *noun*

DIFFERENT KINDS OF MEAT ARE

**bacon    beef    chicken    ham    lamb    pork    turkey
veal    venison**

YOU CAN BUY MEAT IN THE FORM OF

**burgers    chops    joint    mince    sausage    steak**

## medicine *noun*
I need medicine for my cough.
For other words, see **health**

## medium *adjective*
Sam is medium height for his age.
OTHER WORDS YOU MIGHT USE ARE    **average    middling    normal**

## meet *verb*
1  Two roads meet here.
OTHER VERBS YOU MIGHT USE ARE    **to come together    to join    to merge**
2  I met my friend in town.
OTHER VERBS ARE    **to encounter**    (*informal*) **to run into    to see**
3  All the classes met in the hall.
OTHER VERBS ARE    **to assemble    to congregate    to gather**

## meeting *noun*
DIFFERENT KINDS OF MEETING ARE    **assembly    committee    conference
council**

## melt *verb*
The ice melted in the sun.
OTHER VERBS YOU MIGHT USE ARE    **to thaw    to unfreeze**

## mend *verb*
1  The garage mended the car.
OTHER VERBS YOU MIGHT USE ARE    **to fix    to put right    to repair**
2  Dad likes mending old furniture.
OTHER VERBS ARE    **to do up    to renovate    to restore**
3  Sam mended his jeans.
OTHER VERBS ARE    **to darn    to patch    to sew up    to stitch up**

**mention** *verb*
I mentioned that I was hungry.
OTHER VERBS YOU MIGHT USE ARE    **to comment    to remark    to say**

**merciful** *adjective*
The judge was merciful and let him off with a warning.
OTHER WORDS YOU MIGHT USE ARE    **forgiving    kind    sympathetic**
The opposite is **cruel**

**mercy** *noun*
The judge showed mercy.
OTHER WORDS YOU MIGHT USE ARE    **forgiveness    pity**

**merry** *adjective*
a merry tune.
OTHER WORDS YOU MIGHT USE ARE    **cheerful    happy    jolly    lively**
The opposite is **sad**

**mess** *noun*
Clear up this mess!
OTHER WORDS YOU MIGHT USE ARE    **chaos    clutter    confusion    jumble    muddle**

**message** *noun*
I sent a message that I was busy.
OTHER WORDS YOU MIGHT USE ARE    **letter    note**

**metal** *noun*
DIFFERENT METALS ARE
**aluminium    brass    bronze    copper    gold    iron    lead    platinum    silver    steel    tin    uranium    zinc**

**method** *noun*
Our teacher showed us a good method for doing multiplication.
OTHER WORDS YOU MIGHT USE ARE **procedure    system    technique    way**

**middle** *noun*
the middle of the earth.
OTHER WORDS YOU MIGHT USE ARE    **centre    core    heart**

# mild *adjective*

1 mild weather.

    OTHER WORDS YOU MIGHT USE ARE     **gentle**     **pleasant**     **warm**

2 a mild illness.

    ANOTHER WORD IS **slight**

The opposite is **severe**

# mind *noun*

Use your mind!

    OTHER WORDS YOU MIGHT USE ARE     **brain**     **intelligence**     **understanding**

# mind *verb*

1 I'll mind the baby.

    OTHER VERBS YOU MIGHT USE ARE     **to care for**     **to look after**     **to tend**

2 Do you mind about missing the party?

    OTHER VERBS ARE     **to care**     **to worry**

# mine *noun*

a coal mine.

    OTHER WORDS YOU MIGHT USE ARE     **pit**     **shaft**

A place where they dig coal from the Earth's surface is an **opencast mine**.

A place where they dig stone is a **quarry**.

# mischievous *adjective*

The mischievous puppy stole Dad's slippers.

    OTHER WORDS YOU MIGHT USE ARE     **badly behaved**     **naughty**

# miserable *adjective*

1 Jo's miserable when Sam is away.

    OTHER WORDS YOU MIGHT USE ARE     **depressed**     **gloomy**     **sad**     **unhappy**     **wretched**

The opposite is **happy**

2 The refugees live in miserable conditions.

    OTHER WORDS ARE     **awful**     **bad**     **pitiful**     **poor**     **wretched**

# misery *noun*

We can't imagine the misery of the refugees.

    OTHER WORDS YOU MIGHT USE ARE     **distress**     **grief**     **sadness**     **sorrow**     **suffering**     **unhappiness**

# mislead *verb*

She misled us and sent us the wrong way.

    OTHER VERBS YOU MIGHT USE ARE     **to deceive**     **to fool**     **to trick**

## miss *verb*

1  If we leave now we'll miss the rush-hour traffic.
   OTHER VERBS YOU MIGHT USE ARE   **to avoid**   **to dodge**   **to steer clear of**
2  I missed the bus.
The opposite is **catch**
3  Jo missed Sam when he was away.
   ANOTHER VERB IS **to pine for**
4  You can miss out the questions you don't understand.
   OTHER VERBS ARE   **to leave out**   **to omit**   **to skip**

## missing *adjective*

Did you find the missing money?
ANOTHER WORD IS **lost**

## mist *noun*

ANOTHER WORD IS **haze**
A thick mist is **fog**.

## mistake *noun*

spelling mistakes.
OTHER WORDS YOU MIGHT USE ARE   **blunder**   **error**   (*informal*) **slip**

## misty *adjective*

a misty view.
OTHER WORDS YOU MIGHT USE ARE   **blurred**   **dim**   **faint**   **fuzzy**
   **hazy**   **indistinct**   **unclear**
The opposite is **clear**

## mix *verb*

1  Mix the flour, fat, and sugar in a bowl.
   OTHER VERBS YOU MIGHT USE ARE   **to blend**   **to combine**   **to mingle**
   **to stir together**
2  Don't mix two packs of cards!
   OTHER VERBS ARE   **to confuse**   **to jumble**   **to muddle**

## mixture *noun*

I had a mixture of sweets.
OTHER WORDS YOU MIGHT USE ARE   **assortment**   **variety**

## moan *verb*

He moaned with pain.
OTHER VERBS YOU MIGHT USE ARE   **to groan**   **to wail**

## mock *verb*

It's unkind to mock other people.

> OTHER VERBS YOU MIGHT USE ARE   **to laugh at     to make fun of**
> **to ridicule     to sneer at     to taunt     to tease**

## moderate *adjective*

Dad drives at moderate speed.

> OTHER WORDS YOU MIGHT USE ARE   **medium     middling     normal**
> **ordinary     reasonable**

## modern *adjective*

1  Grandad says he doesn't understand modern inventions like computers.

> OTHER WORDS YOU MIGHT USE ARE   **new     recent**

The opposite is **old**

2  Do you like modern clothes?

> OTHER WORDS ARE   **fashionable     stylish     (*informal*) trendy**
> **up-to-date**

The opposite is **old-fashioned**

## modest *adjective*

1  She was modest about winning the prize.

> ANOTHER WORD IS **humble**

The opposite is **conceited**

2  He was too modest to undress on the beach.

> OTHER WORDS YOU MIGHT USE ARE   **bashful     shy**

---

## money *noun*

Money you have in your pocket is **cash** or **change**.

> IT MIGHT BE
> **coins     (*informal*) coppers     notes     silver**

People can also buy things with a **cheque** or a **credit card**.

> A LOT OF MONEY IS
> **a fortune     wealth**

> MONEY YOU GET FOR WORK YOU DO IS
> **earnings     income     pay     salary     wages**

Money you get when you retire from work is a **pension**.
Money you save in the bank is your **savings**.
Money people have to pay to the government is **tax**.

## monster *noun*

FRIGHTENING CREATURES YOU READ ABOUT IN STORIES ARE

| | | | |
|---|---|---|---|
| **beast** | **dragon** | **giant** | **ogre** |
| **troll** | **vampire** | **werewolf** | |

## month *noun*

THE MONTHS OF THE YEAR ARE

| | | | |
|---|---|---|---|
| **January** | **February** | **March** | **April** |
| **May** | **June** | **July** | **August** |
| **September** | **October** | **November** | **December** |

## mood *noun*

Is Dad in a good mood today?

OTHER WORDS YOU MIGHT USE ARE   **humour**   **temper**

## moral *adjective*

a moral person.

OTHER WORDS YOU MIGHT USE ARE   **good**   **honest**   **truthful**   **virtuous**

The opposite is **immoral**

## motive *noun*

What was the motive for the crime?

OTHER WORDS YOU MIGHT USE ARE   **purpose**   **reason**

## motor *noun*

an electric motor.

ANOTHER WORD IS **engine**

## mountain *noun*

The top of a mountain is the **summit** or **peak**.
A line of mountains is a **range** or **ridge**.
A mountain which sometimes sends out hot liquid, gases, or ash is a **volcano**.

## move *verb*

THIS VERB HAS MANY USES. HERE ARE SOME OF THE WAYS YOU CAN USE IT, AND SOME OTHER VERBS YOU COULD CHOOSE

1  to move along.
**to come    to fly    to go    to journey    to march
to pass    to tour    to travel    to walk**

2  to move along quickly.
**to canter    to dart    to dash    to fly    to gallop
to hurry    to race    to run    to rush    to shoot
to speed    to streak    to tear**    (*informal*) **to zoom**

3  to move along slowly.
**to crawl    to dawdle    to stroll**

4  to move along gracefully.
**to dance    to glide    to skate    to skim    to slide
to slip**

5  to move along clumsily.
**to shuffle    to stagger    to stumble    to sway
to totter    to trip**

6  to move along stealthily.
**to crawl    to creep    to slink    to slither**

7  to move away from somewhere.
**to depart    to leave    to quit**

8  to move back.
**to reverse    to withdraw**

9  to move downwards.
**to descend    to drop    to fall    to sink**

10  to move upwards.
**to arise    to climb    to mount    to rise**

11  to move in somewhere.
**to enter**

12  to move round and round.
**to revolve    to roll    to rotate    to spin    to turn
to twirl    to twist    to whirl**

13  to move towards something.
**to advance    to approach**

14  to move restlessly.
**to fidget    to shake    to stir    to toss    to tremble
to twist    to twitch    to wag    to waggle    to wave**

15  to move things.
**to budge    to carry    to shift    to transport**

**mud** *noun*

There was some mud on the road.

OTHER WORDS YOU MIGHT USE ARE    **clay    dirt    muck    slime**

**muddle** *verb*

1 Don't muddle the library books.

OTHER VERBS YOU MIGHT USE ARE    **to jumble    to mix up**

2 You muddle me if you talk fast.

OTHER VERBS ARE    **to bewilder    to confuse**

**murder** *verb*

For other verbs, see **kill**

---

**music** *noun*

DIFFERENT KINDS OF MUSIC ARE

**classical music    disco music    folk music    jazz**
**musicals    opera    pop music    rap**
**reggae    rock**

KINDS OF MUSIC FOR SINGING ARE

**ballad    carol    folk song    hymn**
**lullaby    pop song    shanty    spiritual**

BRASS INSTRUMENTS ARE

**bugle    cornet    horn    trombone**
**trumpet    tuba**

OTHER INSTRUMENTS YOU PLAY BY BLOWING ARE

**bagpipes    bassoon    clarinet    flute**
**harmonica** or **mouthorgan    oboe    pan pipes**
**piccolo    recorder    saxophone**

INSTRUMENTS WITH STRINGS THAT YOU PLAY BY PLUCKING ARE

**banjo    guitar    harp    sitar**

INSTRUMENTS WITH STRINGS THAT YOU CAN PLAY WITH A BOW ARE

**cello    double bass    fiddle    viola**
**violin**

INSTRUMENTS YOU PLAY BY PRESSING KEYS ARE

**harmonium    harpsichord    keyboard    organ**
**piano**

PERCUSSION INSTRUMENTS ARE

| | | | |
|---|---|---|---|
| castanets | chime bars | cymbals | drums |
| glockenspiel | gong | kettledrum | tambourine |
| triangle | tubular bells | xylophone | |

PEOPLE WHO MAKE MUSIC ARE

| | | | |
|---|---|---|---|
| composer | conductor | performer | player |
| singer | | | |

PEOPLE WHO PLAY INSTRUMENTS ARE

| | | | |
|---|---|---|---|
| drummer | fiddler | guitarist | harpist |
| organist | percussionist | pianist | piper |
| trumpeter | violinist | | |

DIFFERENT SINGING VOICES ARE

| | | | |
|---|---|---|---|
| alto | bass | soprano | tenor |
| treble | | | |

People who play or sing on their own are **soloists**.
A singer may also be called a **vocalist**.

GROUPS OF MUSICIANS ARE

| | | | |
|---|---|---|---|
| band | choir or chorus | | ensemble |
| group | orchestra | quartet | quintet |
| trio | | | |

# mysterious *adjective*

1 The doctors didn't know what to do about my mysterious illness.

OTHER WORDS YOU MIGHT USE ARE   **mystifying   puzzling   strange**

2 The castle looked mysterious in the moonlight.

OTHER WORDS ARE   **eerie   ghostly   magical   weird**

# mystery *noun*

The detective solved the mystery.

OTHER WORDS YOU MIGHT USE ARE   **problem   puzzle   riddle**

# Nn

**naked** *adjective*
> OTHER WORDS YOU MIGHT USE ARE   **bare    nude    unclothed
> undressed**

---

**name** *noun*
> The name that you are given when you are born is your **first name**.
> The name that everyone in your family has is your **surname** or **family name**.
> An invented name which friends give you is a **nickname**.
> A name you use instead of your real name is an **alias**.
> A name an author uses instead of a real name is a **pen name**.
> The name of a book is the **title**.
> The name of a particular make of goods is the **brand**.

---

**narrow** *adjective*
> OTHER WORDS YOU MIGHT USE ARE   **fine    slim    thin**
The opposite is **wide**

**nasty** *adjective*
1 nasty weather.
> OTHER WORDS YOU MIGHT USE ARE   **bad    dreadful    horrible
> unpleasant**
2 a nasty mess.
> OTHER WORDS ARE   **dirty    disgusting    filthy    foul    revolting**
3 a nasty person.
> OTHER WORDS ARE   **rude    unfriendly    unkind**
The opposite is **nice**

**nation** *noun*
People from many nations take part in the Olympic Games.
> OTHER WORDS YOU MIGHT USE ARE   **country    race**

## natural *adjective*
It's natural to go to sleep when you are tired.
ANOTHER WORD IS **normal**
The opposite is **unnatural**

## naughty *adjective*
We punished the dog because he had been naughty.
OTHER WORDS YOU MIGHT USE ARE **bad   disobedient   mischievous   wicked**
The opposite is **well-behaved**

## near *adjective* and *adverb*
Our house is near to the shops.
ANOTHER WORD IS **close**

## nearly *adverb*
I've nearly finished.
OTHER WORDS YOU MIGHT USE ARE **almost   not quite   practically**

## neat *adjective*
Jo arranged her books in a neat row.
OTHER WORDS YOU MIGHT USE ARE **orderly   smart   tidy**
The opposite is **untidy**

## necessary *adjective*
It is necessary to water plants in dry weather.
OTHER WORDS YOU MIGHT USE ARE **essential   important   vital**
The opposite is **unnecessary**

## neck *noun*
For other parts of the body, see **body**

## need *verb*
1  We need some butter to make the sandwiches.
OTHER VERBS YOU MIGHT USE ARE **to require   to want**
2  The football team needs Sam to play in goal.
OTHER VERBS ARE **to count on   to depend on   to rely on**

## neglect *verb*
You mustn't neglect your pets when you go on holiday.
OTHER VERBS YOU MIGHT USE ARE **to forget   to ignore   to overlook**
The opposite is **look after**

## nervous *adjective*
Our dog gets nervous when she hears thunder.
OTHER WORDS YOU MIGHT USE ARE   **anxious   edgy   fidgety   jumpy**
The opposite is **calm**

## neutral *adjective*
The referee has to be neutral.
OTHER WORDS YOU MIGHT USE ARE   **impartial   unbiased**

## new *adjective*
1  new clothes.
OTHER WORDS YOU MIGHT USE ARE   **brand new   unused**
2  new bread.
ANOTHER WORD IS **fresh**
3  a new invention.
OTHER WORDS ARE   **modern   recent   up-to-date**
The opposite is **old**

---

## nice *adjective*
THIS WORD HAS MANY USES. HERE ARE SOME OF THE WAYS YOU CAN USE IT, AND SOME OTHER WORDS YOU COULD CHOOSE
1  nice weather.
**beautiful   fine   good   lovely   pleasant**
2  nice food.
**delicious   enjoyable   tasty**
3  a nice person.
**friendly   kind   likeable**

The opposite is **nasty**

---

## noble *adjective*
1  a noble deed.
OTHER WORDS YOU MIGHT USE ARE   **brave   gallant   heroic   worthy**
2  a noble palace.
OTHER WORDS ARE   **grand   majestic   stately**

## noise *noun*
Stop that noise!
OTHER WORDS YOU MIGHT USE ARE   **din   hubbub   (**informal**) racket   row   rumpus   uproar**
For kinds of noise, see **sound**

## noisy *adjective*
The neighbours complained that our music was too noisy.
OTHER WORDS YOU MIGHT USE ARE    **deafening    loud    rowdy**
The opposite is **silent**

## nonsense *noun*
Don't talk nonsense!
ANOTHER WORD IS **rubbish**

## normal *adjective*
1  It's quite normal for people to sweat in hot weather.
OTHER WORDS YOU MIGHT USE ARE    **common    natural    ordinary
usual**
2  The temperature is normal for this time of year.
ANOTHER WORD IS **average**

## nosy *adjective*
The kitten was being nosy and got her head stuck in a tin.
OTHER WORDS YOU MIGHT USE ARE    **curious    inquisitive**

## nothing *noun*
OTHER WORDS YOU MIGHT USE ARE    **nought    zero**
Nothing in cricket is a **duck**.
Nothing in football is **nil**.
Nothing in tennis is **love**.

## notice *noun*
We put up a notice about our play.
OTHER WORDS YOU MIGHT USE ARE    **advertisement    placard    poster
sign**

## notice *verb*
Jo noticed that Mum looked tired.
OTHER VERBS YOU MIGHT USE ARE    **to detect    to observe    to see**

## nude *adjective*
OTHER WORDS YOU MIGHT USE ARE    **bare    naked    unclothed
undressed**

## nuisance *noun*
That dog is a nuisance!
OTHER WORDS YOU MIGHT USE ARE    **bother    pest    trouble    worry**

## number *noun*
We had to add up the numbers.
ANOTHER WORD IS **figure**

## nurse *noun*
For people who help us when we are ill, see **health**

---

### nut *noun*
SOME NUTS YOU CAN EAT ARE

| | | | |
|---|---|---|---|
| almond | brazil | cashew | chestnut |
| coconut | hazelnut | peanut | walnut |

---

# Oo

## obedient *adjective*
an obedient dog.
ANOTHER WORD IS **well-behaved**
The opposite is **disobedient**

## obey *verb*
You have to obey the rules.
PHRASES YOU MIGHT USE ARE    **to abide by**    **to keep to**
The opposite is **disobey**

## object *verb*
We object to bad language.
PHRASES YOU MIGHT USE ARE    **to complain about**    **to disapprove of**
    **to protest about**

## obstinate *adjective*
The donkey was obstinate and refused to move.
OTHER WORDS YOU MIGHT USE ARE    **defiant**    (*informal*) **pig-headed**
    **stubborn**    **unhelpful**
The opposite is **helpful**

## obtain *verb*
For other verbs, see **get**

## obvious *adjective*
Jo thought the answer to the question was obvious.
> OTHER WORDS YOU MIGHT USE ARE    **clear    easy to see    plain**

## occasional *adjective*
We make occasional visits to the pictures.
> OTHER WORDS YOU MIGHT USE ARE    **infrequent    rare**
The opposite is **regular**

## occupation *noun*
1  What's your mother's occupation?
> OTHER WORDS YOU MIGHT USE ARE    **business    employment    job    work**
2  Fishing is a quiet occupation.
> OTHER WORDS YOU MIGHT USE ARE    **activity    hobby    pastime**

## occupy *verb*
1  Six people occupy our house.
> OTHER VERBS YOU MIGHT USE ARE    **to inhabit    to live in**
2  The soldiers occupied the town.
> OTHER VERBS ARE    **to capture    to conquer    to invade    to take over**

## occur *verb*
A nasty accident occurred today.
> OTHER VERBS YOU MIGHT USE ARE    **to happen    to take place**

## odd *adjective*
1  Jo can't explain her dog's odd behaviour.
> OTHER WORDS YOU MIGHT USE ARE    **abnormal    curious    funny    peculiar    queer    strange    uncommon    unusual    weird**
The opposite is **ordinary**
2  Where did this odd sock come from?
> OTHER WORDS YOU MIGHT USE ARE    **extra    single    spare**

## offend *verb*
I offended Jo because I didn't go to her party.
> OTHER VERBS YOU MIGHT USE ARE    **to annoy    to displease    to insult    to upset**
The opposite is **please**

## offensive *adjective*

1  There's an offensive smell in the kitchen.
> OTHER WORDS YOU MIGHT USE ARE    **disgusting    foul    horrible    nasty    unpleasant**
2  Don't use offensive language.
> OTHER WORDS ARE    **improper    indecent    rude**
The opposite is **pleasing**

## offer *verb*

1  I offered some cake to Granny.
> ANOTHER VERB IS **to give**
2  Sam offered to wash up.
> ANOTHER VERB IS **to volunteer**

## often *adverb*

> OTHER WORDS YOU MIGHT USE ARE    **again and again    frequently    regularly    repeatedly**
The opposite is **seldom**

## old *adjective*

1  an old car.
> OTHER WORDS YOU MIGHT USE ARE    **ancient    old-fashioned**
2  an old man.
> OTHER WORDS ARE    **aged    elderly**
3  an old magazine.
> ANOTHER WORD IS **out-of-date**
4  old bread.
> ANOTHER WORD IS **stale**
5  old clothes.
> OTHER WORDS ARE    **shabby    worn-out**
6  valuable old furniture.
> ANOTHER WORD IS **antique**
The opposite is **new**

## omit *verb*

The captain omitted Sam from the team because he was injured.
> OTHER VERBS YOU MIGHT USE ARE    **to drop    to exclude    to leave out**
The opposite is **include**

## open *adjective*

Leave the door open.
> OTHER WORDS YOU MIGHT USE ARE    **unfastened    unlocked**
The opposite is **shut**

# open *verb*
Please open the door.
> OTHER VERBS YOU MIGHT USE ARE    **to undo    to unfasten    to unlock**

The opposite is **close**

# opening *noun*
1  Jo's tortoise crawled through an opening in the fence.
> OTHER WORDS YOU MIGHT USE ARE    **break    crack    gap    hole    space**

2  Sam looks forward to the opening of the football season.
> OTHER WORDS ARE    **beginning    start**

# opinion *noun*
It's my opinion that the dog stole the sausages.
> OTHER WORDS YOU MIGHT USE ARE    **belief    guess    idea    thought    view**

# opposite *adjective*
1  the opposite side of the road.
> ANOTHER WORD IS **facing**

2  the opposite opinion.
> OTHER WORDS YOU MIGHT USE ARE    **contrary    different    opposing**

# order *verb*
1  He ordered us to stand still.
> OTHER VERBS YOU MIGHT USE ARE    **to command    to direct    to instruct    to tell**

2  We ordered fish and chips.
> PHRASES YOU MIGHT USE ARE    **to ask for    to send for**

# ordinary *adjective*
1  We spent the holiday doing ordinary things.
> OTHER WORDS YOU MIGHT USE ARE    **everyday    normal    typical    unexciting    usual**

2  Most of the birds we saw on our walk were just ordinary ones.
> OTHER WORDS ARE    **common    familiar    uninteresting    well-known**

3  I want an ordinary portion of chips.
> OTHER WORDS ARE    **regular    standard**

The opposite is **special**

# organize *verb*
Our teacher organized a trip to the zoo.
> ANOTHER VERB IS **to arrange**

**original** *adjective*

Mum said the ideas in Sam's story were very original.
　　OTHER WORDS YOU MIGHT USE ARE　**fresh**　**imaginative**　**new**
　　**unusual**

**outing** *noun*

We went on an outing to the country park.
　　OTHER WORDS YOU MIGHT USE ARE　**excursion**　**expedition**　**trip**

**oven** *noun*

For things you use to heat or cook food, see **kitchen**

**overgrown** *adjective*

an overgrown garden.
　　OTHER WORDS YOU MIGHT USE ARE　**tangled**　**untidy**

**overturn** *verb*

The boat overturned.
　　ANOTHER VERB IS **to capsize**

**own** *verb*

Do you own a bike?
　　ANOTHER VERB IS **to possess**
**to own up**
　　ANOTHER VERB IS **to confess**

# Pp

**pack** *verb*

We packed everything into the car.
　　OTHER VERBS YOU MIGHT USE ARE　**to load**　**to put**

**packet** *noun*

1　The postman brought an interesting-looking packet.
　　OTHER WORDS ARE　**package**　**parcel**
2　I bought a packet of cornflakes.
　　ANOTHER WORD IS **box**

**page** *noun*
Jo tore a page out of her notebook.
OTHER WORDS YOU MIGHT USE ARE    **leaf    sheet**

**pail** *noun*
a pail of water.
ANOTHER WORD IS **bucket**

**pain** *noun*
OTHER WORDS YOU MIGHT USE ARE    **ache    soreness    sting    twinge**
VERY BAD PAIN IS    **agony    suffering    torture**
For other words, see **hurt**

**painful** *adjective*
The cut on Jo's knee was painful.
OTHER WORDS YOU MIGHT USE ARE    **aching    hurting    smarting    sore
stinging    throbbing**

---

**paint** *noun*
DIFFERENT KINDS OF PAINT ARE
**emulsion    enamel    gloss    oil paint    varnish
watercolour**

---

**pale** *adjective*
1  His face went pale when he heard the bad news.
OTHER WORDS YOU MIGHT USE ARE    **colourless    white**
2  Mum decorated the sitting room in pale colours.
OTHER WORDS ARE    **faint    light**

**pant** *verb*
We were all panting for breath at the end of the race.
OTHER VERBS YOU MIGHT USE ARE    **to gasp    to puff**

---

**paper** *noun*
DIFFERENT KINDS OF PAPER ARE
**card    newspaper    notepaper    tissue paper
toilet paper    wallpaper    wrapping paper
writing paper**

---

## parcel *noun*
The postman came with a parcel.
OTHER WORDS ARE    **package    packet**

## pardon *verb*
The King pardoned the knight who had committed a crime.
OTHER VERBS YOU MIGHT USE ARE    **to excuse    to forgive    to let off    to reprieve    to set free    to spare**

## park *noun*
DIFFERENT KINDS OF PARK ARE    **gardens    recreation ground    safari park    wildlife park**

## part *noun*
1  I don't want it all, only a part of it.
OTHER WORDS YOU MIGHT USE ARE    **bit    fraction    piece    portion    section**
2  They sell food in a different part of the shop.
ANOTHER WORD IS **department**
3  Granny lives in a nice part of the country.
OTHER WORDS ARE    **area    district    region**
4  Which part did you have in the nativity play?
OTHER WORDS ARE    **character    role**

## particular *adjective*
1  Jo has her own particular way of writing.
OTHER WORDS YOU MIGHT USE ARE    **individual    personal**
2  Do you want a particular record, or will any music do?
ANOTHER WORD IS **special**
3  The dog is particular about what he eats.
OTHER WORDS ARE    **choosy    fussy**

## partner *noun*
1  You can take a partner with you when you go to the party.
OTHER WORDS YOU MIGHT USE ARE    **companion    friend**
2  The burglar had a partner.
ANOTHER WORD IS **accomplice**

## party *noun*
DIFFERENT KINDS OF PARTY ARE
**ball    barbecue    birthday party    dance    disco    picnic    social    wedding**

## pass *verb*

1 We waited for the cars to pass before we crossed the road.
OTHER VERBS YOU MIGHT USE ARE    **to go by    to move along**
2 Jo's knee hurt when she cut it, but the pain soon passed.
OTHER VERBS ARE    **to disappear    to go away    to vanish**

## passage *noun*

1 We went in through the front door and waited in the passage.
OTHER WORDS ARE    **corridor    hall**
2 They say there's a secret passage under the castle.
OTHER WORDS ARE    **tunnel    way**
3 I read my favourite passage from the book.
OTHER WORDS YOU MIGHT USE ARE    **extract    piece    quotation**

---

## path *noun*

We walked along the path.
DIFFERENT KINDS OF PATH ARE

**bridleway    cart track    footpath    pavement
towpath    track    trail**

---

## patient *adjective*

Although we had to wait a long time, everyone was very patient.
ANOTHER WORD IS **calm**
The opposite is **impatient**

## pattern *noun*

1 I like the patterns on the wallpaper.
OTHER WORDS YOU MIGHT USE ARE    **decoration    design    shape**
2 Is there a pattern I can copy?
OTHER WORDS ARE    **guide    model**

## pause *noun*

There was a pause before the main film.
OTHER WORDS YOU MIGHT USE ARE    **break    delay    gap    intermission
interruption    interval**

## pause *verb*

We paused to have a drink.
OTHER VERBS ARE    **to rest    to stop    to wait**

**pay** *noun*
>OTHER WORDS YOU MIGHT USE ARE
>**earnings    income    payment**
>
>If you are paid by the week, your pay is **wages**.
>If you get a regular amount each year, your pay is a **salary**.
>The pay for doing one job is a **fee**.

**pay** *verb*
1  Sam paid £10 for his bike.
>OTHER VERBS YOU MIGHT USE ARE    **to give    to hand over    to spend**
2  When can you pay back the money you owe me?
>OTHER VERBS ARE    **to refund    to repay**

**peace** *noun*
1  After the war ended there was peace between the two countries.
>ANOTHER WORD YOU MIGHT USE IS **agreement**
The opposite is **war**
2  We sat by the lake and enjoyed the peace of the evening.
>OTHER WORDS ARE    **calmness    quiet    stillness**
Opposites are **excitement, noise**

**peaceful** *adjective*
It seemed peaceful when the baby went to sleep.
>OTHER WORDS YOU MIGHT USE ARE    **calm    quiet    restful**
The opposite is **noisy**

**pebble** *noun*
>ANOTHER WORD IS **stone**
A lot of pebbles are called **gravel**
Pebbles on a beach are called **shingle**

**peculiar** *adjective*
This drink has a peculiar taste.
>OTHER WORDS YOU MIGHT USE ARE    **funny    odd    queer    special
strange    unusual**

**peel** *noun*
the peel of an orange.
>OTHER WORDS YOU MIGHT USE ARE    **rind    skin**

**pen** *noun*
DIFFERENT KINDS OF PEN ARE
ballpoint    Biro    felt tip    fountain pen    quill pen

## penalty *noun*
For other words, see **punishment**

## people *noun*
For other words, see **person**

## perfect *adjective*
1  It's a perfect day for a picnic.
OTHER WORDS YOU MIGHT USE ARE    **excellent    ideal**
2  Jo's new coat was a perfect fit.
ANOTHER WORD IS **exact**

## perform *verb*
Everyone in the class performed in the concert.
OTHER VERBS YOU MIGHT USE ARE    **to appear    to take part**
DIFFERENT WAYS TO PERFORM ARE    **to act    to dance
to play an instrument    to sing**
For other words, see **entertainment**

## perfume *noun*
Mum used some nice perfume when she went to the party.
ANOTHER WORD IS **scent**
For other words, see **smell**

## period *noun*
For other words, see **time**

## perish *verb*
1  Many birds perish in cold weather.
ANOTHER VERB IS **to die**
2  These pears will perish if you don't use them quickly.
OTHER VERBS YOU MIGHT USE ARE    **to decay    to go bad    to rot**

## permission *noun*
We had the teacher's permission to go home.
OTHER WORDS YOU MIGHT USE ARE    **approval    consent**

**permit** *noun*
You need a permit to go fishing.
OTHER WORDS YOU MIGHT USE ARE    licence    pass    ticket

**permit** *verb*
They don't permit smoking on the bus.
OTHER VERBS YOU MIGHT USE ARE    **to agree to**    **to allow**    **to approve of**

**persist** *verb*
If the pain persists you must go to the doctor.
OTHER VERBS YOU MIGHT USE ARE    **to carry on**    **to continue**

**person** *noun*, see opposite page

**personal** *adjective*
1 Jo keeps her personal belongings in a drawer in her bedroom.
ANOTHER WORD IS **private**
2 Don't make personal remarks.
OTHER WORDS ARE    **cheeky**    **impertinent**

**persuade** *verb*
We tried to persuade the cat to come down from the tree.
OTHER VERBS YOU MIGHT USE ARE    **to coax**    **to tempt**    **to urge**

**pester** *verb*
Don't pester me when I'm busy!
OTHER VERBS YOU MIGHT USE ARE    **to annoy**    **to bother**    **to nag**
**to torment**    **to trouble**    **to worry**

---

**pet** *noun*
ANIMALS OFTEN KEPT AS PETS ARE
**budgerigar    canary    cat    dog    ferret    gerbil
goldfish    guinea pig    hamster    mouse    parrot
pigeon    rabbit    rat    tortoise**

---

**phone** *verb*
I phoned Granny to ask how she was.
OTHER VERBS YOU MIGHT USE ARE    **to call**    **to ring**    **to telephone**

# person *noun*

OTHER WORDS YOU MIGHT USE ARE

**character    human being    individual    mortal**

a fully grown person

**adult    grown-up**

a young person

**baby    boy    child    girl    infant    toddler**

a person who is not a child but is not yet grown up

**adolescent    juvenile    teenager**

a woman who is married

**wife**

an unmarried woman

**spinster**

a woman whose husband has died

**widow**

the man who plays a woman in a pantomime

**dame**

a polite word for a woman

**lady**

a female child

**girl**

Female members of a family

**aunt    daughter    grandmother    mother    niece
stepdaughter    stepmother**

a man who is married

**husband**

a man who is not married

**bachelor**

a man whose wife has died

**widower**

a polite word for a man

**gentleman**

informal words for a man

**bloke    chap    fellow**

a young man

**youth**

a male child

**boy** or **lad**

Male members of a family

**father    grandfather    nephew    son    stepfather
stepson    uncle**

---

## photo, photograph *nouns*

DIFFERENT KINDS OF PHOTOGRAPH ARE

enlargement    negative    print    slide or **transparency**
snapshot

For other words, see **camera**

---

## pick *verb*

1  You can pick any flavour of ice cream.
   OTHER VERBS YOU MIGHT USE ARE    **to choose    to decide on    to select**
2  We picked Sam to be captain.
   OTHER VERBS YOU MIGHT USE ARE    **to elect    to vote for**
3  I picked a lot of blackberries.
   OTHER VERBS ARE    **to collect    to gather    to harvest**

---

## picture *noun*

DIFFERENT KINDS OF PICTURE ARE

**cartoon    collage    drawing    mosaic    mural
painting    photograph    print    sketch
slide** or **transparency**

A picture of countryside is a **landscape**
A picture of a person is a **portrait**
A picture in a book is an **illustration**

---

## piece *noun*

1  Sam had a big piece of cake.
   OTHER WORDS YOU MIGHT USE ARE    **chunk    helping    hunk    lump
   portion    share    slab    slice**
2  Mum told Jo to pick up every single piece of the broken cup.
   OTHER WORDS ARE    **bit    chip    fragment**
3  I need a piece of cloth to clean my bike.
   OTHER WORDS YOU MIGHT USE ARE    **rag    scrap**

## pierce *verb*

The needle pierced my skin.
   OTHER VERBS YOU MIGHT USE ARE    **to go through    to penetrate
   to prick    to puncture**

**pig** *noun*
A male pig is a **hog**.
A female pig is a **sow**.
A baby pig is a **piglet**.

## **pile** *noun*
Who dumped that pile of rubbish in the yard?
OTHER WORDS YOU MIGHT USE ARE    **heap    mound    stack**

## **pillar** *noun*
The roof was held up on pillars.
OTHER WORDS YOU MIGHT USE ARE    **column    post    support**

## **pipe** *noun*
a pipe to carry water.
OTHER WORDS YOU MIGHT USE ARE    **hose    tube**

## **pit** *noun*
A pit where miners dig for coal is a **mine** or **coal mine**.
For other words, see **hole**

## **pity** *noun*
The soldiers showed no pity for their enemies.
OTHER WORDS YOU MIGHT USE ARE    **kindness    mercy    sympathy**

## **place** *noun*
1 The map showed the place where the treasure was hidden.
OTHER WORDS YOU MIGHT USE ARE    **location    point    position    site
situation    spot**
2 This is a nice place to live.
OTHER WORDS ARE    **area    district    neighbourhood    region**
3 Save me a place next to you.
OTHER WORDS ARE    **chair    seat**

## **place** *verb*
1 Place your rubbish in the bin.
OTHER VERBS YOU MIGHT USE ARE    **to deposit    to leave    to put**
2 Place your work on the table.
OTHER VERBS ARE    **to arrange    to lay    to set out**
3 He placed the ladder against the wall.
OTHER VERBS ARE    **to lean    to rest    to stand**

## plain *adjective*

1  She was wearing a plain dress.
OTHER WORDS YOU MIGHT USE ARE  **ordinary**  **simple**
The opposite is **decorated**
2  She gave a plain signal.
OTHER WORDS ARE  **clear**  **definite**
The opposite is **confusing**

## plan *noun*

1  Sam has a plan for making a den in the garden.
OTHER WORDS YOU MIGHT USE ARE  **idea**  **project**  **scheme**
2  We drew a plan of the town to show where we all live.
OTHER WORDS ARE  **diagram**  **map**

## plan *verb*

1  We plan to go to the fair on Saturday.
OTHER VERBS YOU MIGHT USE ARE  **to aim**  **to intend**
2  It took weeks to plan our trip.
OTHER VERBS ARE  **to arrange**  **to organize**  **to prepare for**

## plane *noun*

For other words, see **aircraft**

## planet *noun*

THE PLANETS IN THE SOLAR SYSTEM ARE
**Earth**  **Jupiter**  **Mars**  **Mercury**  **Neptune**
**Pluto**  **Saturn**  **Uranus**  **Venus**

## plant *noun*

DIFFERENT KINDS OF PLANT ARE
**bulb**  **cactus**  **climbing plant**  **fern**  **flower**
**fungus**  **grass**  **moss**  **shrub**  **tree**  **water plant**
**weed**

PLANTS YOU CAN EAT ARE
**cereals**  **herbs**  **vegetables**
You can eat some kinds of **fungus**.

For other words, see **flower, tree, vegetable**

## play *verb*

1  I play with my friends at the weekend.
   OTHER VERBS YOU MIGHT USE ARE     **to amuse yourself     to have fun**
2  Jo played a tune on the piano.
   ANOTHER VERB IS **to perform**

## playful *adjective*

a playful puppy.
   OTHER WORDS YOU MIGHT USE ARE     **frisky     lively**

---

## pleasant *adjective*

THIS WORD HAS MANY USES. HERE ARE SOME OF THE WAYS YOU CAN USE IT, AND SOME OTHER WORDS YOU COULD CHOOSE

1  a pleasant day out.
   **enjoyable     nice     pleasing**
2  a pleasant person.
   **friendly     kind     likeable**
3  pleasant weather.
   **fine     mild     warm**
4  pleasant countryside.
   **attractive     peaceful     pretty**

The opposite is **unpleasant**

---

## pleased *adjective*

Was Mum pleased when you gave her the present?
   OTHER WORDS YOU MIGHT USE ARE     **contented     delighted     grateful
   satisfied     thankful**
For other words, see **happy**
The opposite is **angry**

## pleasure *noun*

Jo's dog whines with pleasure when you tickle his neck.
   OTHER WORDS YOU MIGHT USE ARE     **contentment     delight     enjoyment
   happiness     satisfaction**

## plot *verb*

The robbers plotted to steal some jewels.
   OTHER VERBS YOU MIGHT USE ARE     **to conspire     to plan     to scheme**

## plunge *verb*
She plunged into the water.
OTHER VERBS YOU MIGHT USE ARE     **to dive     to drop     to jump     to leap**

## poem *noun*
OTHER WORDS YOU MIGHT USE ARE     **poetry     rhyme     verse**

## point *noun*
1 Don't hurt yourself on the sharp point.
OTHER WORDS YOU MIGHT USE ARE     **spike     tip**
2 We marked the exact point on the map.
OTHER WORDS ARE     **location     place     position     spot**

## point *verb*
1 The signpost points the way you have to go.
OTHER VERBS YOU MIGHT USE ARE     **to indicate     to show**
2 Don't point that arrow at me!
OTHER VERBS ARE     **to aim     to direct**

## pointed *adjective*
a pointed stick.
ANOTHER WORD IS **sharp**
The opposite is **blunt**

## poisonous *adjective*
Some toadstools are poisonous.
OTHER WORDS YOU MIGHT USE ARE     **deadly     harmful**

## poke *verb*
He poked me in the back with a stick.
OTHER VERBS YOU MIGHT USE ARE     **to dig     to jab     to prod**

## pole *noun*
We pinned our flag to a pole.
OTHER WORDS YOU MIGHT USE ARE     **post     rod     stick**

## police *noun*
DIFFERENT NAMES FOR PEOPLE WHO WORK IN THE POLICE ARE
**constable     detective     inspector     officer
policeman     policewoman     sergeant**

## polish *verb*
Jo helped to polish the car.
ANOTHER VERB IS **to shine**
For ways to clean things, see **clean**

## polite *adjective*
a polite boy.
OTHER WORDS YOU MIGHT USE ARE    **considerate    respectful
well-mannered**
The opposite is **rude**

---

## pool *noun*
A large pool is a **pond** or **lake**.
A small pool is a **puddle**.
A pool made to swim in is a **swimming pool**.

---

## poor *adjective*
1  The poor family didn't have enough to eat.
OTHER WORDS YOU MIGHT USE ARE    **hard up    needy    penniless
poverty-stricken**
The opposite is **rich**
2  Our teacher was angry because we had done poor work.
For other words, see **bad**

## poorly *adjective*
Jo stayed at home because she was poorly.
OTHER WORDS YOU MIGHT USE ARE    **ill    sick    unwell**
The opposite is **healthy**

## popular *adjective*
We sang some popular carols at our concert.
OTHER WORDS YOU MIGHT USE ARE    **famous    favourite    well-known**

## port *noun*
The ship entered port.
For other words, see **harbour**

## portion *noun*
Can I have another portion of pie?
OTHER WORDS YOU MIGHT USE ARE    **helping    piece    share    slice**

## positive *adjective*
Are you positive you saw a ghost?
> OTHER WORDS YOU MIGHT USE ARE  **certain  convinced  definite  sure**

## possess *verb*
Sam only possesses one pair of jeans.
> OTHER VERBS YOU MIGHT USE ARE  **to have  to own**

## possessions *noun*
Jo keeps her personal possessions in her bedroom.
> OTHER WORDS YOU MIGHT USE ARE  **belongings  property**

## possible *adjective*
The opposite is **impossible**

## post *noun*
1 Dad put up some posts to support the fence.
> OTHER WORDS YOU MIGHT USE ARE  **column  pillar  pole  prop  support**
2 The postman brought the post.
> ANOTHER WORD IS **mail**
> THINGS YOU GET IN THE MAIL ARE  **letter  packet  parcel  postcard**

## poster *noun*
We put up a poster to tell people about our concert.
> OTHER WORDS YOU MIGHT USE ARE  **advertisement  notice  placard  sign**

## postpone *verb*
They postponed sports day because it was raining.
> A PHRASE IS **to put off**

## pottery *noun*
> OTHER WORDS YOU MIGHT USE ARE  **crockery  earthenware**
For other words, see **china**

## poultry *noun*
> DIFFERENT KINDS OF POULTRY ARE
> **chicken  cockerel  duck  goose  hen  rooster  turkey**

## **pour** *verb*
1 Water poured through the hole.
    OTHER VERBS YOU MIGHT USE ARE    **to flow**    **to gush**    **to run**    **to stream**
2 I poured the cold tea into the sink.
    OTHER VERBS ARE    **to empty**    **to tip**

## **power** *noun*
1 The police have the power to arrest criminals.
    OTHER WORDS YOU MIGHT USE ARE    **ability**    **authority**    **right**
2 Those big waves have the power to knock you over.
    OTHER WORDS ARE    **energy**    **force**    **might**    **strength**

## **powerful** *adjective*
a powerful giant.
    OTHER WORDS YOU MIGHT USE ARE    **mighty**    **strong**
The opposite is **weak**

## **practical** *adjective*
a practical tool.
    OTHER WORDS YOU MIGHT USE ARE    **efficient**    **handy**    **useful**
The opposite is **useless**

## **practically** *adverb*
I've practically finished.
    OTHER WORDS YOU MIGHT USE ARE    **almost**    **nearly**

---

### **practise** *verb*
If you practise for a concert, you **rehearse**.
If you practise at a sport, you **train** for it.
If you practise for a test, you **revise**.

---

## **praise** *verb*
Our teacher praised us for working hard today.
    OTHER VERBS YOU MIGHT USE ARE    **to compliment**    **to congratulate**
The opposite is **scold**

## **precious** *adjective*
precious jewels.
    OTHER WORDS YOU MIGHT USE ARE    **costly**    **dear**    **expensive**    **priceless**
    **valuable**
The opposite is **worthless**

## precise *adjective*
What is the precise time?
> OTHER WORDS YOU MIGHT USE ARE  **accurate**  **correct**  **exact**  **right**

## prepare *verb*
Jo asked Sam to help her prepare for her party.
> OTHER VERBS YOU MIGHT USE ARE  **to get ready**  **to make arrangements**  **to organize**  **to plan**

## present *noun*
Jo got a present from Grandad.
> ANOTHER WORD IS **gift**

## present *verb*
1 The head presented the prizes on sports day.
> OTHER VERBS YOU MIGHT USE ARE  **to award**  **to give**  **to hand over**
2 Sam presented the songs to the audience.
> ANOTHER VERB IS **to introduce**
3 We presented a nativity play at Christmas.
> OTHER VERBS ARE  **to act**  **to perform**  **to put on**

## preserve *verb*
1 You can preserve food in a freezer.
> OTHER VERBS YOU MIGHT USE ARE  **to keep**  **to save**
2 The museum put the old book in a glass case to preserve it.
> OTHER VERBS ARE  **to look after**  **to protect**

## press *verb*
1 Press the bell.
> ANOTHER VERB IS **to push**
2 Sam pressed his best trousers.
> OTHER VERBS YOU MIGHT USE ARE  **to flatten**  **to iron**  **to smooth**

## pretend *verb*
There are different ways of pretending.
You can **act** or **play** a part in a play.
You can **disguise** yourself as someone else.
You can **imitate** or **impersonate** someone.
You can **deceive** or **trick** someone.

## pretty *adjective*
a pretty dress.
> OTHER WORDS YOU MIGHT USE ARE    **attractive    beautiful    lovely**

The opposite is **ugly**

## prevent *verb*
The snow prevented us from going to Granny's.
> OTHER VERBS YOU MIGHT USE ARE    **to hinder    to stop**

## previously *adverb*
> OTHER WORDS YOU MIGHT USE ARE    **before    earlier**

## price *noun*
Before you buy anything, ask what the price is.
> OTHER WORDS YOU MIGHT USE ARE    **charge    cost    fee    payment**

The price you pay to ride in a bus or train is the **fare**.

## prick *verb*
The doctor pricked my thumb with a needle.
> OTHER VERBS YOU MIGHT USE ARE    **to pierce    to puncture**

## principal *adjective*
This map only shows the principal towns.
> OTHER WORDS YOU MIGHT USE ARE    **chief    important    main**

## principles *noun*
Sam taught Jo the principles of chess.
> OTHER WORDS YOU MIGHT USE ARE    **laws    rules    theory**

---

### prison *noun*
> ANOTHER WORD IS **gaol** or **jail**

A small room where someone can be locked up is a **cell**.
A prison in a castle is a **dungeon**.

### prisoner *noun*
> ANOTHER WORD IS **captive**

A person you keep prisoner until you get what you want is a **hostage**.

## private *adjective*

1  Jo keeps her private things in a drawer in her bedroom.
OTHER WORDS YOU MIGHT USE ARE  **personal  secret**
2  We found a private spot for a picnic.
OTHER WORDS ARE  **hidden  quiet  secluded**
The opposite is **public**

## problem *noun*

1  If you have a problem, tell the teacher.
OTHER WORDS YOU MIGHT USE ARE  **difficulty  worry**
2  The detective had a hard problem to solve.
OTHER WORDS ARE  **mystery  puzzle  question  riddle**

## procession *noun*

There was a big procession through the middle of town.
OTHER WORDS YOU MIGHT USE ARE  **march  parade**

## prod *verb*

Someone prodded me in the back.
OTHER VERBS YOU MIGHT USE ARE  **to dig  to jab  to poke  to push**

## produce *verb*

1  The factory down the road produces television sets.
OTHER VERBS YOU MIGHT USE ARE  **to make  to manufacture**
2  Grandad's garden produces lots of vegetables.
OTHER VERBS ARE  **to grow  to yield**
3  We produce a magazine every term.
OTHER VERBS ARE  **to issue  to publish**
4  The cat produced four kittens.
OTHER VERBS ARE  **to bear  to give birth to**
5  The conjuror produced a rabbit from a hat.
OTHER VERBS YOU MIGHT USE ARE  **to bring out  to present**

## progress *noun*

to make progress
OTHER WORDS YOU MIGHT USE ARE  **advance  move forward  proceed**

## prohibited *adjective*

Smoking is prohibited on the bus.
OTHER WORDS YOU MIGHT USE ARE  **banned  forbidden  illegal**
The opposite is **allowed**

## promise *verb*
You promised to come to my party.
> OTHER VERBS YOU MIGHT USE ARE     **to agree     to give your word to guarantee     to swear     to vow**

## promptly *adverb*
1 Mum replied promptly to Granny's letter.
> OTHER WORDS YOU MIGHT USE ARE     **immediately     quickly**
2 The train arrived promptly.
> OTHER WORDS ARE     **on time     punctually**

## prop *verb*
Jo propped her bike against the wall.
> OTHER VERBS YOU MIGHT USE ARE     **to lean     to rest     to stand to support**

## proper *adjective*
1 Put the library books back in their proper places.
> OTHER WORDS YOU MIGHT USE ARE     **appropriate     correct     right suitable     usual**
The opposite is **wrong**
2 I think it would be proper for you to apologise.
> OTHER WORDS ARE     **decent     polite     respectable**
The opposite is **rude**

## protect *verb*
1 The mother bird tried to protect her babies.
> OTHER VERBS YOU MIGHT USE ARE     **to defend     to guard     to keep safe to look after**
2 The hedge protected us from the wind.
> OTHER VERBS ARE     **to screen     to shield**

## protest *verb*
We protested when they put up the bus fares.
> OTHER VERBS YOU MIGHT USE ARE     **to complain     to object**

## proud *adjective*
1 He was too proud to admit that he was wrong.
> OTHER WORDS YOU MIGHT USE ARE     **boastful**     (*informal*) **cocky conceited**     (*informal*) **stuck up     vain**
The opposite is **modest**
2 Mum was proud when Jo won a prize.
> OTHER WORDS ARE     **happy     pleased**

## prove *verb*
They proved that he was guilty.
<small>OTHER VERBS YOU MIGHT USE ARE</small>   **to demonstrate     to show**

## provide *verb*
Our teacher provided the paper for us to draw on.
<small>OTHER VERBS YOU MIGHT USE ARE</small>   **to give     to supply**

## provoke *verb*
If you provoke the dog, he may bite you.
<small>OTHER VERBS YOU MIGHT USE ARE</small>   **to anger     to annoy     to tease
to torment     to upset     to worry**

## pry *verb*
Don't pry in my affairs!
<small>OTHER WORDS YOU MIGHT USE ARE</small>   **to interfere**
(*informal*) **to poke your nose into**

## publish *verb*
We publish a magazine every term.
<small>OTHER VERBS YOU MIGHT USE ARE</small>   **to bring out     to issue     to produce**

## pudding *noun*
Sam ate so much first course that he didn't have room for pudding.
<small>OTHER WORDS YOU MIGHT USE ARE</small>   (*informal*) **afters     dessert     sweet**

## pull *verb*
1   We pulled the heavy box across the floor.
<small>OTHER VERBS YOU MIGHT USE ARE</small>   **to drag     to haul     to tug**
2   The car was pulling a caravan.
<small>ANOTHER VERB IS</small> **to tow**
3   The horse was pulling a cart.
<small>ANOTHER VERB IS</small> **to draw**

## punch *verb*
For other ways to hit, see **hit**

## punctual *adjective*
The train was punctual.
<small>OTHER WORDS YOU MIGHT USE ARE</small>   **on time     prompt**
The opposite is **late**

## punctuation *noun*

DIFFERENT PUNCTUATION MARKS ARE

| | |
|---|---|
| apostrophe | ' |
| brackets | ( ) |
| colon | : |
| comma | , |
| dash | – |
| exclamation mark | ! |
| full stop | . |
| hyphen | - |
| question mark | ? |
| semi-colon | ; |
| speech marks | "    " |

## punishment *noun*

DIFFERENT KINDS OF PUNISHMENT ARE

a beating    detention    execution    a fine
gaol (or jail) or prison    an imposition    a penalty

## pupil *noun*

OTHER WORDS YOU MIGHT USE ARE    schoolboy    schoolgirl    student

## pure *adjective*

pure water.

OTHER WORDS YOU MIGHT USE ARE    clean    clear    natural

The opposite is **dirty**

## purpose *noun*

He must have a particular purpose to go out in that storm.

OTHER WORDS YOU MIGHT USE ARE    aim    intention    object    plan
reason

**purse** *noun*
Jo put her money in a **purse**.
OTHER THINGS YOU KEEP MONEY IN ARE
**handbag** **money box** **piggy bank** **pocket** **wallet**

**pursue** *verb*
The police pursued the robbers across the town.
OTHER VERBS YOU MIGHT USE ARE **to chase** **to follow** **to hunt**

**push** *verb*
1 The door will open if you push harder.
OTHER VERBS YOU MIGHT USE ARE **to press** **to shove**
2 I pushed my clothes into a drawer.
OTHER VERBS ARE **to crush** **to force** **to squeeze**

**put** *verb*
1 Put your dirty cups in the sink.
OTHER VERBS YOU MIGHT USE ARE **to deposit** **to leave** **to pile**
**to place** **to stack**
2 We put our pictures where everyone could see them.
OTHER VERBS ARE **to arrange** **to lay** **to position** **to set out**
**to put something off**
ANOTHER VERB IS **to postpone**
**to put up with something**
ANOTHER VERB IS **to endure**

**puzzle** *noun*
Can you solve this puzzle?
OTHER WORDS YOU MIGHT USE ARE **mystery** **problem** **question**
**riddle**

**puzzle** *verb*
The riddle puzzled me.
OTHER VERBS YOU MIGHT USE ARE **to bewilder** **to confuse** **to mystify**
**to perplex**

# Qq

**quaint** *adjective*
a quaint thatched cottage.
OTHER WORDS YOU MIGHT USE ARE       **old-fashioned    picturesque**

**quake** *verb*
Jack quaked with fear when he saw the giant.
OTHER VERBS YOU MIGHT USE ARE       **to quiver    to shake    to shudder
to tremble**

**quality** *noun*
Our butcher only sells meat of the best quality.
OTHER WORDS YOU MIGHT USE ARE       **class    grade    standard
value**

**quantity** *noun*
In hot weather the shop sells a large quantity of ice cream.
OTHER WORDS YOU MIGHT USE ARE       **amount    volume**

**quarrel** *verb*
Jo and Sam sometimes quarrel, but they soon make it up.
OTHER VERBS YOU MIGHT USE ARE       **to argue    to disagree    to fall out
to fight    to squabble**

**queer** *adjective*
1  queer shapes. a queer smell.
OTHER WORDS YOU MIGHT USE ARE       (*informal*) **funny    odd    peculiar
strange    unusual**
2  I feel rather queer.
For other words, see **ill**

**queue** *noun*
A queue of cars waited at the level-crossing.
OTHER WORDS YOU MIGHT USE ARE       **line    row**

## quick *adjective*

1 a quick journey.
   OTHER WORDS YOU MIGHT USE ARE   **fast   rapid   speedy   swift**
2 quick dance.
   ANOTHER WORD IS **lively**
3 a quick reply.
   OTHER WORDS ARE   **instant   prompt**
The opposite is **slow**
4 The bus came to a quick halt.
   OTHER WORDS ARE   **hasty   sudden**

## quiet *adjective*

1 Our teacher told us to be quiet.
   ANOTHER WORD IS **silent**
2 I listened to some quiet music.
   OTHER WORDS ARE   **low   soft**
The opposite is **noisy**

## quite *adverb*

1 I'm not quite sure.
   OTHER WORDS YOU MIGHT USE ARE   **absolutely   completely   entirely   totally**
2 I'm quite cold.
   OTHER WORDS ARE   **fairly   moderately   (*informal*) pretty   rather**

## quiver *verb*

For other verbs, see **quake**

# Rr

## radio *noun*

An old-fashioned word is **wireless**.
SOME PROGRAMMES YOU HEAR ON THE RADIO ARE
   **chat shows   interviews   music   news
   phone-in programmes   plays   sport   stories   talks
   weather forecasts**

## rail *noun*
There was a rail to stop people falling into the water.
OTHER WORDS YOU MIGHT USE ARE     **bar     railing**

## railway *noun*, see next page

---

## rain *noun*
Very heavy rain is a **downpour**.
A short period of rain is a **shower**.
Rain coming down in very small drops is **drizzle**.
For other words, see **weather**

---

## raise *verb*
1  A crane raised the car out of the ditch.
OTHER VERBS YOU MIGHT USE ARE     **to hoist     to lift     to pick up**
2  We raised money for charity.
OTHER VERBS ARE     **to collect     to get     to make**

## rapid *adjective*
OTHER WORDS YOU MIGHT USE ARE     **fast     quick     speedy     swift**
The opposite is **slow**

## rare *adjective*
Pandas are rare animals.
OTHER WORDS YOU MIGHT USE ARE     **scarce     uncommon**
The opposite is **common**

## rather *adverb*
I was rather ill yesterday.
OTHER WORDS YOU MIGHT USE ARE     **fairly     moderately**
(*informal*) **pretty     quite**

## ration *noun*
You can't have any more because you've had your ration.
OTHER WORDS YOU MIGHT USE ARE     **portion     share**

## ravenous *adjective*
We were so ravenous that we ate everything!
OTHER WORDS YOU MIGHT USE ARE     **famished     hungry     starving**

## railway *noun*

KINDS OF RAILWAY ARE

**branch line    main line    metro    mountain railway narrow gauge railway    tramline    underground**

KINDS OF TRAIN ARE

**diesel    electric train    express freight train** or **goods train    steam train    tram**

PARTS OF A TRAIN ARE

**buffet car    carriage    coach    locomotive sleeping car    steam engine    wagon**

PARTS OF A RAILWAY LINE MIGHT BE

**electric rail    overhead wires    points    sleepers    rails**

ALONG THE RAILWAY YOU MIGHT SEE

**cutting    embankment    junction    level crossing sidings    signals    signal box    station    tunnel**

THINGS YOU SEE AT A STATION ARE

**booking office** or **ticket office    buffet    platform timetable    waiting room**

PEOPLE WHO WORK ON THE RAILWAY ARE

**booking clerk    conductor    driver    guard    porter signalman    ticket collector**

## ray *noun*

A ray of light shone through the crack in the door.

OTHER WORDS YOU MIGHT USE ARE    **beam    shaft**

## reach *verb*

1 I will hold you if you reach out your hand.

ANOTHER VERB IS **to stretch**

2 We can have something to eat when we reach home.

OTHER VERBS YOU MIGHT USE ARE    **to arrive at    to get to**

## ready *adjective*

1 Are you ready to go?

OTHER WORDS YOU MIGHT USE ARE    **prepared    willing**

2 Have you got your money ready?

OTHER WORDS ARE    **available    handy**

# real *adjective*

1  Are those real diamonds?
   ANOTHER WORD IS **genuine**
The opposite is **artificial**
2  You can trust Sam: he's a real friend.
   ANOTHER WORD IS **true**
The opposite is **false**

# realistic *adjective*

The acting was very realistic.
   OTHER WORDS YOU MIGHT USE ARE   **lifelike    natural**

# realize *verb*

I suddenly realized that everyone was waiting for me.
   OTHER VERBS YOU MIGHT USE ARE   **to know    to see    to sense    to understand**

# rear *noun*

He crashed into the rear of a bus.
   OTHER WORDS YOU MIGHT USE ARE   **back    end**
The opposite is **front**

# rear *verb*

Our cat reared four kittens.
   OTHER VERBS YOU MIGHT USE ARE   **to bring up    to care for    to look after**

# reason *noun*

Was there any reason for Sam's funny behaviour?
   OTHER WORDS YOU MIGHT USE ARE   **cause    excuse    explanation**
The reason why someone commits a crime is the **motive**.

# reasonable *adjective*

1  Dad paid a reasonable price for his car.
   OTHER WORDS YOU MIGHT USE ARE   **fair    moderate**
2  You can't have a reasonable argument with a tiny baby.
   OTHER WORDS ARE   **intelligent    logical    sensible**

# rebel *verb*

The soldiers rebelled because they were so hungry.
   OTHER VERBS YOU MIGHT USE ARE   **to disobey    to revolt**
If sailors rebel on a ship, the word is **mutiny**.

## receive *verb*

1  I received ten birthday cards.
   ANOTHER VERB IS **to get**
2  He received £2 for doing odd jobs.
   ANOTHER VERB IS **to earn**

## recent *adjective*

Have you got any recent CDs?
   OTHER WORDS YOU MIGHT USE ARE   **new      up-to-date**
The opposite is **old**

## reckless *adjective*

Reckless drivers can kill people.
   OTHER WORDS YOU MIGHT USE ARE   **careless      thoughtless**
The opposite is **careful**

## reckon *verb*

1  Jo reckoned how much the shopping cost.
   OTHER VERBS YOU MIGHT USE ARE   **to add up      to calculate      to count
   to work out**
2  I reckon our side will win.
   OTHER VERBS ARE   **to believe      to feel sure      to think**

## recognize *verb*

Would you recognize that man if you saw him again?
   OTHER VERBS YOU MIGHT USE ARE   **to identify      to know      to remember**

## recommend *verb*

Mum recommends the restaurant down the road.
   OTHER VERBS YOU MIGHT USE ARE   **to approve of      to praise
   to speak well of**

## record *noun*

1  We kept a record of the birds we saw on holiday.
   OTHER WORDS YOU MIGHT USE ARE
   **account      description      diary      log**
2  Dad has lots of old pop records.
   KINDS OF GRAMOPHONE RECORD ARE
   **album      LP      single**
   OTHER KINDS OF RECORD ARE
   **cassette      compact disc** or **CD      tape      video**

## recover *verb*
1 Mum recovered slowly after her operation.
     OTHER VERBS YOU MIGHT USE ARE    **to get better    to heal    to improve**
2 Did you recover your lost watch?
     OTHER VERBS ARE    **to find    to get back    to retrieve    to trace**

## reduce *verb*
She reduced speed when she saw the police-car.
     OTHER VERBS YOU MIGHT USE ARE    **to cut    to decrease    to lessen**

## refer *verb*
1 Did Dad refer to the broken window?
     OTHER VERBS YOU MIGHT USE ARE    **to comment on    to mention**
2 I referred to the dictionary to find the spelling.
     OTHER VERBS ARE    **to consult    to look up    to turn to**

## refresh *verb*
The drink refreshed us.
     OTHER VERBS YOU MIGHT USE ARE    **to cool    to quench the thirst
     to revive**

## refuse *noun*
Put the refuse in the bin.
     OTHER WORDS YOU MIGHT USE ARE    **junk    rubbish    waste**

## refuse *verb*
Why did Jo refuse to go to her friend's party?
     ANOTHER VERB IS **to decline**
The opposite is **agree**

## regard *verb*
We regard Sam as the best swimmer in the school.
     OTHER VERBS YOU MIGHT USE ARE    **to consider    to think of**

## region *noun*
The South Pole is a cold region.
     OTHER WORDS YOU MIGHT USE ARE    **area    district    place    zone**

## regret *verb*
Jo regretted saying nasty things about her friend.
     OTHER VERBS YOU MIGHT USE ARE    **to be sad about    to be sorry for
     to repent**

## regular *adjective*

1 Did the postman come at the regular time today?
OTHER WORDS YOU MIGHT USE ARE **customary** **normal** **usual**
2 The drummer kept a regular rhythm.
OTHER WORDS ARE **even** **steady**

## rehearse *verb*

We rehearsed for the concert all afternoon.
OTHER VERBS YOU MIGHT USE ARE **to practise** **to prepare**

## reject *verb*

Jo rejected the invitation to her friend's party.
OTHER VERBS YOU MIGHT USE ARE **to refuse** **to turn down**
The opposite is **accept**

## rejoice *verb*

The crowd rejoiced when their team won the cup.
OTHER VERBS YOU MIGHT USE ARE **to be happy** **to celebrate**

## relation *noun*

For other words, see **family**

## relax *verb*

I like to relax in a hot bath.
OTHER VERBS YOU MIGHT USE ARE **to rest** **to unwind**

## release *verb*

They released the animals from the cage.
OTHER VERBS YOU MIGHT USE ARE **to free** **to let loose** **to let out**
**to liberate** **to set free**

## reliable *adjective*

You can trust Sam: he's a reliable friend.
OTHER WORDS YOU MIGHT USE ARE **faithful** **loyal** **trustworthy**

## relief *noun*

The pills gave me some relief from my headache.
OTHER WORDS YOU MIGHT USE ARE **comfort** **ease** **help**

## relieved *adjective*

We were relieved to hear that Jo's accident was not serious.
OTHER WORDS YOU MIGHT USE ARE **glad** **happy** **thankful**

## religion *noun*

OTHER WORDS YOU MIGHT USE ARE
**belief    creed    faith**

SOME RELIGIONS ARE
**Buddhism    Christianity    Hinduism    Judaism
Islam    Sikhism**

PEOPLE WHO FOLLOW A RELIGION ARE
**Buddhist    Christian    Hindu    Jewish    Muslim
Sikh**

KINDS OF RELIGIOUS SERVICE ARE
**baptism** or **christening    cremation    funeral
Holy Communion    mass    prayers    wedding
worship**

PARTS OF A MEETING FOR WORSHIP MIGHT BE
**anthem    blessing    collection** or **offering    confession
devotions    hymn    meditation    prayers    psalm
reading from scripture    sermon**

PLACES WHERE PEOPLE WORSHIP ARE
**cathedral    chapel    church    mosque    pagoda
shrine    synagogue    temple**

RELIGIOUS LEADERS AND TEACHERS ARE
**archbishop    ayatollah    bishop    cardinal    chaplain
clergyman    curate    druid    guru    imam    lama
minister    missionary    parson    pope    priest
prophet    rabbi    rector    vicar**

ADJECTIVES YOU MIGHT USE TO DESCRIBE RELIGIOUS THINGS ARE
**blessed    consecrated    divine    holy    sacred**

ADJECTIVES YOU MIGHT USE TO DESCRIBE RELIGIOUS PEOPLE ARE
**devout    pious**

A person who thinks there is no God is an **atheist**.
A person who says you can't know whether there is a God or not
is an **agnostic**.

## reluctant *adjective*
I was reluctant to walk home because it was raining.
OTHER WORDS YOU MIGHT USE ARE    **hesitant    unwilling**
The opposite is **enthusiastic**

## rely *verb*

You can rely on Jo to do her best.
> OTHER VERBS YOU MIGHT USE ARE  (*informal*) **to bank on**  **to count on**  **to depend on**  **to trust**

## remain *verb*

He told me to remain where I was.
> OTHER VERBS YOU MIGHT USE ARE  **to stay**  **to stop**

## remains *noun*

1  We explored the remains of the castle.
> ANOTHER WORD IS **ruins**
2  What shall we do with the remains of this stew?
> OTHER WORDS ARE  (*informal*) **leftovers**  **remainder**  **rest**
3  His remains were buried near the church.
> OTHER WORDS ARE  **body**  **corpse**

## remark *verb*

I remarked that it was a nice day.
> OTHER VERBS YOU MIGHT USE ARE  **to comment**  **to mention**  **to say**

## remarkable *adjective*

Our team had a remarkable victory.
> OTHER WORDS YOU MIGHT USE ARE  **amazing**  **extraordinary**  **special**  **surprising**  **unusual**

## remedy *noun*

Do you know a remedy for a cold?
> OTHER WORDS YOU MIGHT USE ARE  **cure**  **medicine**  **treatment**

## remember *verb*

Do you remember our holiday last year?
> OTHER WORDS YOU MIGHT USE ARE  **to recall**  **to recollect**
The opposite is **forget**

## remind *verb*

Jo reminded Mum to buy some sugar.
> A PHRASE YOU MIGHT USE IS **to jog someone's memory**

## remove *verb*

1  Please remove this rubbish.
> OTHER VERBS YOU MIGHT USE ARE  **to carry away**  **to get rid of**  **to move**  **to shift**  **to take away**

2  The dentist removed a tooth.
OTHER VERBS ARE    **to extract**    **to take out**
3  What removes oil from clothes?
ANOTHER VERB IS **to wash off**

# repair *verb*

OTHER VERBS YOU MIGHT USE ARE    (*informal*) **to fix**    **to mend**
**to put right**
to repair clothes
**to darn**    **to patch**    **to sew up**
to repair something old or broken
**to do up**    **to renovate**    **to restore**

# repeat *verb*

Don't repeat everything I say!
OTHER VERBS YOU MIGHT USE ARE    **to go over**    **to say again**

# reply *verb*

I replied to Granny's letter.
OTHER VERBS YOU MIGHT USE ARE    **to answer**    **to respond to**

# report *verb*

1  We reported that we had finished our work.
OTHER VERBS YOU MIGHT USE ARE    **to announce**    **to declare**    **to state**
2  I reported him to the police.
OTHER VERBS ARE    **to complain about**    **to inform against**
(*informal*) **to tell of**

# reproduce *verb*

1  Sam can reproduce a lot of bird calls.
OTHER VERBS YOU MIGHT USE ARE    **to imitate**    **to mimic**
2  We reproduced our work on the copier in the school office.
OTHER VERBS ARE    **to copy**    **to duplicate**    **to photocopy**
3  Rabbits reproduce very quickly.
OTHER VERBS ARE    **to breed**    **to multiply**

---

# reptile *noun*

DIFFERENT KINDS OF REPTILE ARE
**alligator    crocodile    lizard    snake    tortoise
turtle**

## request *verb*
When the work got too hard, we requested help from our teacher.
OTHER VERBS YOU MIGHT USE ARE   **to appeal for**   **to ask for**   **to beg for**

## require *verb*
We required 3 more runs to win.
OTHER VERBS ARE   **to be short of**   **to need**   **to want**

## rescue *verb*
Robin Hood rescued the prisoners from the Sheriff's castle.
OTHER VERBS YOU MIGHT USE ARE   **to free**   **to liberate**   **to release**   **to save**   **to set free**

## resemble *verb*
Sam resembles his father.
OTHER VERBS YOU MIGHT USE ARE   **to be similar to**   **to look like**

## reserve *noun*
We have two reserves who can play on Saturday if necessary.
OTHER WORDS ARE   **deputy**   **stand-in**   **substitute**

## reserve *verb*
1 Jo reserved some sandwiches for people who came late.
OTHER VERBS YOU MIGHT USE ARE   **to keep**   **to save**
2 We reserved our seats on the train.
ANOTHER WORD IS **to book**

## resign *verb*
The manager resigned because the team was doing so badly.
OTHER VERBS YOU MIGHT USE ARE   **to give up**   **to leave**
   (*informal*) **to quit**

## resist *verb*
He made things worse because he resisted the police.
OTHER VERBS YOU MIGHT USE ARE   **to defy**   **to oppose**   **to stand up to**

## respect *noun*
We should show respect to people who work hard for us.
OTHER WORDS YOU MIGHT USE ARE   **admiration**   **consideration**
The respect you show towards religious things is **reverence**.

## responsible *adjective*

1 Who is responsible for this dog?
   A PHRASE IS **in charge of**
2 Jo was responsible for breaking the window.
   A PHRASE IS **guilty of**
3 We need a responsible person to look after the money.
   OTHER WORDS ARE     **dependable     honest     reliable     trustworthy**

## rest *noun*

1 Let's have a rest for a minute.
   OTHER WORDS YOU MIGHT USE ARE     **break     pause**
2 If you have finished, the dog will eat the rest.
   ANOTHER WORD IS **remainder**

## rest *verb*

1 Half way up the hill we sat down to rest.
   OTHER VERBS YOU MIGHT USE ARE     **to relax**     (*informal*) **to take it easy**
   When you are resting you might     **doze     lie down     sleep**
      (*informal*) **take a nap**
2 Rest the ladder against the wall.
   OTHER VERBS YOU MIGHT USE ARE     **to lean     to prop     to stand
   to support**

## restore *verb*

Uncle David restores old cars.
   OTHER VERBS YOU MIGHT USE ARE     (*informal*) **to do up     to mend
   to renovate     to repair**

## result *noun*

The result of getting up late was that I missed the bus.
   OTHER WORDS YOU MIGHT USE ARE     **consequence     effect**

## retreat *verb*

The soldiers retreated when they knew that they were losing.
   OTHER VERBS YOU MIGHT USE ARE     **to go back     to move back
   to run away**

## return *verb*

1 We returned at tea time.
   OTHER VERBS YOU MIGHT USE ARE     **to come back     to go back**
2 Jo returned the pen I lent her.
   OTHER VERBS ARE     **to give back     to repay**

## reveal *verb*

1 We drew back the curtain and revealed the stage.

OTHER VERBS YOU MIGHT USE ARE   **to disclose**   **to show**

2 Don't ever reveal our secret!

PHRASES ARE   **to let out**   **to make known**

## reverse *verb*

Dad damaged the car when he reversed into a wall.

OTHER VERBS ARE   **to back**   **to go backwards**

## revolt *verb*

The players revolted because they thought the rules were not fair.

OTHER VERBS YOU MIGHT USE ARE   **to disobey**   **to rebel**

When sailors revolt the word is **mutiny**.

## revolting *adjective*

The food was so revolting that nobody would eat it.

OTHER WORDS YOU MIGHT USE ARE   **disgusting**   **foul**   **horrible**   **nasty**   **unattractive**

The opposite is **attractive**

## rhythm *noun*

Sam likes music with a strong rhythm.

OTHER WORDS YOU MIGHT USE ARE   **beat**   **pulse**

## rich *adjective*

Rich people can buy what they want.

OTHER WORDS YOU MIGHT USE ARE   **prosperous**   **wealthy**   **well-off**

The opposite is **poor**

## ride *verb*

For other verbs, see **travel**

## ridiculous *adjective*

We laughed at his ridiculous hat.

OTHER WORDS YOU MIGHT USE ARE   **absurd**   **comic**   **funny**   **silly**   **stupid**

## right *adjective*

1 Most people use their right hand to write with.

The opposite is **left**

2 All Jo's answers were right.

OTHER WORDS YOU MIGHT USE ARE   **accurate**   **correct**

3  Is that the right time?
>    OTHER WORDS ARE    **exact    precise    proper    true**

4  It's right to own up when you've been naughty.
>    OTHER WORDS ARE    **fair    honest    moral**

5  A thesaurus helps you to find the right word.
>    OTHER WORDS ARE    **appropriate    suitable**

The opposite is **wrong**

# ring noun

We all stood in a ring.
>    ANOTHER WORD IS **circle**

---

## ring verb

1  I heard a bell ring.

Loud bells **peal**.

A small bell **tinkles**.

An annoying noisy bell **jangles**.

A clock **chimes**.

2  We ring Granny every Sunday.
>    OTHER WORDS ARE
>    **to call    to phone    to telephone**

---

# riot noun

The police were called to control the riot.
>    OTHER WORDS YOU MIGHT USE ARE    **disorder    disturbance    mutiny    revolt**

# rip verb

Sam ripped his jeans.
>    OTHER VERBS YOU MIGHT USE ARE    **to split    to tear**

# rise verb

1  I watched the balloon rise into the sky.
>    OTHER VERBS YOU MIGHT USE ARE    **to ascend    to climb    to go up    to lift**

The opposite is **fall**

2  Bus fares are going to rise next week.
>    ANOTHER VERB IS **to increase**

3  We all rose when the teacher came into the room.
>    OTHER VERBS ARE    **to get up    to stand**

**risk** *noun*

There's a risk of rain today.

OTHER WORDS YOU MIGHT USE ARE **chance    danger    possibility**

**rival** *noun*

The team we played on Saturday were our old rivals.

OTHER WORDS YOU MIGHT USE ARE **enemy    opponent**

**river** *noun*

For other words, see **water**

---

**road** *noun*

BIG ROADS FOR MOTOR TRAFFIC ARE

**bypass    motorway    ring road**

OTHER WORDS YOU MIGHT USE ARE

a road with houses along it
**street**

a road with trees along it
**avenue**

a narrow road between buildings
**alley**

a road where you can only drive one way
**one-way street**

a road closed at one end
**cul-de-sac**

a road that goes up to a house
**drive**

a narrow road in the country
**lane**

a rough road in the country
**track** or **cart track**

a path for horses
**bridleway**

a path along a canal
**towpath**

**robber** *noun*
> ANOTHER WORD IS **thief**
> DIFFERENT KINDS OF ROBBER ARE
>> **burglar    highwayman    mugger    pick-pocket    shoplifter**
> For other words, see **steal**

**rock** *noun*
> ANOTHER WORD IS **stone**
A big piece of rock is a **boulder**.

**rock** *verb*
1 The boat rocked gently in the breeze.
> OTHER VERBS YOU MIGHT USE ARE    **to sway    to swing**
2 The boat rocked violently in the storm.
> OTHER VERBS ARE    **to roll    to toss**

**rod** *noun*
The climbing frame is made of iron rods.
> OTHER WORDS YOU MIGHT USE ARE    **bar    pole    rail**

**rodent** *noun*
> THESE ANIMALS ARE RODENTS:
>> **gerbil    hamster    mouse    rat    squirrel**

**room** *noun*
For different rooms, see **house**

**rope** *noun*
> OTHER WORDS YOU CAN USE ARE    **cord    line**

**rotten** *adjective*
1 rotten wood.
> OTHER WORDS YOU MIGHT USE ARE    **decayed    decomposed**
2 rotten food.
> OTHER WORDS ARE    **bad    mouldy    smelly**
3 Sam is rotten at tennis!
> OTHER WORDS ARE    **bad    hopeless    incompetent    useless**

## rough *adjective*

1 We jolted along the rough road.

    OTHER WORDS YOU MIGHT USE ARE   **bumpy**   **uneven**

The opposite is **smooth**

2 Sandpaper feels rough.

    OTHER WORDS ARE   **coarse**   **harsh**   **scratchy**

The opposite is **soft**

3 The sea was very rough.

    OTHER WORDS ARE   **stormy**   **wild**

The opposite is **calm**

4 I don't like rough games.

    OTHER WORDS ARE   **bad-tempered**   **boisterous**   **rowdy**   **violent**

The opposite is **gentle**

5 At a rough guess it will cost £100 to mend the car.

    ANOTHER WORD IS **approximate**

The opposite is **exact**

---

## round *adjective*

Most coins are round.

    ANOTHER WORD IS **circular**

A flat round shape is a **disc**.

A solid round shape is a **ball** or **globe** or **sphere**.

---

## route *noun*

Sam knows a quick route into town.

    ANOTHER WORD IS **way**

## row *noun* (rhymes with *cow*)

1 Sam and Jo hardly ever have a row.

    OTHER WORDS YOU MIGHT USE ARE   **disagreement**   **quarrel**   **squabble**

2 What was that row in the night?

    OTHER WORDS ARE   **commotion**   **din**   **noise**   **uproar**

## row *noun* (rhymes with *toe*)

We stood in a straight row.

    OTHER WORDS YOU MIGHT USE ARE   **file**   **line**   **queue**

## rubbish *noun*

Throw away that rubbish.

    OTHER WORDS YOU MIGHT USE ARE   (*informal*) **junk**   **litter**   **refuse**
    **scrap**   **waste**

## rude *adjective*

That rude girl shouted at us.

OTHER WORDS YOU MIGHT USE ARE **bad-mannered cheeky disrespectful impertinent impolite impudent insulting offensive**

The opposite is **polite**

## ruin *verb*

The storm ruined the flowers in the garden.

OTHER VERBS YOU MIGHT USE ARE **to destroy to spoil to wreck**

## rule *noun*

When you play a game, you must obey the rules.

OTHER WORDS YOU MIGHT USE ARE **law regulation**

---

## rule *verb*

In the old days, the king used to rule the country.

OTHER VERBS YOU MIGHT USE ARE

**to control to govern to lead to manage to run**

DIFFERENT WORDS FOR PEOPLE WHO RULE OVER THEIR SUBJECTS MIGHT BE

**dictator emperor empress governor king monarch queen president prince princess rajah sovereign sultan tyrant tzar**

Some countries are ruled by a **government** with a **prime minister**.

---

## rumour *noun*

It's not fair to spread stories that are only rumour.

ANOTHER WORD IS **gossip**

---

## run *verb*

DIFFERENT WAYS TO RUN ARE

**to jog to race to scamper to sprint**

For other words, see **rush**.

DIFFERENT WAYS A HORSE RUNS ARE

**canter gallop trot**

**runny** *adjective*
The jelly hasn't set yet - it's still runny.
OTHER WORDS YOU MIGHT USE ARE **liquid sloppy watery**

**rush** *verb*
Jo was hungry, so she rushed home for something to eat.
OTHER VERBS YOU MIGHT USE ARE **to dash to hurry to speed**
For other verbs, see **run**

# Ss

**sacred** *adjective*
The Bible and the Koran are sacred books.
OTHER WORDS YOU MIGHT USE ARE **holy religious**

**sad** *adjective*
1 a sad look on someone's face.
OTHER WORDS YOU MIGHT USE ARE **depressed disappointed gloomy heart-broken melancholy miserable mournful sorrowful tearful troubled unhappy wretched**
2 sad news.
OTHER WORDS YOU MIGHT USE ARE **depressing disappointing distressing tragic upsetting**
The opposite is **happy**

**safe** *adjective*
1 When we got indoors, we felt safe from the storm.
OTHER WORDS YOU MIGHT USE ARE **protected secure**
2 We were glad to get home safe.
ANOTHER WORD IS **unharmed**
3 Is the dog safe?
OTHER WORDS YOU MIGHT USE ARE **harmless tame**

**sailor** *noun*
ANOTHER WORD IS **seaman**
The sailors who sail a ship are the **crew**.

---

**salad** *noun*

THINGS YOU EAT IN SALAD ARE

beetroot    celery    cress    cucumber    lettuce
mustard and cress    onion    potato    radish
tomato    watercress

---

## sample *noun*
Jo showed Dad samples of her work.
OTHER WORDS YOU MIGHT USE ARE    **example    specimen**

## satisfactory *adjective*
We can go out to play if our work is satisfactory.
OTHER WORDS YOU MIGHT USE ARE    **acceptable    all right    good enough**

## satisfy *verb*
He's always grumpy: nothing satisfies him.
OTHER VERBS YOU MIGHT USE ARE    **to content    to make happy
to please**

## savage *adjective*
a savage attack.
OTHER WORDS YOU MIGHT USE ARE    **bloodthirsty    brutal    cruel
fierce    heartless    ruthless    vicious    violent**
The opposite is **gentle**

## save *verb*
1 Robin Hood saved the prisoners.
OTHER VERBS YOU MIGHT USE ARE    **to free    to liberate    to release
to rescue    to set free**
2 I saved some sweets for later.
OTHER VERBS ARE    **to keep    to preserve    to put aside**

## say *verb*
For other verbs, see **talk**

## saying *noun*
'I don't believe it' is a common saying.
OTHER WORDS YOU MIGHT USE ARE    **expression    phrase    remark**
A saying that is supposed to teach a moral, like 'Many hands make light
work', is a **proverb**.

**scarce** *adjective*
1   Water is scarce in the desert.
   A PHRASE IS **in short supply**
The opposite is **plentiful**
2   Snakes are scarce in England.
   OTHER WORDS ARE   **rare**   **uncommon**
The opposite is **common**

**scarcely** *adverb*
I could scarcely believe my eyes!
   OTHER WORDS YOU MIGHT USE ARE   **barely**   **hardly**   **only**   **just**

**scare** *verb*
The sudden noise scared me.
   OTHER VERBS ARE   **to alarm**   **to frighten**   **to shock**   **to startle**
   **to terrify**   **to upset**

**scatter** *verb*
The baby always scatters her toys round the room.
   OTHER VERBS YOU MIGHT USE ARE   **to spread**   **to throw about**

**scent** *noun*
the scent of roses.
   OTHER WORDS YOU MIGHT USE ARE   **fragrance**   **perfume**   **smell**

---

**school** *noun*
   DIFFERENT KINDS OF SCHOOL ARE
   **boarding school**   **comprehensive school**   **first school**
   **infant school**   **junior school**   **kindergarten**
   **middle school**   **nursery school**   **play group**
   **primary school**   **secondary school**

For other words, see **educate, teach**

---

**science** *noun*
   DIFFERENT KINDS OF SCIENCE ARE
   **astronomy**   **biology**   **botany**   **chemistry**
   **electronics**   **engineering**   **geology**   **physics**
   **psychology**   **technology**   **zoology**

## scold *verb*
Jo scolded the dog for eating her chocolate.
> OTHER VERBS YOU MIGHT USE ARE  **to reprimand**  (*informal*) **to tell off** (*informal*) **to tick off**

## scramble *verb*
I scrambled over the rocks.
> OTHER VERBS YOU MIGHT USE ARE  **to clamber**  **to climb**  **to crawl**

## scrap *noun*
1 We put scraps of food out for the birds.
> OTHER WORDS YOU MIGHT USE ARE  **bit**  **crumb**  **piece**
2 Dad took some scrap to the tip.
> OTHER WORDS YOU MIGHT USE ARE  (*informal*) **junk**  **rubbish**  **waste**

## scrape *verb*
1 I scraped my knee on the stones.
> OTHER VERBS YOU MIGHT USE ARE  **to graze**  **to scratch**
2 Jo scraped the mud off her shoe.
> OTHER VERBS ARE  **to clean**  **to rub**  **to scrub**

## scratch *verb*
Dad scratched the car on the gate.
> OTHER VERBS YOU MIGHT USE ARE  **to damage**  **to graze**  **to scrape**

## scream *verb*
Everyone screamed when the ride went faster and faster.
> OTHER VERBS ARE  **to cry out**  **to howl**  **to screech**  **to shriek** **to squeal**  **to yell**

## sculpture *noun*
> OTHER WORDS ARE  **carvings**  **statues**

## sea *noun*
> ANOTHER WORD IS **ocean**

## seal *verb*
Remember to seal the envelope.
> OTHER VERBS YOU MIGHT USE ARE  **to close**  **to fasten**  **to stick down**

## search *verb*
I was searching for my watch.
> OTHER VERBS YOU MIGHT USE ARE  **to hunt for**  **to look for**

**seaside** *noun*

We had a trip to the seaside.

OTHER WORDS YOU MIGHT USE ARE

**beach    coast**

Another word for beach is **shore**.

THINGS YOU MIGHT SEE AT THE SEASIDE ARE

**breakwater    cliffs    pier    promenade    rocks
rock pools    sand    sand dunes    shingle    waves**

THINGS YOU MIGHT FIND ARE

**pebbles    seaweed    shellfish    shells**

---

**season** *noun*

THE SEASONS OF THE YEAR ARE

**spring    summer    autumn    winter**

---

**seat** *noun*

DIFFERENT THINGS YOU SIT ON ARE

**armchair    bench    chair    deckchair    pew
pouffe    rocking chair    settee    sofa    stool**

The seat a king or queen sits on for official occasions is a **throne**.

---

**secret** *adjective*

1 a secret diary.

OTHER WORDS YOU MIGHT USE ARE    **intimate    personal    private**

2 a secret place.

OTHER WORDS ARE    **concealed    hidden    unknown**

The opposite is **public**

**secure** *adjective*

Make sure the ladder is secure before you climb it.

OTHER WORDS YOU MIGHT USE ARE    **firm    fixed    safe    steady**

The opposite is **loose**

## see *verb*
1  Did you see anyone you know?
> OTHER VERBS YOU MIGHT USE ARE  **to make out**   **to notice**
> **to recognize**   **to spot**

To see someone or something very briefly is to **glimpse** it.
2  We saw a good film.
> OTHER VERBS ARE  **to look at**   **to view**   **to watch**
3  If you see an accident, tell the police.
> ANOTHER VERB IS **to witness**

## seem *verb*
Granny seems better today.
> OTHER VERBS YOU MIGHT USE ARE  **to appear**   **to look**

## seize *verb*
1  I seized the end of the rope.
> OTHER VERBS YOU MIGHT USE ARE  (*informal*) **to grab**   **to hold**
> **to snatch**
2  The police seized the thief.
> OTHER VERBS ARE  **to arrest**   **to capture**   **to catch**

## seldom *adverb*
It seldom snows in May.
> ANOTHER WORD IS **rarely**

The opposite is **often**

## select *verb*
1  You can select some sweets from the tin.
> OTHER VERBS YOU MIGHT USE ARE  **to choose**   **to pick**
2  We selected Jo to be captain.
> OTHER VERBS ARE  **to appoint**   **to decide on**   **to vote for**

## selfish *adjective*
It's selfish to keep the best sweets for yourself.
> OTHER WORDS YOU MIGHT USE ARE  **greedy**   **mean**   **thoughtless**

The opposite is **generous**

## send *verb*
We sent a parcel to Grandad.
> OTHER VERBS YOU MIGHT USE ARE  **to dispatch**   **to post**

## sense *noun*

1  If you've got any sense, you won't go out in the rain.
   OTHER WORDS YOU MIGHT USE ARE
   **intelligence    wisdom**
2  We use our five senses to recognize things.
   OUR FIVE SENSES ARE
   **hearing    sight    smell    taste    touch**

## sensible *adjective*

Sensible people stay in when it rains.
   OTHER WORDS YOU MIGHT USE ARE    **reasonable    thoughtful    wise**
The opposite is **silly**

## sensitive *adjective*

Jo has a sensitive skin.
   OTHER WORDS YOU MIGHT USE ARE    **delicate    soft    tender**

## separate *adjective*

1  They kept the sick children separate from the rest of us.
   OTHER WORDS ARE    **apart    divided    isolated    segregated**
2  The infants are in a separate building from the juniors.
   OTHER WORDS ARE    **detached    different    distinct**

## series *noun*

We had a series of accidents.
   OTHER WORDS ARE    **row    sequence    string    succession**

## serious *adjective*

1  Sam takes a serious interest in his work.
   OTHER WORDS YOU MIGHT USE ARE    **careful    sincere    thoughtful**
2  She had a serious look on her face.
   OTHER WORDS ARE    **grave    sad    solemn**
3  Several people were hurt in the serious accident.
   OTHER WORDS ARE    **awful    bad    dreadful    severe    terrible**

## service *noun*

   KINDS OF RELIGIOUS SERVICE ARE
   **baptism** or **christening    funeral    Holy Communion    mass    prayers    wedding service    worship**
For other words, see **religion**

## set *verb*

1 Has the glue set yet?
   ANOTHER VERB IS **to harden**
2 We set out our work for the parents to see.
   OTHER VERBS YOU MIGHT USE ARE   **to arrange**   **to lay out**   **to put out**
3 We set off at breakfast time.
   OTHER VERBS ARE   **to depart**   **to start**

## settle *verb*

Have you settled on what to do?
   OTHER VERBS YOU MIGHT USE ARE   **to agree**   **to decide**   **to fix**

## severe *adjective*

1 a severe teacher.
   OTHER WORDS YOU MIGHT USE ARE   **stern**   **strict**
2 a severe illness.
   OTHER WORDS ARE   **bad**   **serious**
The opposite is **mild**

## sew *verb*

ANOTHER WORD IS **to stitch**
To sew up a hole is **to darn**.
To sew with loose stitches is **to tack**.

## sewing

OTHER WORDS ARE   **embroidery**   **needlework**

## shabby *adjective*

shabby clothes.
   OTHER WORDS YOU MIGHT USE ARE   **faded**   **old**   **ragged**
   (*informal*) **scruffy**   **worn**
The opposite is **smart**

## shade *noun*

1 We sat in the shade of a tree.
   ANOTHER WORD IS **shadow**
2 My coat is a pretty shade of red.
   OTHER WORDS YOU MIGHT USE ARE   **colour**   **hue**   **tinge**

## shady *adjective*

We sat down in a shady place.
   OTHER WORDS YOU MIGHT USE ARE   **shaded**   **shadowy**

## shaggy *adjective*

The dog had a shaggy coat.

OTHER WORDS YOU MIGHT USE ARE    **hairy    rough    woolly**

## shake *verb*

1  I shook with fear.

OTHER VERBS YOU MIGHT USE ARE    **to quake    to quiver    to shiver
to shudder    to tremble**

2  The house shook in the earthquake.

OTHER VERBS ARE    **to rock    to sway    to vibrate    to wobble**

## shallow *adjective*

The opposite is **deep**

## shame *noun*

We'll never forget the shame of losing 14-0!

OTHER WORDS YOU MIGHT USE ARE    **disgrace    embarrassment**

---

### shape *noun*

OTHER WORDS YOU MIGHT USE ARE

**form    outline**

DIFFERENT SHAPES ARE

**circle    heptagon    hexagon    oblong    octagon
oval    pentagon    rectangle    semi-circle    spiral
square    triangle**

DIFFERENT SOLID SHAPES ARE

**cone    cube    cuboid    cylinder    hemisphere    prism
pyramid    sphere    spiral**

---

## share *noun*

1  We all had a share of the money.

OTHER WORDS YOU MIGHT USE ARE    **fraction    part**

2  Mum made sure that everyone had a fair share of the pudding.

OTHER WORDS ARE    **helping    portion    ration**

## share *verb*

We shared the food between us.

OTHER VERBS YOU MIGHT USE ARE    **to deal out    to distribute    to divide
to split**

# sharp *adjective*

1 a sharp stick.
ANOTHER WORD IS **pointed**
2 a sharp knife.
OTHER WORDS YOU MIGHT USE ARE    **keen    razor-sharp**
The opposite is **blunt**
3 a sharp bend in the road.
ANOTHER WORD IS **sudden**
4 a sharp girl.
OTHER WORDS ARE    **bright    clever    intelligent    quick    smart**
The opposite is **dull**

# shed *verb*

A lorry shed its load on the motorway.
OTHER VERBS ARE    **to drop    to scatter**

# sheet *noun*

1 a sheet on a bed.
For things you have on a bed, see **bed**
2 a sheet of paper.
OTHER WORDS YOU MIGHT USE ARE    **leaf    page**

# shelter *noun*

The animals looked for shelter from the storm.
OTHER WORDS ARE    **cover    protection    refuge    safety**

# shelter *verb*

The hedge sheltered us from the wind.
OTHER VERBS YOU MIGHT USE ARE    **to guard    to hide    to protect    to shield**

# shift *verb*

For other verbs, see **move**

# shine *verb*

Things shine in different ways.
THEY CAN:
**blaze    burn    dazzle    flash    flicker    glare    gleam    glimmer    glint    glisten    glitter    glow    shine    sparkle    twinkle**

## shiny *adjective*

a shiny new coin.

OTHER WORDS YOU MIGHT USE ARE    **bright    gleaming    glossy    polished    shining**

The opposite is **dull**

## shiver *verb*

I was shivering with cold.

OTHER VERBS YOU MIGHT USE ARE    **to quiver    to shake    to shudder    to tremble**

## shock *verb*

1  The explosion shocked everyone.

OTHER VERBS YOU MIGHT USE ARE    **to alarm    to frighten    to startle    to stun    to surprise**

2  The swearing shocked us.

OTHER VERBS ARE    **to disgust    to offend    to upset**

---

## shoe *noun*

THINGS YOU WEAR ON YOUR FEET ARE

**boots    clogs    plimsolls    sandals    slippers    trainers    wellingtons**

---

## shoot *verb*

He shot at the target.

OTHER VERBS YOU MIGHT USE ARE    **to aim    to fire**

---

## shop *noun*

ANOTHER WORD IS **store**

BIG SHOPS THAT SELL ALL KINDS OF GOODS ARE

**department store    hypermarket    supermarket**

DIFFERENT KINDS OF SHOP ARE

| | | | |
|---|---|---|---|
| **baker** | **bank** | **barber** | **book shop** |
| **butcher** | **chemist** | **clothes shop** | **dairy** |
| **delicatessen** | **DIY shop** | **fishmonger** | **florist** |
| **greengrocer** | **grocer** | **hairdresser** | **ironmonger** |
| **jeweller** | **launderette** | **newsagent** | **off-licence** |
| **post office** | **shoe shop** | | |

## short *adjective*
1  a short poem.
      ANOTHER WORD IS **brief**
The opposite is **long**
2  a short person.
      OTHER WORDS ARE      **little**    **small**
The opposite is **tall**

## shout *verb*
Sam shouted so loud that the people next door heard him.
      OTHER VERBS YOU MIGHT USE ARE    **to call**    **to cry out**    **to roar**
      **to scream**    **to shriek**    **to yell**

## show *noun*
an art show.
      OTHER WORDS ARE    **display**    **exhibition**

## show *verb*
1  We showed our work to the visitors.
      OTHER VERBS YOU MIGHT USE ARE    **to display**    **to exhibit**    **to present**
2  She showed me how to do it.
      OTHER VERBS ARE    **to explain**    **to teach**    **to tell**
3  We drew pictures to show how people used to dress in Victorian times.
      OTHER VERBS ARE    **to illustrate**    **to portray**    **to represent**

## shrill *adjective*
a shrill whistle.
      OTHER WORDS YOU MIGHT USE ARE    **high**    **piercing**    **sharp**

## shrivel *verb*
The plants shrivelled in the heat.
      OTHER VERBS YOU MIGHT USE ARE    **to dry up**    **to shrink**    **to wither**

## shudder *verb*
I shuddered when I thought of the monster.
      OTHER VERBS YOU MIGHT USE ARE    **to quake**    **to quiver**    **to shake**
      **to tremble**

## shut *verb*
Shut the door.
      OTHER VERBS ARE    **to close**    **to fasten**    **to lock**    **to seal**
To shut a door loudly is to **slam** it.
The opposite is **open**

## shy *adjective*
He was too shy to say that he knew the answer.
> OTHER WORDS YOU MIGHT USE ARE **bashful  modest  nervous  timid**

The opposite is **bold**

## sick *adjective*
Jo was away from school because she was sick.
> OTHER WORDS YOU MIGHT USE ARE **ill** (*informal*) **poorly  unwell**

**to be sick**
> OTHER WORDS ARE (*informal*) **throw up  vomit**

For other words, see **health**

## side *noun*
1  A cube has six sides.
> OTHER WORDS ARE **face  surface**

2  I stood at the side of the road.
> ANOTHER WORD IS **edge**

A grassy side of a road is a **verge**

## sight *noun*
1  The optician says that Sam has good sight.
> OTHER WORDS YOU MIGHT USE ARE **eyesight  vision**

2  The hills are a lovely sight.
> OTHER WORDS ARE **scene  spectacle**

## sign *noun*
1  He gave a sign that it was my turn.
> OTHER WORDS YOU MIGHT USE ARE **hint  reminder  signal**

2  The doctor said that spots might be a sign of measles.
> OTHER WORDS ARE **indication  symptom**

## silent *adjective*
1  During the night the house is completely silent.
> OTHER WORDS YOU MIGHT USE ARE **quiet  soundless**

The opposite is **noisy**
2  Sam was silent when he heard the bad news.
> OTHER WORDS ARE **dumb  speechless**

## silky *adjective*
The cat has a silky coat.
> OTHER WORDS YOU MIGHT USE ARE **sleek  smooth  soft**

The opposite is **rough**

## silly *adjective*
It's silly to go out in the rain.
OTHER WORDS ARE   (*informal*) **daft**   **foolish**   **ridiculous**   **senseless**   **stupid**
The opposite is **sensible**

## similar *adjective*
The two girls had similar dresses.
ANOTHER WORD IS **matching**
The opposite is **different**

## simple *adjective*
1 a simple problem.
OTHER WORDS YOU MIGHT USE ARE   **clear**   **easy**   **straightforward**
The opposite is **complicated**
2 a simple dress.
ANOTHER WORD IS **plain**

## sincere *adjective*
He was sincere when he said he was glad to see us.
OTHER WORDS YOU MIGHT USE ARE   **genuine**   **honest**   **truthful**
The opposite is **dishonest**

---

## singer *noun*
ANOTHER WORD IS **vocalist**
A group of singers is a **choir** or a **chorus**.
Someone who sings on their own is a **soloist**.
SINGERS WITH DIFFERENT KINDS OF VOICE ARE
**alto**   **bass**   **contralto**   **soprano**   **tenor**   **treble**

For other words to do with music, see **music**

---

## single *adjective*
There wasn't a single sweet left!
ANOTHER WORD IS **solitary**

## site *noun*
We found a nice site to put up the tent.
OTHER WORDS YOU MIGHT USE ARE   **plot**   **position**   **situation**   **spot**

## situation *noun*
1 My house is in a nice situation.
    OTHER WORDS YOU MIGHT USE ARE    **place**    **position**    **spot**
2 I was in an awkward situation when I lost my money.
    ANOTHER WORD IS **position**

## size *noun*
For other words, see **measurement**

## skate *verb*
He skated gracefully over the ice.
    OTHER VERBS YOU MIGHT USE ARE    **to glide**    **to skim**    **to slide**

## skeleton *noun*
For other parts of the body, see **body**

## skid *verb*
The car skidded on the ice.
    OTHER VERBS YOU CAN USE ARE    **to slide**    **to slip**

## skilful *adjective*
a skilful player.
    OTHER WORDS YOU MIGHT USE ARE    **clever**    **expert**    **talented**

## skill *noun*
Sam admired the player's skill.
    OTHER WORDS YOU MIGHT USE ARE    **ability**    **cleverness**    **talent**

## skin *noun*
    WORDS FOR ANIMALS' SKIN ARE    **fur**    **hide**
Words for the skin of an orange are **peel** or **rind**.

## skip *verb*
The lambs skipped about the field.
    OTHER VERBS ARE    **to dance**    **to frisk**    **to hop**    **to jump**    **to leap**
    **to prance**    **to spring**

## slanting *adjective*
a slanting line.
    OTHER WORDS ARE    **sloping**    **tilting**

## slay *verb*
For other verbs, see **kill**

## sledge *noun*
OTHER WORDS ARE    sleigh    toboggan

---

### sleep *verb*
DIFFERENT WAYS TO GO TO SLEEP ARE

to doze    (*informal*) **to drop off**    **to nod off**    **to slumber**
**to snooze**    (*informal*) **to take a nap**

When animals sleep for a long time in the winter, they **hibernate**.

---

## sleepy *adjective*
I was sleepy so I went to bed.
OTHER WORDS YOU MIGHT USE ARE    **drowsy**    **tired**    **weary**

## slender *adjective*
She has a slender figure.
ANOTHER WORD IS **graceful**
For other words, see **slim**

## slide *verb*
We slid on the ice.
OTHER VERBS YOU MIGHT USE ARE    **to glide**    **to skate**    **to skid**    **to slip**

## slight *adjective*
a slight accident.
OTHER WORDS YOU MIGHT USE ARE    **minor**    **small**    **unimportant**
The opposite is **serious**

## slim *adjective*
He could get through the hole in the fence because he was so slim.
OTHER WORDS YOU MIGHT USE ARE    **lean**    **slender**    **slight**    **thin**
The opposite is **fat**

## slip *verb*
Sam slipped and fell over.
OTHER VERBS YOU MIGHT USE ARE    **to skid**    **to slide**

## slippery *adjective*
Take care: the floor is slippery.
OTHER WORDS ARE    **greasy**    **icy**    **oily**    **slimy**    **slithery**    **smooth**

## slope *noun*

It's hard to run up a steep slope.

OTHER WORDS ARE　**bank**　**gradient**　**hill**　**ramp**　**rise**

## slope *verb*

The beach slopes down to the sea.

ANOTHER VERB IS **to slant**

## slot *noun*

I put a coin in the slot.

OTHER WORDS YOU MIGHT USE ARE　**groove**　**opening**　**slit**

## slow *adjective*

1 There was a slow change in the weather.

ANOTHER WORD IS **gradual**

2 I'm sorry I'm late, but my watch is slow.

The opposite is **fast**

## sly *adjective*

They say the fox is a sly animal.

OTHER WORDS ARE　**crafty**　**cunning**　(*informal*) **sneaky**　**wily**

## smack *verb*

For other verbs, see **hit**

## small *adjective*

1 The book was small enough to put in my pocket.

OTHER WORDS YOU MIGHT USE ARE　**compact**　**little**　**minute**　**tiny**

2 Sam made a small model of the castle.

ANOTHER WORD IS **miniature**

3 She gave us small helpings.

OTHER WORDS ARE　**mean**　(*informal*) **measly**　**stingy**

4 We had a small problem.

OTHER WORDS ARE　**minor**　**slight**　**unimportant**

The opposite is **big**

## smart *adjective*

1 He looked smart in his new clothes.

OTHER WORDS YOU MIGHT USE ARE　**neat**　**posh**　**tidy**　**well-dressed**

The opposite is **untidy**

2 That's a smart dog if he understands what you say.

OTHER WORDS YOU MIGHT USE ARE　**bright**　**clever**　**intelligent**

The opposite is **stupid**

## smart *verb*

The wasp sting made Sam's hand smart.

OTHER VERBS YOU MIGHT USE ARE     **to hurt     to sting     to throb**

## smear *verb*

I smeared ointment on the sore place.

OTHER VERBS YOU MIGHT USE ARE     **to rub     to spread     to wipe**

## smell *noun*

ANOTHER WORD IS **odour**

WORDS FOR A NICE SMELL ARE     **aroma     fragrance     perfume     scent**

A word for a nasty smell is **stink**.

A word for a slight smell is **whiff**.

## smile *verb*

For other verbs, see **laugh**

## smoke *noun*

the smoke from an engine.

OTHER WORDS YOU MIGHT USE ARE     **exhaust     fumes**

## smooth *adjective*

1 a smooth surface.

OTHER WORDS YOU MIGHT USE ARE     **even     flat     level**

The opposite is **rough**

2 a smooth sea.

ANOTHER WORD IS **calm**

The opposite is **stormy**

## smudge *noun*

I smudged the wet paint.

OTHER WORDS YOU MIGHT USE ARE     **smear     streak**

## snatch *verb*

The dog snatched the sandwich out of my hand.

OTHER VERBS YOU MIGHT USE ARE     **to grab     to seize     to take**

## sneak *verb*

She sneaked up behind me and made me jump.

OTHER VERBS YOU MIGHT USE ARE     **to creep     to steal**

## soft *adjective*
1  The baby cuddled a soft toy.
OTHER WORDS TO DESCRIBE SOFT THINGS ARE    **flexible    floppy    limp    spongy    springy    squashy**
The opposite is **hard**
2  Jo's dress is made of soft material.
OTHER WORDS YOU MIGHT USE ARE    **silky    smooth    velvety**
The opposite is **rough**
3  They played soft music when we went into church.
OTHER WORDS YOU MIGHT USE ARE    **gentle    low    quiet    restful**
The opposite is **loud**

## soil *noun*
Sam planted his seeds in the soil.
OTHER WORDS YOU MIGHT USE ARE    **earth    ground**

---

### soldier *noun*
ANOTHER WORD IS **serviceman** or **servicewoman**
Soldiers who go on horseback are the **cavalry**.
Soldiers who go on foot are the **infantry**.
A soldier trained for specially daring raids is a **commando**.
A soldier trained to fight on land or at sea is a **marine**.
A soldier who goes into battle by parachute is a **paratrooper**.
WORDS FOR A LOT OF SOLDIERS ARE
**army    troops**

For other fighters, see **fight**

---

## solemn *adjective*
They looked solemn when they heard the news.
OTHER WORDS YOU MIGHT USE ARE    **grave    serious    thoughtful**

## solid *adjective*
1  Cricket balls are solid.
The opposite is **hollow**
2  We were glad to get out of the mud onto solid ground.
OTHER WORDS YOU MIGHT USE ARE    **firm    hard**
The opposite is **soft**

## solution *noun*
Did you get the solution to the puzzle?
OTHER WORDS YOU MIGHT USE ARE    **answer    explanation**

**solve** *verb*

Jo solved the puzzle in a couple of minutes.

OTHER VERBS YOU MIGHT USE ARE **to answer** **to explain** **to work out**

---

**song** *noun*

DIFFERENT KINDS OF MUSIC FOR SINGING ARE

**ballad** **carol** **folksong** **hymn** **lullaby** **pop song** **shanty**

For other words to do with music, see **music**

---

**soothe** *verb*

Quiet music soothes your nerves.

OTHER VERBS YOU MIGHT USE ARE **to calm** **to comfort** **to relax**

The opposite is **disturb**

**sore** *adjective*

Jo had a sore place on her knee.

OTHER WORDS YOU MIGHT USE ARE **aching** **inflamed** **painful** **raw** **red** **tender**

**sorrow** *noun*

Jo was full of sorrow when his dog died.

OTHER WORDS YOU MIGHT USE ARE **grief** **misery** **sadness** **unhappiness**

**sorry** *adjective*

1 He was sorry when he saw the damage he had done.

OTHER WORDS ARE **apologetic** **ashamed** **regretful** **repentant**

2 Jo was sorry for the sick boy.

OTHER WORDS ARE **sad** **sympathetic**

**sort** *noun*

1 Which sort of cake do you like?

OTHER WORDS YOU MIGHT USE ARE **brand** **kind** **type** **variety**

2 What sort of dog is that?

OTHER WORDS ARE **breed** **species**

**sort** *verb*

Sam sorted the library books.

OTHER VERBS YOU MIGHT USE ARE **to arrange** **to classify** **to organize**

## sound *adjective*

1 Jo's dog is in a sound condition.

OTHER WORDS YOU MIGHT USE ARE **healthy strong**

2 The teacher said we had done sound work.

OTHER WORDS YOU MIGHT USE ARE **correct good reasonable**

## sound *noun* and *verb*, see opposite page

## sour *adjective*

a sour taste.

OTHER WORDS YOU MIGHT USE ARE **acid sharp tangy tart**

The opposite is **sweet**

## source *noun*

the source of a river.

OTHER WORDS ARE **beginning origin starting point**

## space *noun*

1 Give me a bit of space.

ANOTHER WORD IS **room**

2 Write your answer in the space.

ANOTHER WORD IS **blank**

3 What goes in that empty space?

OTHER WORDS YOU MIGHT USE ARE **gap hole opening**

## spacecraft *noun*

DIFFERENT KINDS OF SPACECRAFT ARE **rocket spaceship space shuttle**

## spare *adjective*

Take some spare socks in case you get your feet wet.

OTHER WORDS YOU MIGHT USE ARE **additional extra**

## spare *verb*

The cruel soldier would not spare his enemy.

OTHER VERBS YOU MIGHT USE ARE **to be merciful to to forgive to let off to pardon to reprieve to save**

## sparkle *verb*

The firework sparkled in the dark.

OTHER VERBS YOU MIGHT USE ARE **to flash to spark**

## speak *verb*

For other verbs, see **talk**

# sound *noun* and *verb*

DIFFERENT SOUNDS WE CAN MAKE ARE

| | | | |
|---|---|---|---|
| bawl | boo | clap | cry |
| groan | hiccup | hiss | jeer |
| lisp | moan | scream | shout |
| shriek | sigh | sniff | snore |
| sob | wail | whistle | yell |

For other sounds we make, see **talk**

DIFFERENT SOUNDS ANIMALS MAKE ARE

| | | | |
|---|---|---|---|
| bark | bellow | bleat | bray |
| croak | growl | grunt | howl |
| jabber | low | miaow | moo |
| neigh | purr | roar | screech |
| snarl | snort | squeak | squeal |
| whine | whinny | yap | |

SOUNDS DIFFERENT BIRDS MAKE ARE

| | | | |
|---|---|---|---|
| cackle | chirp | cluck | coo |
| crow | hoot | quack | screech |
| squawk | twitter | warble | |

SOUNDS INSECTS MAKE ARE

| | | | |
|---|---|---|---|
| buzz | drone | hum | murmur |

DIFFERENT SOUNDS THINGS MAKE ARE

| | | | |
|---|---|---|---|
| bang | blare | bleep | boom |
| chime | clang | clank | clash |
| clatter | click | clink | crack |
| crackle | crash | creak | jangle |
| jingle | peal | ping | plop |
| pop | rattle | ring | rumble |
| rustle | sizzle | slam | snap |
| splutter | swish | throb | thud |
| thunder | tick | tinkle | twang |
| whiz | | | |

For other words, see **music, noise**

> ### spear *noun*
> A spear used by knights in old times was a **lance**.
> A spear used to kill whales is a **harpoon**.
> A spear you throw as a sport is a **javelin**.

## special *adjective*
1   Your birthday is a special day.
    ANOTHER WORD IS **important**
2   Petrol has a special smell.
    OTHER WORDS ARE    **different    distinct**
3   Jo has tea in her special mug.
    OTHER WORDS YOU MIGHT USE ARE    **individual    particular    personal**

## specimen *noun*
Show me a specimen of your work.
    OTHER WORDS YOU MIGHT USE ARE    **example    illustration    sample**

## speck *noun*
a speck of dust.
    OTHER WORDS ARE    **bit    dot    grain    spot**

## speckled *adjective*
a speckled pattern.
    OTHER WORDS ARE    **dotted    mottled    spotty**

## spectacular *adjective*
a spectacular fireworks display.
    OTHER WORDS YOU MIGHT USE ARE    **big    exciting    impressive**

## speech *noun*
We listened to the speech.
    OTHER WORDS YOU MIGHT USE ARE    **lecture    talk**

## speed *noun*
We walked at an ordinary speed.
    OTHER WORDS YOU MIGHT USE ARE    **pace    rate**

## spell *noun*
a magic spell.
    OTHER WORDS YOU MIGHT USE ARE    **charm    enchantment**

## spend *verb*

1 How much money did you spend?
OTHER VERBS YOU MIGHT USE ARE   **to pay**   **to use**
2 We spent a nice day by the sea.
ANOTHER VERB IS **to pass**

## spike *noun*

There were spikes along the top of the railings.
OTHER WORDS YOU MIGHT USE ARE   **point**   **prong**

## spill *verb*

Who spilt the milk on the carpet?
OTHER VERBS YOU MIGHT USE ARE   **to drop**   **to slop**   **to tip**   **to upset**

## spin *verb*

The top spun round and round.
OTHER VERBS ARE   **to revolve**   **to turn**   **to twirl**   **to whirl**

---

## spirit *noun*

Another word for your spirit is your **soul**.
SPIRITS YOU READ ABOUT IN STORIES ARE
**demon**   **devil**   **fairy**   **genie**   **ghost**   **gremlin**
**imp**   **phantom**   **poltergeist**   (*informal*) **spook**

---

## spiteful *adjective*

Jo doesn't like people who make spiteful remarks.
OTHER WORDS YOU MIGHT USE ARE   (*informal*) **catty**   **hurtful**   **nasty**
**unkind**
The opposite is **kind**

## splash *verb*

The car splashed water over us.
OTHER VERBS YOU MIGHT USE ARE   **to shower**   **to slop**   **to spatter**

## splendid *adjective*

1 The soldiers wore splendid uniforms.
OTHER WORDS YOU MIGHT USE ARE   **brilliant**   **gorgeous**   **grand**
**impressive**   **magnificent**
2 We had a splendid holiday.
For other words, see **good**

## split *verb*

1 He split the log with an axe.
   OTHER VERBS YOU MIGHT USE ARE    **to chop**    **to crack**    **to cut**    **to slice**
2 We split into two teams.
   OTHER VERBS ARE    **to divide**    **to separate**

## spoil *verb*

The stain has spoilt my new dress.
   OTHER VERBS YOU MIGHT USE ARE    **to damage**    (*informal*) **to mess up**    **to ruin**    **to wreck**

---

### sport *noun*

DIFFERENT SPORTS ARE

| | | | |
|---|---|---|---|
| athletics | baseball | basketball | boxing |
| climbing | cricket | darts | fishing |
| football | golf | gymnastics | hockey |
| ice hockey | rounders | rugby | running |
| sailing | showjumping | skating | skiing |
| snooker | soccer | squash | surfing |
| surf-riding | swimming | table tennis | tennis |
| volleyball | water-skiing | windsurfing | wrestling |
| yachting | | | |

---

### spot *noun*

1 You've got a dirty spot on your new trousers.
   OTHER WORDS YOU MIGHT USE ARE
   **blot**    **dot**    **mark**    **speck**    **stain**
2 I've got spots on my face.
   DIFFERENT KINDS OF SPOTS ARE
   **boil**    **freckle**    **mole**    **pimple**
A spot on your eyelid is a **sty**.
A large number of spots is a **rash**.

3 Here's a nice spot for a picnic.
   OTHER WORDS ARE
   **place**    **position**    **situation**

## spray *verb*

The bus sprayed us with water when it went through the puddle.

OTHER VERBS YOU MIGHT USE ARE **to scatter** **to shower** **to spatter** **to splash** **to sprinkle**

## spread *verb*

We spread the map on the table.

OTHER VERBS YOU MIGHT USE ARE **to lay out** **to open out** **to unfold**

## spring *verb*

1 The cat crouched, ready to spring on the mouse.

OTHER VERBS YOU MIGHT USE ARE **to jump** **to leap** **to pounce**

2 Weeds sprang up all over the garden.

OTHER VERBS ARE **to grow** **to shoot**

## sprout *verb*

The seeds began to sprout.

OTHER VERBS YOU MIGHT USE ARE **to grow** **to shoot up** **to spring up**

## squabble *verb*

Those boys are always squabbling.

OTHER VERBS YOU MIGHT USE ARE **to argue** **to fight** **to quarrel**

## squeeze *verb*

1 I squeezed an orange to make some juice.

OTHER VERBS YOU MIGHT USE ARE **to crush** **to press**

2 They squeezed us into a little room.

OTHER VERBS ARE **to crowd** **to push** **to shove** **to squash**

## squirt *verb*

Water squirted out of the hole.

OTHER VERBS YOU MIGHT USE ARE **to pour** **to spout** **to spurt** **to stream**

## stack *noun*

a stack of books.

OTHER WORDS ARE **heap** **mound** **pile**

## stage *noun*

1 We stood on the stage to sing.

ANOTHER WORD IS **platform**

2 Baby is at the crawling stage.

OTHER WORDS ARE **period** **phase**

## stain *noun*

What's that stain on your shirt?
OTHER WORDS ARE    **blot    mark    smudge    spot**

## stairs *noun*

OTHER WORDS YOU MIGHT USE ARE    **staircase    steps**

## stale *adjective*

1 stale bread.
OTHER WORDS YOU MIGHT USE ARE    **dry    old**
2 stale news.
ANOTHER WORD IS **out-of-date**
The opposite is **fresh**

## stalk *noun*

a flower on a stalk.
ANOTHER WORD IS **stem**

## stand *verb*

1 We all stood when the visitors arrived.
OTHER VERBS YOU MIGHT USE ARE    **to get up    to rise**
2 I stood my books on the shelf.
OTHER VERBS ARE    **to arrange    to place    to position**

## standard *noun*

Our teacher expects a high standard of work.
OTHER WORDS YOU MIGHT USE ARE    **level    quality**

## stare *verb*

For other verbs, see **look**

## start *verb*

1 What time does the film start?
OTHER VERBS YOU MIGHT USE ARE    **to begin    to commence**
2 Our teacher has started a chess club.
OTHER VERBS ARE    **to create    to introduce    to set up**
3 They started on their journey at dawn.
OTHER VERBS ARE    **to depart    to embark    to set off    to set out**

## startle *verb*

The explosion startled us.
OTHER VERBS YOU MIGHT USE ARE    **to alarm    to frighten    to shock    to surprise    to upset**

## starving *adjective*
For other words, see **hungry**

## state *verb*
Dad stated that he had no money.
> OTHER VERBS YOU MIGHT USE ARE    **to announce    to declare    to report    to say**

## statement *noun*
The police issued a statement about the burglary.
> OTHER WORDS YOU MIGHT USE ARE    **announcement    communication**

## statue *noun*
We saw some statues in the museum.
> OTHER WORDS YOU MIGHT USE ARE    **carving    figure    sculpture**

## stay *verb*
1  Stay here until I come back.
> OTHER VERBS YOU MIGHT USE ARE    **to remain    to stop    to wait**

2  Stay on the path.
> OTHER VERBS ARE    **to carry on    to continue    to keep on**

3  Jo went to stay with Granny.
> ANOTHER WORD IS **to visit**

## steady *adjective*
1  Make sure the ladder is steady.
> OTHER WORDS YOU MIGHT USE ARE    **firm    secure    solid**

2  The music had a steady rhythm.
> OTHER WORDS ARE    **constant    continuous    even    regular**

---

## steal *verb*
> OTHER VERBS YOU MIGHT USE ARE
> *(informal)* **to pinch    to take**

Someone who steals things is a **robber** or a **thief**.
Someone who steals things from someone's house is a **burglar**.
Someone who steals things in a riot is a **looter**.
Someone who steals things from a shop is a **shoplifter**.
Someone who steals by attacking people in the street is a **mugger**.
Someone who steals things out of your pocket is a **pickpocket**.
Someone who used to steal things from travellers was a **highwayman**.

**step** *noun*

1   We all moved forwards one step.
> OTHER WORDS YOU MIGHT USE ARE     **pace**     **stride**

2   I climbed up the steps.
> ANOTHER WORD IS **stair**

**stern** *adjective*

She had a stern look on her face.
> OTHER WORDS YOU MIGHT USE ARE     **angry     grim     severe     strict**

---

**stick** *noun*

> DIFFERENT KINDS OF STICK ARE:

a long straight stick
> **pole     rod**

a stick that is part of a plant
> **branch     stalk     twig**

a stick used in a relay race or by the conductor of a band
> **baton**

a stick used to support plants
> **bamboo     cane**

a stick used as a weapon
> **club     truncheon**

a stick used to help someone walk
> **crutch     walking stick**

a magician's stick
> **wand**

---

**stick** *verb*

1   The door has stuck.
> ANOTHER VERB IS **to jam**

2   This glue will stick plastic.
> OTHER VERBS YOU MIGHT USE ARE     **to fasten     to fix     to glue**

3   She stuck a pin in me!
> OTHER VERBS ARE     **to jab     to stab**

**stiff** *adjective*

1   stiff cardboard.
> OTHER WORDS YOU MIGHT USE ARE     **hard     rigid**

2  stiff paste.
    ANOTHER WORD IS **thick**

## still *adjective*
It was a very still evening.
    OTHER WORDS ARE    **calm**    **peaceful**    **quiet**

## stir *verb*
1  Sam stirred the cake mixture.
    OTHER VERBS YOU MIGHT USE ARE    **to beat**    **to mix**    **to whisk**
2  Mum called Jo and said it was time to stir.
    OTHER VERBS ARE    **to get going**    **to get up**    **to move**

## stitch *noun*
For other words, see **sew**

## stomach *noun*
    AN INFORMAL WORD IS **tummy**
A word some people think is impolite is **belly**.

## stone *noun*
    DIFFERENT KINDS OF STONE ARE    **boulder**    **cobble**    **gravel**    **jewel**
    **pebble**    **rock**

## stoop *verb*
I stooped down to pull up my sock.
    OTHER VERBS YOU MIGHT USE ARE    **to bend**    **to bow**    **to crouch**
    **to kneel**

## stop *verb*
1  The policeman stopped the traffic.
    OTHER VERBS YOU MIGHT USE ARE    **to check**    **to halt**    **to hold up**
2  The bus stopped.
    OTHER VERBS ARE    **to draw up**    **to halt**    **to pull up**
3  The noise suddenly stopped.
    OTHER VERBS ARE    **to cease**    **to end**    **to finish**
4  You can stop for tea.
    ANOTHER VERB IS **to stay**

## store *verb*
We store food in the fridge.
    OTHER VERBS YOU MIGHT USE ARE    **to keep**    **to put away**    **to save**

## storm *noun*

DIFFERENT KINDS OF STORM:

a violent storm
> **tempest**

a snow storm
> **blizzard**

a storm with a lot of wind
> **gale    hurricane    tornado    whirlwind**

a storm with a lot of rain
> **deluge    downpour    rainstorm**

a storm with thunder and lightning
> **thunderstorm**

For other words, see **weather**


## story *noun*

OTHER WORDS YOU MIGHT USE ARE
> **narrative    tale**

DIFFERENT KINDS OF STORY ARE
> **adventure story    comedy    fable    fairy tale    fantasy
> folk tale    legend    love story    myth    novel
> parable    romance**


## stout *adjective*

a stout person.
> OTHER WORDS YOU MIGHT USE ARE    **fat    overweight    plump**
> (*informal*) **tubby**
The opposite is **thin**


## straight *adjective*

a straight line. a straight road.
> ANOTHER WORD IS **direct**
The opposite is **crooked**

## strain *verb*

1 He strained to escape from the monster's grip.
> OTHER VERBS YOU MIGHT USE ARE    **to make an effort**    **to struggle**
> **to try hard**

2 Jo strained a muscle when she was running.
> OTHER VERBS ARE    **to damage**    **to hurt**    **to injure**

3 Don't strain yourself!
> OTHER VERBS ARE    **to exhaust**    **to tire out**    **to wear out**

## strange *adjective*

1 When I woke up I was in a strange place.
> OTHER WORDS YOU MIGHT USE ARE    **different**    **foreign**    **new**
> **unfamiliar**    **unknown**

The opposite is **familiar**

2 A strange thing happened.
> OTHER WORDS ARE    **curious**    **extraordinary**    **funny**
> **mysterious**    **odd**    **peculiar**    **puzzling**    **queer**    **surprising**
> **unusual**

The opposite is **ordinary**

## stranger *noun*

Please show me the way, because I am a stranger here.
A stranger might be a **foreigner** or a **visitor**.

## stray *verb*

Whatever you do, don't stray in the forest.
> OTHER VERBS YOU MIGHT USE ARE    **to get lost**    **to roam about**
> **to wander**

## streak *noun*

The plane left a white streak in the sky.
> OTHER WORDS YOU MIGHT USE ARE    **line**    **stripe**

## stream *noun*

We paddled across a stream.
> ANOTHER WORD IS **brook**

A big stream is a **river**.
For other words, see **water**

## strength *noun*

Have you got the strength to lift this box?
> OTHER WORDS ARE    **force**    **might**    **power**

## strengthen *verb*
Dad put in some posts to strengthen the fence.
> OTHER VERBS YOU MIGHT USE ARE     **to reinforce     to support**

The opposite is **weaken**

## stretch *verb*
You can stretch elastic.
> OTHER VERBS YOU MIGHT USE ARE     **to lengthen     to pull out**

## strict *adjective*
a strict teacher.
> OTHER WORDS YOU MIGHT USE ARE     **firm     severe     stern**

---

## string *noun*
> OTHER THINGS YOU MIGHT USE TO TIE THINGS UP ARE
> **cord     lace     line     ribbon     rope     wire**

---

## strip *verb*
We stripped off our clothes to go swimming.
> OTHER VERBS YOU MIGHT USE ARE     **to peel off     to remove     to take off**

## stripe *noun*
Sam's football shirt has red and white stripes.
> OTHER WORDS ARE     **band     line     strip**

## strong *adjective*
1 a strong person.
> OTHER WORDS YOU MIGHT USE ARE     **healthy     muscular     sturdy     tough     wiry**

2 a strong rope. strong walking shoes.
> OTHER WORDS ARE     **sound     stout     thick**

The opposite is **weak**

## struggle *verb*
1 The thief struggled to get away.
> OTHER VERBS YOU MIGHT USE ARE     **to fight     to wrestle**

2 We struggled to put the tent up.
> OTHER VERBS ARE     **to exert yourself     to make an effort     to strive     to try**

## stubborn *adjective*
The stubborn animal refused to move.
> OTHER WORDS YOU MIGHT USE ARE    **defiant**    **disobedient**    **obstinate**

## study *verb*
1 Mum is studying for an exam.
> OTHER VERBS YOU MIGHT USE ARE    **to learn**    **to revise**    (*informal*) **to swot**

2 The police studied the evidence.
> OTHER VERBS ARE    **to analyse**    **to consider**    **to examine**
> **to investigate**    **to think about**

## stuff *noun*
1 What's this stuff in the jar?
> ANOTHER WORD IS **substance**

2 What's that stuff in the attic?
> OTHER WORDS ARE    **articles**    **odds and ends**    **things**

3 I put my stuff in a box.
> OTHER WORDS ARE    **belongings**    **possessions**

## stuffy *adjective*
a stuffy room.
> OTHER WORDS YOU MIGHT USE ARE    **close**    **muggy**    **stifling**    **warm**

## stumble *verb*
I stumbled over a big stone.
> OTHER VERBS YOU MIGHT USE ARE    **to blunder**    **to stagger**    **to trip**

## stun *verb*
1 The hit on the head stunned her.
> OTHER VERBS YOU MIGHT USE ARE    **to daze**    **to knock out**

2 The unexpected news stunned us.
> OTHER VERBS ARE    **to amaze**    **to astonish**    **to shock**    **to surprise**

## stupid *adjective*
1 a stupid idea.
> OTHER WORDS YOU MIGHT USE ARE    **crazy**    **foolish**    **idiotic**    **silly**

2 a stupid person.
> OTHER WORDS ARE    **dense**    **dim**    **dull**    **slow**    (*informal*) **thick**
The opposite is **clever**

## style *noun*
Jo likes the new style of dancing.
> OTHER WORDS YOU MIGHT USE ARE    **fashion**    **way**

## subject *noun*
Sam chose an interesting subject for his project.
> OTHER WORDS YOU MIGHT USE ARE　**theme**　**topic**

## submit *verb*
1　The wrestler submitted to his opponent.
> OTHER VERBS YOU MIGHT USE ARE　**to give in**　**to surrender**　**to yield**
2　We must submit our work today.
> OTHER VERBS ARE　**to give in**　**to hand in**　**to present**

## substance *noun*
What's this sticky substance?
> OTHER WORDS YOU MIGHT USE ARE　**material**　**stuff**

## subtract *verb*
Our teacher subtracts marks for untidy work.
> OTHER VERBS YOU MIGHT USE ARE　**to deduct**　**to take away**

## succeed *verb*
1　Jo succeeded in winning the race.
> OTHER VERBS YOU MIGHT USE ARE　**to be successful**　**to do well**
2　Did your plan succeed?
> ANOTHER VERB IS **to work**

## sudden *adjective*
The car came to a sudden halt.
> OTHER WORDS YOU MIGHT USE ARE　**abrupt**　**hasty**　**quick**　**unexpected**
The opposite is **gradual**

## suffer *verb*
I hate to see animals suffer pain.
> OTHER VERBS YOU MIGHT USE ARE　**to bear**　**to endure**　**to go through**　**to put up with**　**to stand**

## suffering *noun*
For other words, see **pain**

## sufficient *adjective*
Have you got sufficient money for your journey?
> OTHER WORDS YOU MIGHT USE ARE　**adequate**　**enough**

## suggest *verb*
What do you suggest we should do?

OTHER VERBS YOU MIGHT USE ARE        **to advise        to propose
to recommend**

## suitable *adjective*
Is this dress suitable for a wedding?

OTHER WORDS YOU MIGHT USE ARE        **appropriate        proper        right**

## sulky *adjective*
After Mum told him off he was sulky for hours.

OTHER WORDS ARE        **bad-tempered        cross        gloomy        moody
sullen**

The opposite is **cheerful**

## sunny *adjective*
sunny weather.

OTHER WORDS YOU MIGHT USE ARE        **bright        clear        cloudless        fine**

## supply *noun*
There's a supply of paper in the cupboard.

OTHER WORDS YOU MIGHT USE ARE        **reserve        stock**

## supply *verb*
We took our own sandwiches, and our teacher supplied the drinks.

OTHER VERBS YOU MIGHT USE ARE        **to contribute        to give        to provide**

## support *verb*
1 Those pillars support the roof.

OTHER VERBS YOU MIGHT USE ARE        **to bear        to hold up        to prop up**

2 Our friends supported us when we were in trouble.

OTHER VERBS ARE        **to aid        to assist        to encourage        to help
to stand up for**

## supporter *noun*
Sam is a supporter of the local team.

OTHER WORDS ARE        **fan        follower**

## suppose *verb*
Let's suppose that Jo's the queen.

OTHER VERBS YOU MIGHT USE ARE        **to assume        to believe        to imagine
to pretend**

**sure** *adjective*
   1  I'm sure he will come.
         OTHER WORDS YOU MIGHT USE ARE    **certain    confident    convinced
         definite    positive**
   2  He's sure to come.
         ANOTHER WORD IS **bound**

**surprise** *verb*
   The unexpected news surprised us.
         OTHER VERBS YOU MIGHT USE ARE    **to amaze    to astonish    to shock
         to startle    to stun**

**surrender** *verb*
   After a long fight, the army surrendered.
         OTHER VERBS YOU MIGHT USE ARE    **to give in    to submit    to yield**

**survey** *noun*
   We did a survey to find out who comes to school by car.
         OTHER WORDS YOU MIGHT USE ARE    **investigation    study**

**survive** *verb*
   Some plants don't survive through the winter.
         OTHER VERBS YOU MIGHT USE ARE    **to keep going    to last    to live**

**suspect** *verb*
   Mum suspects that I broke her mug.
         OTHER VERBS ARE    **to guess    to have a feeling    to think**

**swamp** *noun*
   The lorry got stuck in the swamp.
         OTHER WORDS ARE    **bog    marsh**

**swarm** *noun*
   For other words, see **group**

**swear** *verb*
   1  Do you swear that you'll tell the truth?
         OTHER VERBS YOU MIGHT USE ARE    **to give your word    to promise
         to vow**
   2  He swore when he hit his finger.
         ANOTHER VERB IS **to curse**

## sweep *verb*
I swept the floor.
> ANOTHER VERB IS **to brush**

For ways to clean things, see **clean**

## sweet *adjective*
For other words to describe how things taste, see **taste**
The opposite is **sour**

## swell *verb*
You can see the tyre swell while you pump it up.
> OTHER VERBS ARE   **to blow up**   **to bulge**   **to get bigger**   **to grow**   **to puff up**

## swelling *noun*
I got a nasty swelling where the wasp stung me.
> OTHER WORDS YOU MIGHT USE ARE   **bulge**   **bump**   **lump**

## swift *adjective*
a swift journey.
> OTHER WORDS YOU MIGHT USE ARE   **fast**   **quick**   **rapid**   **speedy**

The opposite is **slow**

## swill *verb*
Swill the plates under the tap.
> OTHER VERBS YOU MIGHT USE ARE   **to rinse**   **to wash**

## swindle *verb*
He swindled us and made us pay too much.
> OTHER VERBS YOU MIGHT USE ARE   **to cheat**   **to deceive**   **to fool**   **to trick**

## swing *verb*
The branches swung to and fro in the wind.
> ANOTHER VERB IS **to sway**

## switch *verb*
I switched places with my friend.   OTHER VERBS YOU MIGHT USE ARE   **to change**   **to exchange**   **to swap**

## swoop *verb*
The owl swooped down on its prey.
> OTHER VERBS ARE   **to dive**   **to pounce**

**sympathy** *noun*

He didn't have much sympathy when I was ill!

OTHER WORDS YOU MIGHT USE ARE   **consideration**   **feeling**   **mercy**
**pity**

**symptom** *noun*

Spots might be a symptom of measles.

OTHER WORDS ARE   **indication**   **sign**

# Tt

**take** *verb*

1  Take my hand.

OTHER VERBS YOU MIGHT USE ARE   **to clasp**   **to get hold of**   **to grasp**
**to hold**   **to seize**

2  The bus takes you into town.

OTHER VERBS ARE   **to bring**   **to carry**   **to transport**

3  The army took many prisoners.

OTHER VERBS ARE   **to capture**   **to catch**   **to seize**

4  The burglar took the jewels.

OTHER VERBS ARE   **to remove**   **to steal**

5  The dentist took out one of my teeth.

OTHER VERBS ARE   **to extract**   **to remove**

**talent** *noun*

Sam has great talent in football.

OTHER WORDS YOU MIGHT USE ARE   **ability**   **skill**

**talented** *adjective*

Jo is a talented musician.

OTHER WORDS YOU MIGHT USE ARE   **clever**   **expert**   **gifted**   **skilful**

**talk** *noun*

1  I had a nice talk with Granny.

OTHER WORDS YOU MIGHT USE ARE   **chat**   **conversation**   **discussion**

2  The head gave us a long talk.

OTHER WORDS ARE   **address**   **lecture**   **speech**

**talk** *verb*

OTHER VERBS YOU MIGHT USE ARE

to communicate    to express yourself    to say something
to speak

THERE ARE DIFFERENT WAYS OF TALKING. YOU CAN

| | | | |
|---|---|---|---|
| call out | chat | chatter | exclaim |
| gossip | have a conversation | | lisp |
| mumble | murmur | mutter | prattle |
| recite a poem | scream | screech | shout |
| shriek | snap at someone | | snarl |
| splutter | stammer | stutter | whisper |
| yell | | | |

**tall** *adjective*

a tall tower.

ANOTHER WORD IS **high**

The opposite is **low** or **short**

**tame** *adjective*

These animals are very tame.

OTHER WORDS YOU MIGHT USE ARE    **gentle    meek    obedient
safe**

The opposite is **dangerous** or **wild**

**tangled** *adjective*

tangled string.

OTHER WORDS YOU MIGHT USE ARE    **knotted    muddled    twisted**

**tank** *noun*

A tank to keep fish in is an **aquarium**.

**tap** *verb*

She tapped on the door.

OTHER VERBS YOU MIGHT USE ARE    **to knock    to rap**

**task** *noun*

OTHER WORDS YOU MIGHT USE ARE    **job    work**

**taste** *noun*
1 Do you like the taste of this?
ANOTHER WORD IS **flavour**
2 Can I have a taste of your ice cream?
OTHER WORDS YOU MIGHT USE ARE
**bit    lick    mouthful    nibble    piece**

WORDS TO DESCRIBE THINGS THAT TASTE NICE ARE
**appetizing    delicious    luscious    tasty**

WORDS TO DESCRIBE THINGS THAT TASTE NASTY ARE
**bad**    (*informal*) **off    stale    uneatable**

OTHER WORDS TO DESCRIBE HOW THINGS TASTE ARE
**acid    bitter    creamy    fruity    hot    meaty
peppery    salty    savoury    sharp    sour    spicy
sugary    sweet    tangy**

**taste** *verb*
Taste a bit of this!
OTHER VERBS YOU MIGHT USE ARE    **to nibble    to sample    to sip    to try**

**teach** *verb*
OTHER WORDS YOU MIGHT USE ARE
to teach someone in school
    **educate**
to teach someone to do a job
    **instruct    train**
to teach someone to be good at a sport
    **coach**

**teacher** *noun*
DIFFERENT KINDS OF TEACHER ARE    **lecturer    professor    schoolteacher
tutor**
a person who teaches us to play games properly    **coach    trainer**
a person who teaches you how to do a particular thing **instructor**

**team** *noun*
a football team.
ANOTHER WORD IS **side**

## tear *verb*

Sam tore his jeans.

> OTHER VERBS ARE    **to rip**    **to slit**    **to split**

## tease *verb*

If you tease the cat she'll scratch.

> OTHER VERBS YOU MIGHT USE ARE    **to annoy**    **to laugh at**
> **to make fun of**    **to pester**    **to torment**

## telephone *verb*

I telephoned Grandad to ask him to come to tea.

> OTHER VERBS YOU MIGHT USE ARE    **to call**    **to dial**    **to phone**    **to ring**

---

## television *noun*

> DIFFERENT KINDS OF TV PROGRAMME ARE
>
> **cartoons    chat shows    comedy    commercials    films
> interviews    music    nature programmes    news
> plays    quiz shows    serials    sport**

---

## tell *verb*

1  He told me he'd be home for tea.
> OTHER VERBS YOU MIGHT USE ARE    **to inform**    **to promise**

2  Our teacher told the story.
> OTHER VERBS ARE    **to narrate**    **to relate**

3  I told the police what happened.
> OTHER VERBS ARE    **to describe to someone**    **to explain to someone**

4  Mum told us to stop shouting.
> OTHER VERBS ARE    **to command**    **to instruct**    **to order**

**to tell someone off**
> OTHER VERBS YOU MIGHT USE ARE    **to reprimand**    **to scold**
> (*informal*) **to tick off**

## temper *noun*

1  Is Dad in a good temper?
> ANOTHER WORD IS **mood**

2  Baby yells when she's in a temper.
> OTHER WORDS YOU MIGHT USE ARE    **rage    tantrum**

**to lose your temper**
> A PHRASE IS **get angry**

## tend *verb*

1 Grandad tends to fall asleep in the evening.
A PHRASE YOU MIGHT USE IS **to be liable to**
2 Nurses tend sick people.
OTHER VERBS YOU MIGHT USE ARE **to care for** **to look after** **to mind**

## tender *adjective*

1 I gave the baby a tender smile.
OTHER WORDS YOU MIGHT USE ARE **affectionate** **fond** **gentle** **kind** **loving**
The opposite is **cruel**
2 The baby has tender skin.
OTHER WORDS ARE **delicate** **soft**
The opposite is **tough**
3 I had a tender place where I hit my head.
OTHER WORDS ARE **sensitive** **sore**

## terrible *adjective*

There was a terrible storm.
OTHER WORDS YOU MIGHT USE ARE **alarming** **awful** **bad** **dreadful** **frightening** **horrible** (*informal*) **scary** **terrific**

## terrific *adjective*

1 I had a terrific idea.
For other words, see **good**
2 There was a terrific storm.
For other words, see **terrible**

## terrify *verb*

The dog terrified the baby.
OTHER VERBS YOU MIGHT USE ARE **to alarm** **to frighten** **to scare** **to upset**

## terror *noun*

People ran away from the fire in terror.
OTHER WORDS YOU MIGHT USE ARE **alarm** **fear** **fright** **panic**

## test *noun*

1 a spelling test. a driving test.
ANOTHER WORD IS **exam** or **examination**
2 a scientific test.
OTHER WORDS YOU MIGHT USE ARE **experiment** **research** **trial**

## thankful *adjective*

I was thankful it wasn't raining.

OTHER WORDS YOU MIGHT USE ARE     **grateful     pleased**

## thaw *verb*

The snow thawed when the sun came out.

OTHER VERBS YOU MIGHT USE ARE     **to melt     to unfreeze**

The opposite is **freeze**

---

## theatre *noun*

We went to the theatre for a Christmas treat.

OTHER WORDS YOU MIGHT USE ARE     **performance     show**

THINGS YOU SEE IN A THEATRE ARE

**ballet     comedy     drama     musical     opera
pantomime     play**

For other words, see **entertainment**

---

## thick *adjective*

1 a thick line.

OTHER WORDS YOU MIGHT USE ARE     **broad     wide**

2 a thick slice of cake.

AN INFORMAL WORD IS **chunky**

The opposite is **thin**

3 thick gravy.

The opposite is **runny**

## thief *noun*

For different kinds of thief, see **steal**

## thin *adjective*

1 a thin line.

OTHER WORDS YOU MIGHT USE ARE     **fine     narrow**

The opposite is **thick**

2 a thin person.

KIND WORDS YOU MIGHT USE ARE     **lean     slender     slim**

AN UNKIND WORD IS **skinny**

The opposite is **fat**

3 thin gravy.

OTHER WORDS ARE     **runny     watery**

The opposite is **thick**

## thing *noun*

1   What are these things in the cupboard?
OTHER WORDS YOU MIGHT USE ARE   **article   item   object**
2   I've got several things on my mind.
OTHER WORDS ARE   **idea   thought   worry**
3   I saw a funny thing today.
ANOTHER WORD IS **happening**

## think *verb*

1   If you think, you won't make a mistake.
OTHER VERBS YOU MIGHT USE ARE   **to attend   to concentrate**
2   We thought about what to do.
OTHER VERBS ARE   **to consider   to reflect**
3   I think you are right.
OTHER VERBS ARE   **to believe   to feel   to guess   to suppose**

## thorough *adjective*

1   a thorough job.
OTHER WORDS YOU MIGHT USE ARE   **careful   proper**
2   a thorough mess.
OTHER WORDS ARE   **absolute   complete   utter**

## thoughtful *adjective*

1   You look thoughtful today.
OTHER WORDS YOU MIGHT USE ARE   **serious   solemn**
2   It's thoughtful of you to wash up.
OTHER WORDS ARE   **considerate   friendly   helpful   unselfish**

## threaten *verb*

For other verbs, see **frighten**

## thrilling *adjective*

The band played thrilling music.
OTHER WORDS ARE   **exciting   rousing   stirring**

## throw *verb*

She threw a stone and broke the glass.
OTHER VERBS YOU MIGHT USE ARE   **to bowl   to cast   (*informal*) to chuck
to fling   to hurl   to lob   to pitch   to sling   to toss**

## tidy *adjective*

Mum asked Jo to make her room tidy.
OTHER WORDS YOU MIGHT USE ARE   **neat   orderly   smart   trim**

## tie *verb*

1  Can you tie this string?
   ANOTHER VERB IS **to knot**
2  I tied a bandage round my leg.
   OTHER VERBS YOU MIGHT USE ARE    **to bind    to fasten    to fix    to wind**
3  They tied up the boat.
   OTHER VERBS ARE    **to anchor    to moor**
4  The farmer tied up the bull.
   ANOTHER VERB IS **to tether**

## tight *adjective*

1  Make sure the lid is tight.
   OTHER WORDS YOU MIGHT USE ARE    **firm    fixed    secure**
2  These shoes are a bit tight.
   OTHER WORDS ARE    **close-fitting    small**
The opposite is **loose**

## tilt *verb*

The boat tilted to one side.
   OTHER VERBS ARE    **to lean    to slant    to slope    to tip**

## time *noun*, see next page

## timid *adjective*

He was too timid to ask for more.
   OTHER WORDS ARE    **cowardly    fearful    nervous    shy**
The opposite is **brave**

## tiny *adjective*

Some insects are tiny.
   OTHER WORDS ARE    **little    microscopic    minute    small**
The opposite is **big**

## tip *noun*

1  the tip of a pencil.
   OTHER WORDS ARE    **end    point**
2  the tip of an iceberg.
   OTHER WORDS ARE    **head    top**

## tip *verb*

A big wave tipped the boat over.
   OTHER VERBS YOU MIGHT USE ARE    **to capsize    to overturn    to turn over    to upset**

## time *noun*

1   Is this a good time to ring Granny?

OTHER WORDS YOU MIGHT USE ARE

**moment    opportunity**

2   Shakespeare lived in the time of Elizabeth I.

OTHER WORDS ARE

**age    era    period**

UNITS USED TO MEASURE TIME ARE

**centuries    days    fortnights    hours    minutes months    seconds    weeks    years**

DIFFERENT TIMES OF THE DAY ARE

**afternoon    bedtime    dawn    dusk    evening midday    midnight    morning    night    noon sunrise    sunset    twilight**

THE SEASONS OF THE YEAR ARE

**spring    summer    autumn    winter**

SPECIAL TIMES OF THE YEAR ARE

**an anniversary    your birthday    Christmas    Diwali Easter    Hallowe'en    Hogmanay    Midsummer New Year    Passover    Ramadan    St Valentine's Day Yom Kippur**

THINGS WE USE TO MEASURE TIME ARE

**calendar    clock    digital watch    hourglass    sundial watch**

## tired *adjective*

1   We were tired after our walk.

OTHER WORDS YOU MIGHT USE ARE    **exhausted    weary    worn out**

2   Go to bed: you look tired.

OTHER WORDS ARE    **drowsy    sleepy**

## tiring *adjective*

tiring work.

OTHER WORDS YOU MIGHT USE ARE    **exhausting    hard**

The opposite is **easy**

## toilet *noun*

OTHER WORDS YOU MIGHT USE ARE    **lavatory**    (*informal*) **loo    WC**

## token *noun*

I've got a token for a free drink.

OTHER WORDS ARE    counter    coupon    voucher

## tomb *noun*

OTHER WORDS ARE    grave    gravestone    memorial    monument    tombstone

## tone *noun*

Her voice had a gentle tone.

OTHER WORDS YOU MIGHT USE ARE    expression    note    sound

---

## tool *noun*

Dad has tools for every job.

OTHER WORDS YOU MIGHT USE ARE

device    gadget    implement    instrument

TOOLS USED FOR WOODWORK ARE

chisel    clamp    drill    hammer    pincers    plane
saw    vice

TOOLS YOU MIGHT USE ON THE CAR ARE

jack    lever    oil can    pliers    screwdriver    spanner

TOOLS USED IN THE GARDEN ARE

broom    fork    hoe    lawn-mower    rake    shears
spade    trowel    watering can

OTHER TOOLS PEOPLE USE ARE

axe    chopper    crowbar    file    ladder    pick
shovel    sledgehammer    wrench

---

## top *noun*

1 the top of a hill.

OTHER WORDS YOU MIGHT USE ARE    head    peak    summit    tip

The opposite is **bottom**

2 the top of a jar.

OTHER WORDS ARE    cap    cover    lid

## topic *noun*

We all wrote about different topics.

OTHER WORDS YOU MIGHT USE ARE    subject    theme

## torment *verb*
1 I hate it when people torment animals.
OTHER VERBS YOU MIGHT USE ARE **to annoy** **to distress** **to tease**
2 Sam saw a big boy tormenting some little ones.
OTHER VERBS ARE **to bully** **to victimize**

## torture *verb*
It's horrible to think of people torturing each other.
OTHER VERBS ARE **to be cruel to** **to hurt**

## total *adjective*
Because it rained, the picnic was a total disaster.
OTHER WORDS YOU MIGHT USE ARE **absolute** **complete**

## total *noun*
Count the money and tell me the total.
OTHER WORDS ARE **amount** **answer** **sum**

## touch *verb*
OTHER VERBS YOU MIGHT USE ARE
**to contact** **to feel** **to handle**

DIFFERENT WAYS TO TOUCH PEOPLE OR ANIMALS ARE
**to caress** **to cuddle** **to embrace** **to fondle** **to kiss**
**to pat** **to rub** **to stroke** **to tickle**

DIFFERENT WAYS TO TOUCH THINGS ARE
**to fiddle with** **to fidget with** **to finger** **to handle**
**to hold**

## tough *adjective*
You need tough shoes to walk in the hills.
OTHER WORDS YOU MIGHT USE ARE **hard-wearing** **stout** **strong**
**sturdy**

## tour *verb*
We toured the castle before we had our picnic.
OTHER VERBS ARE **to go round** **to visit**

## tow *verb*
The car was towing a caravan.
OTHER VERBS YOU MIGHT USE ARE **to haul** **to pull**

## town *noun*

A big town is a **city.**
A small town is a **village.**
The areas at the edge of a town are the **outskirts** or **suburbs.**

THINGS YOU OFTEN FIND IN A TOWN ARE

**bank   bus station   café   car park   church   cinema
college   factory   flats   hotel   leisure centre
library   museum   offices   park   police station
post office   railway station   school   shopping centre
supermarket   theatre   town hall**

For other words, see **shop**

IN THE OUTSKIRTS OF A TOWN YOU MIGHT FIND

**housing estate   industrial estate   retail park**

## track *verb*

The hounds tracked the fox across the fields.

OTHER VERBS YOU MIGHT USE ARE   **to chase   to follow   to hunt
to pursue   to trail**

## traffic *noun*

TRAFFIC YOU SEE ON THE ROADS INCLUDES

**bicycles   buses   cars   coaches   lorries
motorbikes** or **motorcycles   taxis   vans**

For other words, see **travel**

## tragedy *noun*

The plane crash was a terrible tragedy.

OTHER WORDS YOU MIGHT USE ARE   **calamity   catastrophe   disaster
misfortune**

## trail *noun*

For other words, see **path**

## trail *verb*

1 The police trailed him for miles.
For other verbs, see **track**
2 Jo's scarf is so long that it trails in the mud.

ANOTHER VERB IS **to drag**

## train *noun*
We went to London on the train.
For other words, see **railway**

## train *verb*
1 Jo's Dad trains the school team.
OTHER VERBS YOU MIGHT USE ARE   **to coach**   **to instruct**   **to teach**
2 The team trains every Thursday.
OTHER VERBS ARE   **to exercise**   **to practise**

## trainer *noun*
1 Sam's feet are too big for his old trainers.
For other things you wear on your feet, see **shoe**
2 Our team has a new trainer.
ANOTHER WORD IS **coach**

## transfer *verb*
1 A bus transferred us from the airport to the hotel.
OTHER VERBS YOU MIGHT USE ARE   **to carry**   **to take**   **to transport**
2 The goalkeeper was transferred to another team.
OTHER VERBS ARE   **to move**   **to switch**

## transform *verb*
The fairy transformed the pumpkin into a coach.
OTHER VERBS YOU MIGHT USE ARE   **to change**   **to turn**

## transport *noun*
For different kinds of transport, see **travel**

## trap *verb*
We trapped the mouse in a box.
OTHER VERBS YOU MIGHT USE ARE   **to capture**   **to catch**   **to corner**

## travel *verb*, see opposite page

## treacherous *adjective*
Take care: that dog's treacherous.
OTHER WORDS YOU MIGHT USE ARE   **dangerous**   **untrustworthy**
The opposite is **loyal**

## tread *verb*
Don't tread on the flowers.
OTHER VERBS YOU MIGHT USE ARE   **to step**   **to trample**   **to walk**

# travel *verb*

DIFFERENT WAYS TO TRAVEL ARE

**cruise    cycle    drive    fly    hitch-hike    ride    sail    walk**

DIFFERENT KINDS OF JOURNEY ARE

**cruise    drive    expedition    flight    hike    outing    pilgrimage    ramble    ride    safari    tour    trek    trip    voyage    walk**

A person who travels is a **traveller**.

OTHER WORDS FOR PEOPLE WHO TRAVEL ARE

a person who drives a car: **motorist**

a person who travels while someone else drives: **passenger**

a person who goes on foot

**hiker    pedestrian    rambler    walker**

a person who travels to work every day: **commuter**

a traveller to a holy place: **pilgrim**

a person who travels on holiday

**holidaymaker    tourist**

a person who travels in a boat

**sailor    yachtsman    yachtswoman**

a person who travels to find somewhere new: **explorer**

people who travel about because that's how they like to live

**gypsies    nomads    tramps    travellers**

Something you travel in is a **vehicle**.

DIFFERENT VEHICLES THAT PEOPLE TRAVEL IN ON THE ROADS ARE

**bus    car    coach    jeep    minibus    motorbike** or **motorcycle    taxi    tram**

OTHER FORMS OF TRANSPORT FOR PASSENGERS ARE

**aeroplane    bicycle    ferry    railway    underground**

WAYS PEOPLE USED TO TRAVEL ARE

**carriage    horse    stagecoach**

VEHICLES THAT CARRY GOODS ARE

**articulated lorry    cart    lorry    pick-up truck    truck    van    wagon**

OTHER KINDS OF TRANSPORT FOR GOODS ARE

**aircraft    goods train    ship**

VEHICLES MADE TO DO SPECIAL JOBS ARE

**ambulance    bulldozer    caravan    digger    dustcart    fire engine    horsebox    milk float    police car    steamroller    tanker    tractor**

For other words, see **aircraft, boat, car, railway**

## treat *verb*
1 Treat your pets well.
OTHER VERBS YOU MIGHT USE ARE **to care for**  **to look after**
2 How shall we treat this problem?
OTHER VERBS ARE **to attend to**  **to deal with**  **to tackle**

---

## tree *noun*
DIFFERENT KINDS OF TREE ARE
**ash  beech  birch  cedar  chestnut  elm  fir
holly  larch  lime  maple  oak  palm tree  pine
plane  poplar  sycamore  willow  yew**

---

## tremble *verb*
I trembled with fear.
OTHER VERBS YOU MIGHT USE ARE **to quake  to quiver  to shake
to shiver  to shudder**

## tremendous *adjective*
1 We heard a tremendous explosion.
OTHER WORDS ARE **alarming  awful  fearful  frightful  terrible
terrific**
2 Granny gave us tremendous helpings of dinner.
OTHER WORDS ARE **big  enormous  huge  large**

## trick *noun*
1 That was a nasty trick!
OTHER WORDS YOU MIGHT USE ARE **cheat  deception  fraud  hoax**
2 The dolphins did some amazing tricks.
ANOTHER WORD IS **stunt**

## trick *verb*
He tricked us into buying rubbish.
OTHER VERBS YOU MIGHT USE ARE **to cheat  to fool  to hoax
to mislead  to swindle**

## trickle *verb*
Water trickled out of the crack.
OTHER VERBS YOU MIGHT USE ARE **to dribble  to drip  to leak
to ooze  to run  to seep**

## trip *noun*

a trip to the seaside.

OTHER WORDS YOU MIGHT USE ARE    **excursion    expedition    outing
visit**

For other words, see **travel**

## trouble *noun*

1 Mum had a lot of trouble lately.

OTHER WORDS YOU MIGHT USE ARE    **distress    grief    hardship    misery
misfortune    problems    sadness    worry**

2 There was some trouble in the playground at dinner time.

OTHER WORDS ARE    **bother    commotion    disorder    fighting
fuss    row**

3 Sam takes trouble with his work.

OTHER WORDS ARE    **care    effort**

## trouble *verb*

Do wasps trouble you?

OTHER VERBS YOU MIGHT USE ARE    **to annoy    to bother    to upset
to worry**

## trousers *noun*

For other words, see **clothes**

## true *adjective*

1 Is that story true?

OTHER WORDS YOU MIGHT USE ARE    **correct    factual    genuine    real**

2 Jo is a true friend.

OTHER WORDS ARE    **faithful    loyal    reliable    trustworthy**

## trust *verb*

You can trust Jo to do her best.

PHRASES YOU MIGHT USE ARE    (*informal*) **to bank on    to be sure of
to count on    to depend on    to have faith in    to rely on**

## try *verb*

1 Sam tried to swim ten lengths.

OTHER VERBS ARE    **to aim    to attempt    to endeavour
to exert yourself    to make an effort    to strive**

2 Can I try the cake?

ANOTHER VERB IS **to sample**

3 Try the brakes before you ride your bike.

OTHER VERBS ARE    **to experiment with    to test**

**tube** *noun*
> ANOTHER WORD IS **pipe**
> A tube to take water from the tap to where you want it is a **hose**.

**tune** *noun*
> Jo played a well-known tune.
> > ANOTHER WORD IS **melody**

**tunnel** *noun*
> A tunnel that a rabbit makes is a **burrow**.
> A tunnel under a road is a **subway** or **underpass**.

**turn** *noun*
> It's your turn to play next.
> > OTHER WORDS ARE    **chance    go    opportunity**

**turn** *verb*
> 1  The wheel began to turn.
> > OTHER VERBS YOU MIGHT USE ARE    **to revolve    to rotate    to spin    to twirl    to whirl**
> For other verbs, see **twist**
> 2  Tadpoles turn into frogs.
> > OTHER VERBS ARE    **to become    to change into**
> 3  We turned the attic into a playroom.
> > OTHER VERBS ARE    **to convert    to transform**

**twinkle** *verb*
> The lights twinkled in the distance.
> > OTHER VERBS ARE    **to flicker    to shine    to sparkle**
> For other verbs, see **light**

**twist** *verb*
> 1  The road twisted up the hill.
> > OTHER VERBS YOU MIGHT USE ARE    **to bend    to curve    to zig-zag**
> 2  I twisted the wires round each other.
> > OTHER VERBS ARE    **to coil    to curl    to loop    to turn    to wind**

**type** *noun*
> 1  What type of music do you like?
> > OTHER WORDS YOU MIGHT USE ARE    **kind    sort**
> 2  What type of dog is that?
> > OTHER WORDS ARE    **breed    species    variety**

**typical** *adjective*
In England, showers are typical April weather.
OTHER WORDS YOU MIGHT USE ARE    **common    normal    ordinary
usual**
The opposite is **unusual**

# Uu

**ugly** *adjective*
We screamed when we saw the ugly monster.
OTHER WORDS YOU MIGHT USE ARE    **foul    frightful    hideous
monstrous    repulsive    unattractive**
The opposite is **beautiful**

**uncommon** *adjective*
Eagles are uncommon in this country.
OTHER WORDS YOU MIGHT USE ARE    **infrequent    rare
unusual**
The opposite is **common**

**unconscious** *adjective*
If you are unconscious, you may be **knocked out** or you may have
**fainted**.
The opposite is **conscious**

**understand** *verb*
Do you understand what I mean?
OTHER VERBS YOU MIGHT USE ARE    **to follow    to grasp    to know
to realize    to see**

**undo** *verb*
Jo undid the parcel.
OTHER VERBS YOU MIGHT USE ARE    **to unfasten    to untie**

**unemployed** *adjective*
PHRASES ARE    **on the dole    out of work**

## uneven *adjective*
1  We jolted along the uneven road.
> OTHER WORDS YOU MIGHT USE ARE   **bumpy**   **rough**

The opposite is **smooth**

2  The music had an uneven beat.
> ANOTHER WORD IS **irregular**

The opposite is **regular**

## unfair *adjective*
1  It's unfair if she gets more than me.
> OTHER WORDS YOU MIGHT USE ARE   **unjust**   **unreasonable**   **wrong**

2  We complained that the referee was unfair.
> OTHER WORDS YOU MIGHT USE ARE   **biased**   **prejudiced**

The opposite is **fair**

## unfriendly *adjective*
Mum was upset by our neighbour's unfriendly remarks.
> OTHER WORDS YOU MIGHT USE ARE   **aggressive**   **angry**   **disagreeable**
> **hostile**   **nasty**   **offensive**   **rude**

For other words, see **unkind**
The opposite is **friendly**

## unhappy *adjective*
He was unhappy after his dog died.
> OTHER WORDS ARE   **depressed**   **gloomy**   **glum**   **heart-broken**
> **miserable**   **sorrowful**   **tearful**   **troubled**   **wretched**

The opposite is **happy**

## unite *verb*
We united to sing the last song.
> OTHER VERBS YOU MIGHT USE ARE   **to combine**   **to join together**

## unkind *noun*
Jo hates to see people being unkind to animals.
> OTHER WORDS ARE   **cruel**   **heartless**   **spiteful**   **thoughtless**

For other words, see **unfriendly**
The opposite is **kind**

## unlikely *adjective*
I don't believe his unlikely story.
> OTHER WORDS YOU MIGHT USE ARE   **far-fetched**   **improbable**
> **incredible**   **unconvincing**

The opposite is **likely**

## unlucky *adjective*

We were unlucky to miss the bus.
ANOTHER WORD IS **unfortunate**
The opposite is **lucky**

## unpleasant *adjective*

1　The accident was an unpleasant experience.
　　OTHER WORDS YOU MIGHT USE ARE **awful　dreadful　frightening painful　terrible　upsetting**
2　I hate touching unpleasant things.
　　OTHER WORDS ARE **disgusting　horrible　nasty　objectionable**
3　The noisy neighbours were very unpleasant.
　　OTHER WORDS ARE **rude　unfriendly**
The opposite is **pleasant**

## untidy *adjective*

1　Our teacher hates untidy work.
　　OTHER WORDS YOU MIGHT USE ARE **careless　disorganized　scruffy**
2　Everything was in an untidy pile on the floor.
　　OTHER WORDS ARE **confused　disorderly　jumbled　muddled**
The opposite is **tidy**

## unusual *adjective*

It's unusual to have snow in May.
　　OTHER WORDS YOU MIGHT USE ARE **extraordinary　odd　peculiar strange　surprising　uncommon**
The opposite is **common**

## upset *verb*

1　The thunder upset the dog.
　　OTHER VERBS YOU MIGHT USE ARE **to alarm　to bother　to distress to frighten　to trouble　to worry**
2　Sam upset the milk.
　　OTHER VERBS ARE **to knock over　to overturn　to spill**

## urge *noun*

I had an urge to giggle.
　　OTHER WORDS ARE **desire　wish**

## urge *verb*

Mum urged us to be quick.
　　OTHER VERBS YOU MIGHT USE ARE **to appeal to　to beg　to encourage to entreat　to plead with**

## use *verb*
1 They used the most up-to-date machines to dig the tunnel.
ANOTHER VERB IS **to employ**
2 Have we used all the milk?
OTHER VERBS YOU MIGHT USE ARE    **to consume**    **to finish**

## useful *adjective*
1 Dad's penknife is a useful tool.
OTHER WORDS YOU MIGHT USE ARE    **convenient**    **handy**    **practical**
2 Sam is a useful member of the team.
OTHER WORDS ARE    **helpful**    **valuable**
The opposite is **useless**

## useless *adjective*
1 A car is useless without petrol.
ANOTHER WORD IS **unusable**
2 He was a useless goalkeeper.
OTHER WORDS ARE    **incompetent**    **worthless**
The opposite is **useful**

## usual *adjective*
1 Ten o'clock is my usual bedtime.
OTHER WORDS YOU MIGHT USE ARE    **normal**    **ordinary**    **regular**
2 It's usual to put milk in tea.
OTHER WORDS ARE    **common**    **expected**    **typical**
The opposite is **unusual**

# Vv

## vague *adjective*
1 He made some vague comments, but nothing definite.
OTHER WORDS YOU MIGHT USE ARE    **broad**    **general**
2 He was a vague sort of person.
OTHER WORDS ARE    **absent-minded**    **forgetful**    **scatterbrained**
The opposite is **definite**

## vain *adjective*

He's so vain that he's always looking in the mirror.
OTHER WORDS ARE **boastful    conceited    proud**
The opposite is **modest**

## valuable *adjective*

1  valuable jewels.
OTHER WORDS YOU MIGHT USE ARE    **expensive    precious    priceless**
The opposite is **worthless**
2  He gave me some valuable advice.
OTHER WORDS ARE    **helpful    useful    worthwhile**
The opposite is **useless**

## vanish *verb*

The robber vanished into the crowd.
ANOTHER VERB IS **to disappear**

## variety *noun*

1  There's a variety of things to eat.
OTHER WORDS YOU MIGHT USE ARE    **assortment    mixture**
2  Mum grows many varieties of flowers.
OTHER WORDS ARE    **kind    sort    type**

## various *adjective*

We made various sandwiches.
OTHER WORDS YOU MIGHT USE ARE    **assorted    different    mixed**

## vary *verb*

The date of Easter varies each year.
OTHER VERBS YOU MIGHT USE ARE    **to alter    to change**

---

## vegetable *noun*

VEGETABLES PEOPLE EAT INCLUDE

**asparagus    beans    Brussels sprouts    cabbage
carrot    cauliflower    greens    leek    marrow    nuts
onion    parsnip    pea    potato    pumpkin    spinach
swede    turnip**

---

## vehicle *noun*

For other words, see **travel**

## version *noun*

1 Jo's version of the accident is different from Sam's.
OTHER WORDS YOU MIGHT USE ARE    **account    description    story**
2 Mum makes a vegetarian version of shepherd's pie.
OTHER WORDS ARE    **kind    sort    type**

## vertical *adjective*

The opposite is **horizontal**

## vessel *noun*

For other words, see **boat**

## vibrate *verb*

When the engine started we felt the boat vibrate.
OTHER VERBS YOU MIGHT USE ARE    **to quiver    to shake    to shudder    to throb**

## victory *noun*

We celebrated our team's victory.
OTHER WORDS YOU MIGHT USE ARE    **success    triumph    win**
The opposite is **defeat**

## view *verb*

We viewed the the stars through a telescope.
OTHER VERBS YOU MIGHT USE ARE    **to look at    to watch**

## vigorous *adjective*

1 Jo took her dog out for some vigorous exercise.
OTHER WORDS YOU MIGHT USE ARE    **active    energetic**
2 You need to use fertilizer if you want to grow vigorous plants.
OTHER WORDS ARE    **healthy    strong**

## villain *noun*

I guessed he was the villain at the very beginning of the film.
OTHER WORDS ARE    (*informal*) **baddy    rascal    scoundrel**
The opposite is **hero**

## violent *adjective*

1 a violent attack.
OTHER WORDS ARE    **cruel    ferocious    fierce    savage**
2 a violent storm.
OTHER WORDS ARE    **rough    severe    strong**
The opposite is **gentle**

## visible *adjective*
Is the ink stain still visible?

OTHER WORDS ARE    **clear    noticeable    obvious    plain**

The opposite is **invisible**

## visit *verb*
Granny visited us on Sunday.

OTHER VERBS YOU MIGHT USE ARE    **to call**    (*informal*) **to drop in**

## visitor *noun*
Are you expecting a visitor?

OTHER WORDS ARE    **caller    guest**

## vivid *adjective*
1  vivid colours.

OTHER WORDS YOU MIGHT USE ARE    **bright    brilliant    colourful**

2  a vivid imagination.

ANOTHER WORD IS **lively**

3  a vivid dream.

OTHER WORDS ARE    **clear    lifelike**

The opposite is **dull**

## voice *noun*
For different ways you can use your voice, see **talk**

## volume *noun*
1  The tank holds a large volume of oil.

OTHER WORDS ARE    **amount    mass    quantity**

2  How many volumes are there in the library?

ANOTHER WORD IS **book**

## volunteer *verb*
Sam volunteered to wash up.

ANOTHER VERB IS **to offer**

## vote *verb*
Who did you vote for?

OTHER VERBS YOU MIGHT USE ARE    **to choose    to pick    to select**

## vow *verb*
He vowed never to do it again.

OTHER VERBS YOU MIGHT USE ARE    **to give your word    to guarantee    to promise    to swear**

**voyage** *noun*
For other words, see **travel**

**vulgar** *adjective*
We don't like vulgar language.
OTHER WORDS YOU MIGHT USE ARE    **bad-mannered    coarse    impolite
improper    indecent    rude**
The opposite is **polite**

# **Ww**

**wait** *verb*
1 Wait there!
OTHER VERBS YOU MIGHT USE ARE    **to halt    to keep still    to remain
to rest    to stay    to stop**
2 Don't wait: get on with it!
OTHER VERBS ARE    **to delay    to hesitate    to pause**

**wake** *verb*
I asked Mum to wake me early.
OTHER VERBS YOU MIGHT USE ARE    **to call    to rouse**

---

**walk** *verb*
DIFFERENT WAYS TO WALK ARE

| | | | |
|---|---|---|---|
| **to creep** | **to hobble** | **to limp** | **to march** |
| **to plod** | **to prowl** | **to shuffle** | **to stagger** |
| **to stride** | **to strut** | **to stumble** | **to totter** |
| **to trot** | **to trudge** | | |

to go for a gentle walk: **to stroll**
to go for a long country walk
    **to hike    to ramble    to trek**

When a baby tries to walk it **crawls**.

DIFFERENT WORDS FOR A WALKER ARE
a person who walks in the street: **pedestrian**
a person who goes for a walk in the country
    **hiker    rambler**

## wander *verb*
The sheep wander about the hills.

OTHER VERBS YOU MIGHT USE ARE    **to ramble    to roam    to stray**

## want *verb*
You can't always have what you want.

OTHER VERBS YOU MIGHT USE ARE    **to desire    to fancy    to long for
to wish for    to yearn for**

---

## war *noun*
THINGS THAT HAPPEN IN WAR ARE:

**ambush    attack    battle    fighting    invasion
retreat    siege    surrender**

For other words, see **weapon**

---

## warm *adjective*
If something is very warm it is **hot**.
If something is slightly warm it is **luke-warm** or **tepid**.

WORDS TO DESCRIBE WARM WEATHER ARE    **close    humid    sultry**

## warn *verb*
The policeman warned him not to do it again.

ANOTHER VERB IS **to caution**

---

## wash *verb*
DIFFERENT WAYS TO WASH THINGS ARE

**to bath    to mop    to rinse    to scrub    to shampoo
to sponge down    to swill    to wipe**

---

## waste *noun*
Put the waste in the bin.

OTHER WORDS YOU MIGHT USE ARE    **junk    litter    refuse    rubbish**

## watch *verb*
1  I watched the ducks on the lake.

OTHER VERBS ARE    **to gaze at    to look at    to observe    to stare at**

2  Will you watch my things while I go for a swim?

OTHER VERBS YOU MIGHT USE ARE    **to guard    to look after    to mind**

**water** *noun*

KINDS OF WATER YOU CAN DRINK ARE
**mineral water    spring water    tap water**

OTHER KINDS OF WATER ARE

big stretches of water
**lake    ocean    reservoir    sea**

small areas of water
**pond    puddle**

water that spreads over land that is usually dry
**flood**

water which goes along a channel
**brook    canal    ditch    river    stream    waterway**

water which rushes over rocks
**cascade    cataract    rapids    waterfall**

places where water comes out of the ground
**spring    well**

water which spurts out of a hole
**fountain    jet    spray**

A place where water seems to spin round and round is
a **whirlpool**.

**wave** *noun*
Big waves are **breakers** or **surf**.
Small waves are **ripples**.

**wave** *verb*
The flags waved in the breeze.
OTHER VERBS YOU MIGHT USE ARE    **to flap    to flutter    to shake**

**way** *noun*
1 Sam thinks his way of building a den is the best.
OTHER WORDS YOU MIGHT USE ARE    **method    technique**
2 She does her hair in a pretty way.
OTHER WORDS ARE    **fashion    manner    style**
3 What is the best way home?
ANOTHER WORD IS **route**

## weak *adjective*
1 a weak person.
> OTHER WORDS YOU MIGHT USE ARE **delicate feeble frail**

For other words, see **ill**

2 a weak branch.
> OTHER WORDS YOU MIGHT USE ARE **brittle flimsy fragile thin**

3 weak tea.
> OTHER WORDS YOU MIGHT USE ARE **tasteless watery**

The opposite is **strong**

## wealthy *adjective*
a wealthy millionaire.
> OTHER WORDS YOU MIGHT USE ARE **prosperous rich well-off**

The opposite is **poor**

---

## weapon *noun*

WEAPONS WHICH FIRE THINGS ARE
**airgun bow and arrow cannon catapult
crossbow machinegun musket pistol revolver
rifle shotgun**

WEAPONS WHICH BLOW UP ARE
**bomb grenade mine missile nuclear weapons
time bomb torpedo**

WEAPONS WHICH CUT WITH A SHARP EDGE ARE
**cutlass dagger sabre sword**

WEAPONS WITH A SHARP POINT ARE
**bayonet harpoon javelin lance spear**

---

## weary *adjective*
I was weary after the long walk.
> OTHER WORDS YOU MIGHT USE ARE **exhausted tired worn out**

## weather *noun*, see next page

## weep *verb*
He wept when his dog died.
> OTHER VERBS YOU MIGHT USE ARE **to cry to shed tears to sob**

# weather *noun*

WORDS TO DO WITH DIFFERENT KINDS OF WEATHER ARE

| | | | | |
|---|---|---|---|---|
| cloud | drought | fog | frost | hail |
| heatwave | ice | lightning | mist | rain |
| rainbow | snow | storm | sunshine | thaw |
| thunder | wind | | | |

WORDS FOR DIFFERENT KINDS OF RAIN

a short fall of rain
   **shower**
very heavy rain
   **downpour**
very fine light rain
   **drizzle**
mixed rain and snow
   **sleet**

DIFFERENT KINDS OF WIND

a very strong wind
   **gale**
a gentle wind
   **breeze**
a sudden puff of wind
   **gust**

DIFFERENT KINDS OF STORM

a violent storm
   **tempest**
a snow storm
   **blizzard**
a storm with a lot of wind
   **gale    hurricane    tornado    whirlwind**
a storm with a lot of rain
   **deluge    rainstorm**
a storm with thunder and lightning
   **thunderstorm**

WORDS YOU MIGHT USE TO DESCRIBE THE WEATHER ARE

| | | | | |
|---|---|---|---|---|
| blustery | bright | clear | cloudless | cloudy |
| cold | drizzly | dull | fair | fine |
| foggy | freezing | frosty | hazy | hot |
| icy | misty | rainy | showery | snowy |
| stormy | sultry | sunny | thundery | wet |
| windy | wintry | | | |

## weird *adjective*

1 What a weird thing to do!

OTHER WORDS YOU MIGHT USE ARE    **curious    funny    odd    peculiar    queer    strange**

2 There was a weird atmosphere in the castle.

OTHER WORDS ARE    (*informal*) **creepy    ghostly    (*informal*) scary**

## welcome *verb*

We welcomed the guests at the door.

OTHER VERBS YOU MIGHT USE ARE    **to greet    to receive**

## well *adjective*

I hope you are well.

OTHER WORDS ARE    **fit    healthy**

The opposite is **ill**

## well-known *adjective*

a well-known pop star.

OTHER WORDS YOU MIGHT USE ARE    **familiar    famous**

## wet *adjective*

1 I got wet in the storm.

OTHER WORDS YOU MIGHT USE ARE    **drenched    soaked**

2 The field is too wet to play on.

OTHER WORDS ARE    **muddy    soggy    waterlogged**

3 It was a wet day.

OTHER WORDS ARE    **drizzly    rainy    showery**

If something is slightly wet it is **damp** or **moist**.

The opposite is **dry**

## whip *verb*

For other verbs, see **hit**

## whirl *verb*

The wheel whirled round.

OTHER VERBS YOU MIGHT USE ARE    **to revolve    to rotate    to spin    to turn    to twirl**

## whiskers *noun*

OTHER WORDS ARE    **hairs    bristles**

## whisper *verb*

For other verbs, see **talk**

## **whole** *adjective*

1 We ate the whole cake.

OTHER WORDS YOU MIGHT USE ARE **complete entire**

2 Yasmin dropped the cake but it stayed whole.

OTHER WORDS ARE **intact undamaged**

## **wicked** *adjective*

It's wicked to take food from starving people.

OTHER WORDS YOU MIGHT USE ARE **bad evil immoral sinful wrong**

The opposite is **good**

## **wide** *adjective*

1 The stream was too wide to jump.

ANOTHER WORD IS **broad**

2 There's a wide gap between the two scores.

ANOTHER WORD IS **large**

## **wild** *adjective*

1 wild animals.

OTHER WORDS YOU MIGHT USE ARE **free natural untamed**

The opposite is **tame**

2 wild weather.

OTHER WORDS ARE **rough stormy violent windy**

The opposite is **calm**

3 wild behaviour.

OTHER WORDS ARE **boisterous disorderly excited noisy rowdy unruly**

The opposite is **orderly**

## **willing** *adjective*

1 Sam is willing to help us.

OTHER WORDS YOU MIGHT USE ARE **happy prepared ready**

2 Jo is a willing worker, too.

OTHER WORDS ARE **cooperative helpful obliging**

The opposite is **reluctant**

## **win** *verb*

1 Jo won first prize.

OTHER VERBS YOU MIGHT USE ARE **to earn to gain to receive**

2 The better team won.

OTHER VERBS ARE **to come first to succeed to triumph**

The opposite is **lose**

**wind** (rhymes with *tinned*) *noun*
KINDS OF WIND ARE
a very strong wind
**gale**
a gentle wind
**breeze**
a sudden puff of wind
**gust**

A **whirlwind** blows round and round and can do a lot of damage.

For other words, see **weather**
A kind of wind you feel if someone leaves a door open indoors is a **draught**.

**wind** (rhymes with *find*) *verb*
I wound the string into a ball.
OTHER VERBS YOU MIGHT USE ARE    **to coil    to curl    to loop    to turn to twist**

**windy**, **wintry** *adjectives*
For other words, see **weather**

**wipe** *verb*
DIFFERENT WAYS TO WIPE THINGS ARE    **to dry    to dust    to mop to polish    to rub    to scour    to sponge    to wash**

**wire** *noun*
an electric wire.
OTHER WORDS YOU MIGHT USE ARE    **cable    flex    lead**

**wise** *adjective*
If you're wise you won't go out in the rain.
OTHER WORDS YOU MIGHT USE ARE    **intelligent    reasonable    sensible thoughtful**
The opposite is **silly**

**wish** *verb*
For other verbs, see **want**

## wither *verb*

The plants withered in the dry weather.

OTHER VERBS YOU MIGHT USE ARE    **to dry up**    **to shrink**
**to shrivel    to wilt**

## wobble *verb*

1 Jo wobbled a bit when she first rode a bike.

OTHER VERBS YOU MIGHT USE ARE    **to be unsteady    to sway
to waver**

2 The jelly wobbles when you move the plate.

OTHER VERBS ARE    **to shake    to tremble**

---

## woman *noun*

OTHER WORDS YOU MIGHT USE ARE

a polite word
  **lady**
a married woman
  **wife**
a woman who is not married
  **spinster**
a woman whose husband has died
  **widow**
a woman who has children
  **mother**
a young woman
  **girl**

The man who plays a woman in a pantomime is the **dame**.

---

## wonder *verb*

I wonder if it will be fine tomorrow.

ANOTHER VERB IS **to ask yourself**

## wonderful *adjective*

We had a wonderful time.

OTHER WORDS YOU MIGHT USE ARE    **amazing    excellent**
(*informal*) **fabulous    marvellous    special**
The opposite is **dreadful**

## wood *noun*

1  Dad bought some wood to make a table.
   ANOTHER WORD IS **timber**
   KINDS OF TIMBER ARE
   **beams    boards    planks    posts**
2  We went for a walk in the wood.
   ANOTHER WORD IS **woodland**
A large wood is a **forest**.
A small wood is a **copse** or **grove** or **thicket**.
A place where fruit trees are growing is an **orchard**.

**word** *noun*, see next page

## work *noun*

1  Keeping a garden tidy takes a lot of work.
   OTHER WORDS YOU MIGHT USE ARE    **effort    exertion    labour    toil**
2  What kind of work does Dad do?
   OTHER WORDS ARE    **job    occupation    profession    trade**
3  Our teacher set us work to do.
   OTHER WORDS ARE    **assignment    project    task**

## work *verb*

1  We worked hard all morning.
   OTHER VERBS YOU MIGHT USE ARE    **to labour**    (*informal*) **to slave away**
   **to toil**
2  Does your watch work?
   ANOTHER VERB IS **to go**
3  Can you work this machine?
   ANOTHER VERB IS **to operate**

## worry *verb*

1  Don't worry; everything will be all right.
   PHRASES YOU MIGHT USE ARE    **to be anxious    to be concerned**
   **to be troubled    to feel uneasy**
2  Don't worry the cat when she's sleeping.
   OTHER VERBS ARE    **to annoy    to bother    to disturb    to pester**
   **to trouble    to upset**

## worship *verb*

Jo worships her Grandad.
   OTHER VERBS YOU MIGHT USE ARE    **to adore    to love**

## word *noun*

Different words do different jobs and so they belong to different groups called parts of speech.

THE EIGHT PARTS OF SPEECH ARE
**adjective    adverb    conjunction
interjection** or **exclamation    noun    preposition
pronoun    verb**

Words which are the names of people, things, or ideas are nouns.
For example: *girl*, *animal*, and *happiness* are all nouns.

A word which you use instead of a noun is a pronoun.
For example: *I, you, she,* and *it* are pronouns.

A word which describes a noun is an adjective.
In the phrase '*an old green car*' *old* and *green* are adjectives.

A word which goes in front of a noun to make a phrase is a preposition.
In the phrases '*near my house*' and '*under the table*' *near* and *under* are prepositions.

Words which show what someone does or what happens are verbs.
In the sentences '*Jo ran home*' and '*The rain stopped*' *ran* and *stopped* are verbs.

A word which tells you how, when, or where something happens is an adverb.
For example: in the sentences '*Jo ran home quickly*' and '*Put it here*' *quickly* and *here* are adverbs.

Words like *and* or *but* which we use to join words or ideas are conjunctions.

A word like *Hello!* or *Well!* is an interjection or exclamation.

## worthless *adjective*
worthless rubbish.
> ANOTHER WORD IS **useless**

The opposite is **valuable**

---

## wound *verb*
Was anyone wounded in the accident?
> OTHER VERBS YOU MIGHT USE ARE **to harm** **to hurt** **to injure**
> THERE ARE DIFFERENT WAYS YOU CAN BE WOUNDED

An animal can **bite** you.
A knock or fall can **bruise** you.
Something very hot **burns** you.
A knife will **cut** you.
You can **break** or **fracture** a bone.
You can **graze** your skin on something rough.
A gun can **shoot** you.
You can **sprain** a joint by twisting it.
A dagger can **stab** you.
Some insects can **sting** you.

---

## wrap *verb*
I wrapped the parcel in paper.
> OTHER VERBS YOU MIGHT USE ARE **to cover** **to enclose**

## wreck *verb*
The accident wrecked the car.
> OTHER VERBS YOU MIGHT USE ARE **to break up** **to destroy** **to ruin**
> **to shatter** **to smash**

## write *verb*, see next page

## wrong *adjective*
1 I gave a wrong answer.
> OTHER WORDS YOU MIGHT USE ARE **false** **inaccurate** **incorrect**
> **mistaken** **untrue**

2 It is wrong to steal.
> OTHER WORDS ARE **dishonest** **illegal** **immoral**

3 Cruelty to animals is wrong.
> OTHER WORDS ARE **evil** **wicked**

The opposite is **right**

**write** *verb*

THERE ARE DIFFERENT WAYS TO WRITE THINGS

Musicians **compose** music.
When you are bored, you **doodle**.
You **jot** down rough notes.
People **print** books and newspapers.
When you are in a hurry you **scrawl** or **scribble**.
You can **type** things or use a wordprocessor.

DIFFERENT KINDS OF WRITING

**articles** for a magazine or paper    **diary**    **essays**    **films**
**letters**    **novels**    **plays**    **poems**    **stories**
**programmes** for radio and TV

Another word for a writer is **author**.

DIFFERENT KINDS OF WRITER ARE

a writer of novels
**novelist**
a writer for a newspaper
**journalist**
a person who writes poetry
**poet**
a person who writes for radio or TV
**scriptwriter**
a person who writes plays
**dramatist** or **playwright**

Someone who writes music is a **composer**.

# Xx Yy

**xylophone** *noun*
For other musical instruments, see **instrument**

**yell** *verb*
He yelled angrily at me.
OTHER VERBS YOU MIGHT USE ARE    **to call**    **to shout**

**young** *adjective*

SOMETIMES THERE ARE SPECIAL WORDS FOR YOUNG THINGS

A young tree is a **sapling**.
A young plant is a **seedling**.

A young bird is a **fledgling** or **nestling**.
A young duck is a **duckling**.
A young goose is a **gosling**.
A young hen is a **chick** or **pullet**.
A young swan is a **cygnet**.

A young bear is a **cub**.
A young cat is a **kitten**.
A young cow or whale is a **calf**.
A young deer is a **fawn**.
A young dog is a **puppy**.
A young goat is a **kid**.
A young horse is a **foal**.
A young pig is a **piglet**.
A young sheep is a **lamb**.

A young person
   **baby**   **boy**   **child**   **girl**   **infant**   **toddler**

A person who is not a child but is not yet grown up
   **adolescent**   **juvenile**   **teenager**

# Zz

**zero**

OTHER WORDS YOU MIGHT USE ARE   **nil**   **nothing**   **nought**

**zigzag** *noun*
   a zigzag line.

OTHER WORDS YOU MIGHT USE ARE   **bendy**   **crooked**